New Hope

For Children and Teens with Bipolar Disorder

OTHER BOOKS IN THE NEW HOPE SERIES

New Hope for People with Weight Problems

New Hope for People with Lupus

New Hope for People with Fibromyalgia

New Hope for Couples with Infertility Problems

New Hope for People with Diabetes

New Hope for People with Borderline Personality Disorder

New Hope for People with Bipolar Disorder

New Hope for People with Depression

New Hope for People with Alzheimer's and Their Caregivers

NewHope

For Children and Teens with Bipolar Disorder

Your Friendly, Authoritative Guide to the Latest
in Traditional and Complementary Solutions

BORIS BIRMAHER, M.D.

 THREE RIVERS PRESS • NEW YORK

Published by Three Rivers Press, New York, New York.
Member of the Crown Publishing Group, a division of Random House, Inc.
www.crownpublishing.com

THREE RIVERS PRESS and the Tugboat design are registered trademarks of Random House, Inc.

Printed in the United States of America

Library of Congress Cataloging-in-Publication Data
Birmaher, Boris.
    New hope for children and teens with bipolar disorder : your friendly, authoritative guide to the latest in traditional and complementary solutions / Boris Birmaher.
    — (New hope series)
Includes bibliographical references and index.
    1. Manic-depressive illness in children—Popular works.   2. Manic-depressive illness in adolescence—Popular works.   I. Title.   II. Series.
    RJ506.D4B58 2003
    618.92'895—dc21

2003006864

ISBN 0-761-52718-4

10 9 8 7 6 5 4

First Edition

To all the parents of children with bipolar disorder,
particularly those who attend our Children and Adolescents
Bipolar Services (CABS) and our monthly parent meetings,
thank you for constantly teaching me, giving me ideas about
what to include in this book, and motivating me to continue
with this endeavor. It is to your children and families,
and to my family, staff, colleagues, and teachers, that I,
with great pleasure and with all of my heart,
dedicate this book.

Contents

Foreword

IF YOU HAVE BOUGHT or are considering buying or reading this book, a child you care about has probably been given the diagnosis of bipolar disorder. Or perhaps a professional has entertained the diagnosis in your child. Or perhaps one form or another of the media has exposed you to the term bipolar disorder and its symptoms as they might appear in children or adolescents and you want to know more. Considering the subject barely warranted a chapter in a textbook 20 years ago, it is a testimony to the growth of interest in this condition in young people that there are now a burgeoning number of popular books on the subject.

However, interest in the subject of bipolar disorder in children isn't new. Indeed, 50 years ago one could find papers in professional journals arguing about the occurrence and manifestations of manic depression (the older term) in young people. The interest has mirrored, to some extent, the discovery of treatments, effective in adults, that are hoped to be effective in children. Such was the case in the late 1940s and early 1950s and is the case now.

In my clinical experience, people greet the diagnosis of bipolar disorder with widely varying responses. One is dread. The idea that a child could possibly have a lifetime disorder, dooming them to taking medication "for the rest of their lives," can be sobering. Another is relief. "Now that we know what is wrong, we can give the child a medication and s/he'll be fine!" Part of the current popularity of the diagnosis appears to be related to the "no fault" clause inherent in a genetic disorder where one doesn't have to feel blamed for the fact that a child has inherited whatever it is that causes bipolar disorder. For those inclined to feel guilty, of course, one feels guilt at having perpetuated the gene(s).

When the effectiveness of lithium for treating manic-depressive illness/bipolar disorder was understood 40 years ago, the mental health profession did its usual hammer and nail routine. (When your only tool is a hammer, everything looks like a nail.) While this medication revolutionized (and continues to revolutionize) many lives, it became clear that not everyone with episodes of mania and depression responded to acute lithium treatment. Antipsychotic medications were needed to help subdue the manic periods. Antidepressants sometimes helped depressive episodes, though sometimes at the cost of inciting another mania. Early experience with both lithium and antipsychotics in children with mania look-alikes did not encourage us to think that a magic bullet had been found for the condition in children, either.

The efforts to find and treat bipolar disorder uncovered the fact that a wide variety of problems could be subsumed under the umbrella of bipolar disorder, and interest has grown in finding other treatments for the condition. Those of us who treat young people have long been aware of the fact that any serious disorder that starts in childhood represents a special challenge and special opportunity. The disorder is usually more complicated to diagnose, more protracted when it occurs, and often more difficult to treat, but the opportunity to decrease and prevent long-term suffering is even greater than in adults. Thus, there is sometimes an enthusiasm to label and treat even though the knowledge base isn't as solid as we would like. We simply cannot put the child on ice until all the data are there to be sure. On the other hand, it is the wise consumer who understands the shortcomings of our knowledge base.

Dr. Birmaher's book is thorough, accurate, and enlightening. He brings to it a combination of many years of research and clinical treatment of children with mood disorders. The book is substantial because the subject matter is not easy to summarize. The diagnosis is not simply a check-off list of symptoms. The treatment isn't simply the administration of a drug. Although the disorder is largely genetic, families have the responsibility to treat it. And the flip side of a genetic disorder is that parents often have it as well, which additionally complicates treatment.

The final message of the book is a refrain that underlies virtually all medical conditions in the twenty-first century. The consumer must be informed enough to know what the issues are, what questions need to be asked, and what the limitations are to our knowledge base. And because one's clinician should be at least one step ahead of the consumer, Dr. Birmaher's book is a must-read not only for people who might have a child with bipolar disorder, it is also a must-read for the mental health professionals caring for such disorders.

Gabrielle A. Carlson, M.D.
Professor of Psychiatry and Pediatrics
Director, Child and Adolescent Psychiatry
State University of New York at Stony Brook

Acknowledgments

I WOULD LIKE TO THANK the many people who helped and supported me through this endeavor. My daughter, Vered, despite being very busy with her own studies, spent many hours reading this book, correcting my "Spanglish," reorganizing the chapters, posing inquisitive questions regarding the content of the book, and calling me daily to give me support. Without my daughter's assistance, I would never have been able to write this book. To my wife, Sara, I cannot fully express my gratitude to you for always supporting me and helping create an environment in which I could write this book in peace. Thank you for your company while I typed away frantically on the computer, for editing these chapters, for sending me to work with a home-cooked lunch, and for making sure I took care of myself, got enough rest, and got out once in a while. To my sons, Samuel and Shai, thanks for continuously showing me support and patience, as well as giving me very good editing advice. Samuel, the figures you made for this book look great!

Carol Kostek, thank you for typing these chapters, for reviewing them, and for making sure I still got other things done while writing this book. Without your help, this book would have taken years to be ready. Mary Kay Gill, R.N., it was wonderful to have you reading many of the chapters of this book. You gave me invaluable, sensible editing ideas. This book would not have been written if it were not for Nancy Rosenfeld. Writing a book about youth with bipolar disorder was your idea, and your persistence, enthusiasm, and editorial support got this project going and ensured its completion. Thanks, Nancy!

In addition, I would like to express my gratitude to Marlene Cully, M.Ed., for enriching the section about psychotherapy as well as other chapters of this book; Kim Poling, M.S.W., for revising the chapter about suicide; Kathy Kalas, R.N., and Kelly Monk, R.N., for checking the section on the management of side effects; and Maura Paczan, Ph.D., and Mary Margaret Kerr, Ph.D., for reviewing the tips for helping children who have bipolar disorder with academic problems. These coworkers gave me the crucial feedback of others who are also "in the trenches" working with children and teens with psychiatric problems. I would also like to thank Sonia Chehil, M.D., a last-year psychiatric resident from Halifax, Canada, who, while rotating at our bipolar clinic, wrote most of the sections on medications included in chapters 6 and 9; Steve Edwards, Ph.D., for thoroughly reviewing and allowing the use of the 4R's principles for chapter 10; Laurie Jones and Lisa Brown, who understand what parents go through when dealing with insurance companies and for using their experience and expertise to write a critical chapter regarding the management of health insurance issues for bipolar children; David Axelson, M.D., for sharing the arduous but gratifying daily work with bipolar youth; and David Brent, M.D., and David Koppen for their continuous support.

I would also like to thank my editors at Prima Publishing and Three Rivers Press, who believed in this project and fine-tuned my words: Marjorie Lery, Theresa Foy DiGeronimo, Laura Larson, and Orly Trieber.

Introduction

WHEN I WAS FIRST offered the opportunity to write this book, I hesitated, thinking, "Who needs another book about bipolar disorder?" However, the more I considered it, the more enthusiastic I became, eager to share with you over two decades of my clinical and research experience with children, adolescents, and adults with various psychiatric disorders, including bipolar disorder. This is my chance to summarize what we know, what we do not know, and the current controversies regarding bipolar disorder in children and teens from the perspective of a child psychiatrist who is in the "trenches," evaluating and treating youth with bipolar disorder as well as conducting leading research with this population.

My parents used to tell me that the best of all universities is life. Years of practice have taught me to simplify the diagnostic process and treatment of youth with psychiatric disorders and to become a partner with parents in the treatment of their children. I see myself as a "coach" and the parents as "coaching assistants," helping the child "play" through life. However, for parents to become partners, they need to be up-to-date on the clinical manifestations, outcome, consequences, and treatment of bipolar disorder. These are the main objectives of this book. I believe that I will have accomplished my goal if you read this book and, at the end, you are able to say, "I understand the controversies regarding the diagnosis and treatment of children with bipolar disorder, and I am better equipped to make knowledgeable decisions about the diagnosis and treatment of my child. This book is like a road map to guide me through the rough course of managing my child's bipolar disorder."

WHO WILL BENEFIT FROM THIS BOOK?

This book is written for you—the parents of a child who has been diagnosed with bipolar disorder or who has symptoms that make you wonder if he or she might have this complex psychological condition. By understanding the manifestations, causes, long-term outcome, and treatment of bipolar disorder in youth, you can become active partners in your child's treatment. You will want to understand what is happening in order to stay actively involved and help define a viable solution for your child.

Although this book is mainly written for parents, its simplicity and thoroughness will benefit highly motivated children and teens, grandparents and other relatives, mental health workers, psychiatric residents, psychologists, medical students, psychiatrists, teachers, and other people interested in learning about bipolar disorder in youth.

WHAT WILL YOU LEARN?

The primary goal of this book is to provide you with a summary of *what we know and what we do not know* about bipolar disorder in children and teens. The book is divided into four sections, each focusing on different aspects of bipolar disorder:

About Bipolar Disorder

The first two chapters describe the diagnosis of bipolar disorder in children and the differences among bipolar disorder, other psychiatric disorders, and normal mood and behaviors. Chapter 3 focuses on the course and outcome of bipolar disorder in youth, and chapter 4 reviews the causes of bipolar disorder.

Assessment and Treatment of Bipolar Disorder

Chapter 5 outlines the assessment process, including the information you should observe or obtain in preparation for the initial and subsequent appointments. Chapter 6 details the current biological treatment (medications and other types of treatments) and how to manage the side effects of the medications, while chapter 7 reviews psychosocial therapy (talking therapy and counseling). Chapter 8 focuses on integrating pharmacological and psychosocial therapies to treat acute symptoms and to prevent or at least diminish recurrences of bipolar disorder, and it emphasizes the importance of education and support for the treatment of children and teens with bipolar disorder. Chapter 9 explains the treatments of other psychiatric disorders that often accompany bipolar disorder. Chapter 10 describes the recognition and response to suicidal ideation and behaviors that often occur in youth.

Other Helpful Tips

Suggestions to manage your child's behavior problems at home and school and how to help your child with his or her academic problems can be found in chapters 11 and 12. Chapter 13 deals with handling your child's health insurance issues.

Appendices

In the appendices, you will learn about clinics that specialize in the assessment and treatment of bipolar youth and national organizations, Web sites, and books for parents, children, and clinicians regarding bipolar disorder and related issues. Current research studies and some references of published works about children and teens diagnosed with bipolar disorder are also listed. Finally, some questionnaires that may be useful in evaluating your child's mood, anxiety, and behavior problems are included.

It is my hope that the information provided in this book will help parents and other caretakers develop more realistic expectations regarding their child's disorder and treatment program to make educated decisions about the treatment of bipolar disorder in children and teenagers.

Note: Throughout this book, the words *"child"* and *"youth,"* unless otherwise indicated, imply both children and teens. All clinical cases presented in this book describe actual patients, but their identities have been changed to protect confidentiality.

CHAPTER 1

Does My Child Have Bipolar Disorder?

MARK IS A TEEN who has been experiencing severe mood swings, fluctuating between extreme sadness and extreme happiness, since early childhood. During periods of sadness, Mark is irritable and gets in frequent arguments with his parents and teachers. He has a hard time concentrating, feels tired, and spends much of his time sulking alone in his room. Often, during these episodes of depression, he feels so miserable that he considers committing suicide.

After several weeks of feeling very down, Mark suddenly, without any warning or apparent reason, becomes exaggeratedly happy for one to two weeks. During periods of an elevated or "high" mood, he becomes very talkative, impulsive, and so energetic that he needs to sleep only a couple hours a night to feel rested the next morning. He usually also feels invincible, to the point of putting himself in dangerous situations such as driving recklessly on the freeway. Like approximately 1 percent of the teenagers[1] in the United States (or about 400,000 teens), Mark is experiencing typical symptoms of *bipolar disorder*.[2,3]

Formerly known as *manic-depressive illness*, bipolar (*bi*, meaning "two") indicates that mood cycles or swings between two opposite poles: mania and depression. A child's mood is like a roller coaster with unpredictable ups and downs or highs and lows. As an analogy, when a child is in the "north pole," she or he experiences an episode of mania or "high" mood and, in the "south pole," an episode of depression or "low" mood.

Formerly known as manic-depressive illness, bipolar (bi, meaning "two") indicates that mood cycles or swings between two opposite poles: mania and depression.

Bipolar disorder is a lifelong illness that affects approximately 1 percent of the world's adult population of all sexes, ethnic backgrounds, and economic levels.[1-5] It is most interesting that up to 60 percent of adults with bipolar disorder report experiencing symptoms of the disorder as children. For example, they remember having had long periods of being extremely quiet or isolative, with poor concentration and low motivation. Other times they felt excessively active, outgoing, talkative, and even bossy or very silly. Still, until recently, many professionals did not believe that young people could have bipolar disorder.

Children and teens with bipolar disorder have been frequently misdiagnosed with other psychiatric conditions, such as attention deficit hyperactivity disorder (ADHD) or behavior problems, or parents were blamed for their children's misbehaviors. However, thanks to the recent interest and research in bipolar disorder in youth, it is now clear that this disorder can affect a person at any age.

The Cost of Bipolar Disorder

Bipolar disorder is very costly to the individual, the family, and society in general. It is ranked among the ten most disabling conditions in the world, but up to 40 percent of adults with bipolar disorder and an even higher percentage of youth go untreated. Moreover, it typically takes approximately 8 to 10 years after the first signs of bipolar disorder to receive the appropriate diagnosis and treatment.[2,3]

Recent media attention has helped parents and professionals become more knowledgeable about the problem of children and teens with bipolar disorder, but it also has created some alarming misconceptions regarding symptoms and treatment of childhood bipolar disorder. Parents of children with severe behavior and mood problems are bringing their sons and daughters in for evaluation, but at our clinic we are finding that only around 50 percent of all children and teens referred for assessment actually have the disorder. The remainder of the children have other psychiatric disorders that mimic bipolar, such as ADHD, anxiety disorders, oppositional defiant, conduct disorders, or Asperger's disorder (mild autism). (These will be discussed further in chapter 2.)

Separating the diagnosis of bipolar disorder from these other similar disorders is critical. Unfortunately, laboratory tests and/or specific brain exams for diagnosing bipolar disorder do not yet exist. We can rely only on direct observation of a child's behavior and moods during clinic visits. But observations during an appointment are limited by time and by the fact that children usually do not show their symptoms in the office unless their disorder is severe.

If your child is misdiagnosed with bipolar disorder, he or she will be treated with medication specific for bipolar management, which will, as expected, fail to help and will expose your child to unnecessary medication side effects. Conversely, if your child has bipolar disorder and is not correctly diagnosed, he or she will be treated with inappropriate medications and may suffer needlessly for many years. Therefore, it is crucial that you are aware of and understand the symptoms and subtypes of bipolar disorder discussed in this chapter and become familiar with the controversies regarding its diagnosis. With this information in hand, you can better work closely with your child's clinicians to accurately assess your child's symptoms. If untreated or inadequately treated, bipolar disorder can affect the normal cognitive thinking and the emotional and social development of a child, increasing the risk for suicide, legal problems, and abuse of illegal drugs.

Before discussing the symptoms of bipolar disorder in children and teens, it is important that you understand the fact that the severity of symptoms may vary greatly from child to child. The situation is similar

The Meaning of *Clinician*
The word *clinician*, unless otherwise specified, includes child psychiatrists, psychologists, and other mental health-care workers.

to a case of the flu. If your child has mild flu symptoms with no fever, he or she can still run around and enjoy normal activity. On the other hand, a severe case with fever, muscular pain, and chills will keep your child in bed. The same range of symptoms is found in bipolar disorder; they can be mild, moderate, or severe. The decision for treatment depends mainly on whether the symptoms affect the child's normal development and functioning at home, at school, and with his or her friends.

Although we know that bipolar disorder exists in children and teens, there is controversy regarding the way the symptoms appear in youth. Several studies are ongoing to clarify these diagnostic issues. Until further research is completed, many researchers and clinicians believe that the symptoms of bipolar disorder in young people may be divided into the groups and subgroups described in this chapter and summarized in the sidebar, "Bipolar Disorder Symptoms in Children and Adolescents."

Bipolar Disorder Symptoms in Children and Adolescents

The following is a general summary of ways that the symptoms of bipolar disorder may appear in children and adolescents:[3,7]

- **Typical.** Children with typical periods of mania, hypomania, depression, mixed (mania and depression), and rapid cycles (rapid cycles of mania and depression).
- **Typical, short duration.** Children with typical bipolar symptoms, but the symptoms only occur for short periods of time.
- **Severe mood lability.** Children without typical symptoms, but with severe mood lability, irritability, mood swings, temper tantrums, impulsivity, and hyperactivity.

TYPICAL OR CLASSICAL SYMPTOMS OF BIPOLAR DISORDER

The typical or classical bipolar disorder is manifested by repeated episodes of *mania*, *hypomania*, *depression*, or *subtypes* that include *mixed episodes* and *rapid cycling*. Look carefully at the descriptions of each of these symptoms that follow to help you determine if your child's symptoms fall in this "typical" category.

Symptoms of Mania

According to the American Psychiatric Association's *Diagnostic and Statistical Manual of Mental Disorders,* fourth edition *(DSM-IV)*, mania is indicated by the following symptoms:

⊙ *Persistent* elevated, expansive, euphoric, or irritable mood for at least 1 week and at least three (four if the mood is irritable) of the following symptoms:

- Inflated self-esteem or grandiosity
- Decreased need for sleep
- ⊙ Talkativeness
- ⊙ Racing thoughts
- Distractibility
- ⊙ Increased activity or <u>agitation</u>
- Daring behaviors

⊙ These symptoms are impairing the child's academic, social, or family functioning.

- These symptoms are *not* due to other psychiatric and medical conditions.[1]

Episodes of Mania

Symptoms of mania include persistent elevated, expansive, euphoric, or irritable mood for at least one week and at least three (or four if the mood is irritable) of these symptoms: (1) inflated self-esteem or grandiosity, (2) decreased need for sleep, (3) talkativeness, (4) racing thoughts, (5) distractibility, (6) increased activity or agitation, and (7) daring behaviors. *These symptoms are severe enough to impair the child's academic, social or family functioning.*[1] (The symptoms of mania are summarized in the sidebar, "Symptoms of Mania.")

Episodes of mania, which are distinguished by high energy levels, will affect your child's mood (feelings), cognition (thinking), behavior, and some biological functions (sleep, appetite, sexual drive) and impair his or her functioning and normal development.

Mania: Mood

During periods of mania, your child's mood will be elevated or very irritable. He or she can become very silly, goofy, bold, and overly happy. Of course, it is normal for children and teens to be silly or happy at times. Everyone gets excited when hearing good news, receiving an award, going to a party, departing on vacation, or sharing a special event with a group of friends. However, in the case of mania, *the elevated mood or excitement is above and beyond what is expected for the child's age and out of proportion to whatever is happening.*

Extreme happiness or elevated mood is called *euphoria* or *elation*. Euphoria is very noticeable, even by the child's companions. A friend of a euphoric child may ask whether she or he is on drugs. While euphoric, children may also feel on top of the world, with high self-esteem and overconfidence. They may think that nothing bad can happen to them, that they are better than others, and often they appear very bossy. These children may persistently

> *E*pisodes of mania, which are distinguished by high energy levels, will affect your child's mood (feelings), cognition (thinking), behavior, and some biological functions (sleep, appetite, sexual drive) and impair his or her functioning and normal development.

laugh in class or become very humorous at inappropriate times. Initially, their laughter may seem amusing to others, but after a while this behavior becomes annoying. The euphoric child is out of control and cannot stop talking, laughing, or acting out.

During a manic episode, *irritability and short temper* are also symptomatic, particularly when the child feels misunderstood (if he or she is interrupted or feels frustrated). In these cases, your child can become verbally or physically aggressive and exhibit severe temper tantrums.

Ten-year-old Larry is a child who has manic episodes. He begins laughing for no apparent reason, making jokes at inappropriate times during school, and is constantly joking with family and friends. Larry frequently talks about feeling "supergreat." He "gets into people's faces" and is constantly interrupting. When asked to be quiet, he becomes irritable, swears, and oftentimes gets into fistfights.

Another example of childhood mania is found in the case of Rachel, a 12-year-old. When she becomes euphoric, she gets very silly. Although she is naturally outgoing, she laughs without control and makes sexual jokes during class. At the mall with her friends, she gets even more excitable, making inappropriate noises and talking very loudly. Her girlfriends were the first to notice these changes in her mood because Rachel was not able to control herself whenever they would ask her to be quiet.

Mania: Cognition (Thinking)

Since the high-energy state produced by a manic episode affects all psychological functions, the mind works or runs very fast. So many thoughts may simultaneously pop into your child's mind that he or she becomes unable to think or express ideas clearly. Manic children jump from one topic to another, symptomatically known as having a more than passing *"flight of ideas."* Topics may be connected, but seldom do they have any relationship.

During periods of mania, it is impossible for your child to carry through with any train of thought because he or she is so easily distracted. A manic child may change subjects quickly or have ideas that are unrealistic and/or unfeasible. Or, perhaps, the manic episode may be so intense that the child's ideas become disorganized.

For example, when 16-year-old Mary talked about her vacations, she answered too quickly and without finishing her sentences: "I went swimming. The waves were . . . I love the . . . It was lovely to dance at the nightclub, but the airport so . . . The music was cool." At first, although she was talking quickly and in fragments, all the issues were related to her vacation. However, as the mania got worse, she switched to talking about school and the weather just a few seconds later, then a television program, the physician's tie, and her relationship with her boyfriend.

During periods of mania or hypomania, children can also be very creative, inventing something new, creating poetry, a painting, or a song. As discussed further in chapter 3, many people with bipolar disorder are known to be great artists and inventors. For example, when Suzanne, age 13, begins to have manic symptoms, she can accomplish all her weekly homework in the space of a few days. She writes beautiful poems and paints excellent pictures. Similarly, John can build great cars and airplane models when he is mildly manic. Unfortunately, when the symptoms of mania or hypomania get worse, the child's functioning deteriorates. For example, when Suzanne becomes more manic, it is impossible for her to concentrate more than a few minutes at any given time. Her writing then becomes disorganized and illegible, and she makes no sense. John's creativity, too, is affected by worsening symptoms; then he puts the pieces together incorrectly and eventually destroys or abandons the model altogether.

> *During periods of mania or hypomania, children can also be very creative, inventing something new, creating poetry, a painting, or a song.*

While manic, children and teens usually have poor judgment. This lack of judgment, coupled with their impulsivity, can have disastrous consequences. They may do things that are out of character and may even end up breaking the law. Some become involved in robberies, vandalism, or poor business enterprises. Others become irresponsible in handling money. This symptom is illustrated by the following cases: Harry's relatives gave him a total of $200 for his middle school graduation; he spent it all in just 30 minutes buying candy. Jamal, a 16-year-old boy, stole two cars and wrecked them without ever thinking about the consequences of his acts. Seventeen-year-old Maria had been saving her money for years; she spent all her savings on different types of musical instruments that she could not play. Sixteen-year-old Allen purchased six pairs of designer shoes, not all of which were his size.

During a manic period, your child may have increased self-esteem and unrealistic beliefs in his or her abilities to the point of feeling invincible. These children may dare to do things they would not normally consider. They usually feel that nothing bad will happen to them. They may cross the street without watching for cars, jump off the balcony of an apartment building, drive their car at record speeds, or do dangerous stunts on their skateboards or bicycles. Sam, for example, was feeling very "high" and confident in class. He did not like how his teacher was explaining gravity. He stood up and began to "explain" Einstein's theories to his friends. Another student, Mike, went to talk with the school principal about firing the science teacher when that teacher interrupted him in class. Kathy's impulsivity and lack of judgment led her to spend her last dime on an airplane ticket to Paris and then return later the same day when she decided the weather in Paris was "too cold."

In severe cases, children and teens may become *delusional* (holding false beliefs or ideas that are not shared by their relatives or community and that are very difficult or impossible to change even with reasoning). In some cases, we classify these children as having a *manic episode with psychotic features*. The most common delusions during the manic period are *grandiose delusions* or *ideations* (an exaggerated or unrealistic belief that the person is very important, has special powers, or is on a particular mission) or *paranoid ideations*. For example, while Pedro, a 15-year old boy, was in a manic phase, he developed grandiose ideations and thought he was the Messiah. He misinterpreted other people's remarks and the way that people looked at him. Pedro thought people were looking up at him with awe because they "knew" he was the Messiah. Pedro would say, "Everyone's looking at me because they know I am their salvation. Don't you see that guy nodding his head? Of course you do! He's approving of what I am saying to you." When people looked at him, Pedro grew more suspicious and thought that they were after him. He could not sleep at night because he set his alarm clock to sound every thirty minutes to alert him to check the sky "for a divine sign" or to check if people were waiting outside to see him.

Mania with psychotic features can also be diagnosed when a child is experiencing *hallucinations*. The child can see, hear, and, at times, smell or feel things that other people do not experience. Nora "heard" the voice of an old woman day and night telling her that she would be the most important person in the world. Sixteen-year-old Josh "heard" and "saw" a man who told him that he could take as many objects from a retail store as he wanted because he was the owner.

Delusions Versus Normal Fears

It is important to differentiate between delusions and normal fears and normal fantasies or imagination, particularly in young children.

Mania: Behavior

The high level of energy experienced during an episode of mania increases a child's activity level. Your child may be very agitated and unable to sit still, pacing or running about. During a manic state, John cannot sit quietly for a minute; he cannot go to school, church, or restaurants because he runs, touches everything, and disrupts others. Dave keeps jumping in his bed until 2 or 3 A.M. and sings for hours. Allison never seems tired; she is very active, keeps phoning her friends late at night, and repeatedly cleans her parents' house to keep herself busy. When Allen gets manic, he spends hours cleaning his room and then he cleans the kitchen, the garage, and his parents' bedroom. During manic episodes, children can also become very talkative and get into trouble because they cannot stop talking at school or in other places where proper decorum is indicated, such as houses of worship.

Mania: Biological Functions

During a manic episode, the energy level is so high that your child's *need for sleep is sharply decreased*. When Ed, age 9, is in a manic episode, he needs only 1 to 2 hours sleep per night. He plays video and computer games, takes showers late at night, and phones his friends at 2 A.M. When he gets up the next day, he claims not to be tired at all. He runs around, talks fast, and has many ideas about how his favorite football team should play.

During an episode of mania, appetite can increase or diminish, but sometimes the child becomes so hyperactive that he or she does not seem to have the time to sit and eat. Children and teens are also prone to *hypersexuality* without any prior history of sexual abuse or exposure to X-rated movies. While 16-year-old Cori was in a manic episode, she had unsafe sex with multiple partners, some of whom were peers at school and others people she did not even know. Mary behaved similarly and knew that her behavior was wrong, but she had no control over herself. When her manic phase was over, Mary experienced profound guilt and shame. She became suicidal and dropped out of school.

Another example is John, a 14-year-old who began to make persistent sexual remarks to his sister and sometimes touched her buttocks and breasts. Ed frequently "humps" other people's legs during a manic period as if he were a dog. Another 15-year-old boy masturbates at home in the family room, even in the company of his parents. Sometimes when manic, he touches his mother and sisters inappropriately. After the manic episode subsides, these boys all feel ashamed of their behavior.

Episodes of Hypomania

Hypomania has symptoms similar to the ones described for mania, but they are less intense. Hypomania affects your child's functioning less extensively than a manic episode. In fact, sometimes hypomanic symptoms may even improve his or her ability to function because the hypomanic individual is better able to concentrate, often works harder, and is more creative, more outgoing, and social.

For example, when Helene is hypomanic, she is humorous and gregarious, functions on little sleep, and performs at a high level at school. Normally shy, when hypomanic she is extroverted and enjoys being the center of attention. At this time she also is her most creative and energetic. Her friends see the change and question her about her use of drugs. In class, she sometimes babbles incessantly, laughs too much, and gets in trouble, but she is still functioning and does not have to be removed from the classroom.

> *In contrast with mania, major depression is manifested by low energy levels that permeate your child's mood (feelings), cognition (thinking), behaviors, and biological functions (sleep, appetite, and sexual drive).*

Episodes of Major Depression

In contrast with mania, major depression is manifested by *low* energy levels that permeate your child's mood (feelings), cognition (thinking), behaviors, and biological functions (sleep, appetite, and sexual drive). (The symptoms of major depression are summarized in the sidebar, "Symptoms of Major Depression.")

Depression: Mood

During phases of depression, bipolar children are *sad and/or very irritable*. They do not enjoy activities that they usually like (or enjoy much less), such as dancing, playing sports, and reading. They may not complain about being sad, but they may be whiny, tearful, and constantly complaining about being bored. The motivation to do things, in particular those things that require some effort or sustained attention (such as homework), is diminished or absent. For example, Ryan, a 10-year-old, denies being depressed but does not enjoy activities that he once loved and becomes easily bored. He has a very low tolerance for frustration and has severe recurrent temper outbursts. These tantrums usually are triggered by minor problems but can also occur without an apparent reason. During the depression phase, your child may experience high levels of anxiety or an exacerbation of prior anxiety problems, such as difficulty separating from parents, extreme shyness, and episodes of acute anxiety or panic attacks (sudden palpitations, shortness of breath, pressure in the chest, abdominal pain, headaches, and tremor). In addition, your child may experience exaggerated feelings of guilt for minor faults.

Symptoms of Major Depression

The *DSM-IV* states that major depression is characterized (or manifested) in the following symptoms:

- At least five of the following symptoms have occurred during the same time for a period of at least 2 weeks. One of the symptoms needs to be either (1) depression or irritability or (2) lack of enjoyment, interest, or pleasure.
  - Depressed or irritable mood *most of the time*
  - Diminished or lack of enjoyment, interest, or pleasure
  - Insomnia or too much sleep (hypersomnia)
  - Lack or increased appetite nearly everyday; change in weight
  - Slow movements/speech or agitation
  - Poor concentration, diminished ability to think, indecisiveness
  - Lack of energy or tiredness
  - Feelings of worthlessness or exaggerated feelings of guilt
  - Death wishes, suicidal thoughts or behaviors
- The symptoms are most of the day and nearly every day.
- These symptoms need to cause impairment in the child's social, family, and/or academic functioning.
- These symptoms are *not* due to other psychiatric and medical conditions.[1]

Jessica is an excellent and well-behaved student in a private school. When she is depressed, she feels she is wasting her parents' money because she's a "bad" student who "misbehaves." When 12-year-old Kathy was very depressed, she believed that her depression was a punishment from God because she had "bad thoughts." She burned her hands because she once touched a boy and felt so guilty.

Depression: Cognition

Depression often affects the way a child thinks. Your child's mind may seem to be working in slow motion. It is hard to be creative or do any task that requires concentration. *Thoughts are colored by the depressed mood*, and he or she often feels hopeless, negative, and pessimistic about life. During the depressive period of bipolar disorder, children may have negative thoughts about themselves, their past, present, and future and lose trust in their ability to perform. They may think that they are not good for anything and must have somehow failed. Conversely, positive qualities may be denied, and the negative aspects of their personality or body may become exaggerated (e.g., "I am too ugly, obese, annoying").

Seasonal Depression

The symptoms of depression sometimes appear mainly during the fall, winter, or beginning of spring. These depressions are called *seasonal depressions* and may respond to specific treatment, such as light therapy (as explained in chapter 6).

A child may even become so hopeless that he or she lacks any motivation to live and becomes suicidal. In severe cases, the child may even attempt suicide. (See chapters 3 and 10 for more information about suicide.) Children may exhibit self-injurious behaviors, such as cutting and scratching themselves, and also aggressive ideations (hurting others, homicidal thoughts). Such thoughts and actions may or may not be carried out.

Melissa, a 13-year-old, first displayed symptoms of bipolar disorder at age 8. Her manic symptoms are now well controlled with medication, but her periods of depression continue. During these periods she cannot concentrate, her motivation is poor, and her school grades drop dramatically. Filled with hopelessness, she loses all will to live. On multiple occasions she has tried to cut her wrists. Suzanne's parents found her searching for her father's gun so she could kill herself. Even young children can experience suicidal thoughts and attempt to carry them out. A 6-year-old depressed boy tried to commit suicide several times by holding his breath and submerging his head in a bathtub filled with water. An 8-year-old boy wanted to die and stopped eating and drinking for "2 days and 2 nights." Despite seriously wanting to die, fortunately these two young children could not find an efficacious method to commit suicide due to their immature cognitive level. Nevertheless, these suicide attempts should be taken seriously.

Children suffering depression may have multiple *somatic complaints*, such as stomachaches and headaches. They don't fib about these pains; they really feel them. Parents usually take these children to visit their pediatricians, but the child's doctor frequently finds nothing physically wrong.

On other occasions, especially during a severe depressive episode, children may experience *delusions* (false beliefs) and/or *hallucinations*. They may actually believe that they committed a sin or that everybody is out to get them because they are so bad. They may "hear" voices telling them how bad they are or to hurt themselves or others. For example, Janiki, during a depressive episode at age 11, frequently thought that she saw the devil. The devil told her that she was a "bad" girl and deserved to be punished. She was very afraid and avoided sleeping or staying alone in her room. She refused to go to school because her parents would not be there to protect her. When her depression lifted, the hallucinations disappeared, and Janiki returned to normal life. Another child, Ed, when he is depressed, hears a voice telling him that he is annoying and that he should die.

Depression: Behavior

During the depressive phase of bipolar disorder, your child may become tired, quiet, and slow and, in severe cases, prefer to stay in bed. Mike, a 16-year-old with bipolar disorder, became very depressed after a severe episode of mania. He felt tired and slow and remained in bed

*E*specially during a
severe depressive
episode, children may
experience delusions
(false beliefs) and/or
hallucinations.

most of the day for 2 weeks. He refused to go to school or talk to his friends. The depressed child can isolate from friends, withdraw from activities, stop taking care of her or his hygiene, talk slowly or refuse to talk at all, and sometimes be verbally or physically aggressive. When 17-year-old Martha enters one of her depressive periods, she won't pick up the telephone when it rings, refuses all outings with friends, and won't eat in the same room with her family. She spends most of the time alone in her bedroom. She does not turn on the light, does not comb her hair or brush her teeth, and rarely bathes. When her parents attempt to intervene, Martha acts out inappropriately by becoming very aggressive. She screams, swears, and breaks things.

Sometimes, depressed children become overly agitated; they pace the floor and are unable to sit still. When 16-year-old Therese gets depressed, she paces around, unable to lie down in bed or sit still at school. If her depression is severe, she screams and in some occasions gets violent, requiring hospitalization.

Depression: Biological Functions

During an attack of depression, bodily functions such as sleep patterns, appetite, and sexual drive can be altered.

When your child suffers the symptom of depression he or she may experience *insomnia*: having problems falling asleep, waking up several times during the night, or waking up very early in the morning. The sleep schedule may also change; your child may become a "night owl" and sleep during the day. (Such changes in sleep patterns are sometimes difficult to diagnose because teens in general do not have regular sleeping habits.) While depressed, some children can experience *hyper-somnia*, or seeking too much sleep during the day or night instead of less sleep. One 14-year-old girl became so depressed that she slept 12 to 14 hours a day for two consecutive weeks. In contrast, another child, Ashley, went to bed at 11 P.M., could not fall asleep until one the next morning, and woke spontaneously at 5 A.M. She tried to fall asleep again, but without success.

Appetite can also decrease or increase during periods of depression. John lost 10 pounds in 6 weeks while depressed. In contrast, when Sheri was depressed she gained 15 pounds in 7 weeks because she stuffed herself with candy and ice cream. Some children also crave carbohydrates.

Sexual desire (or sexual enjoyment) usually decreases during depression. This can add to the feeling of inadequacy and poor self-esteem found in people with depression.

SUBTYPES OF BIPOLAR DISORDER

The symptoms of mania, hypomania, and depression may appear in different combinations. For example, a child may have a period of mania followed by a depression, hypomania followed by a depression, or mania and depression at the same time (called *mixed episodes*). Or, a child may have very frequent episodes of mania and depression (called *rapid cycling*). This chapter section (summarized in the sidebar, "Subtypes of Typical Bipolar Disorder") will explain several subtypes of classical bipolar disorder, characterized by the intensity, quality, and duration of the manic and depressive symptoms. This information is important for you to know since you will hear mental health professionals discussing these subtypes of bipolar disorder and the differences in treatment. For example, we know that it is more difficult to treat mixed or rapid cycling episodes and that these subtypes may respond better to certain types of mood stabilizing medications than to others.

Bipolar I Disorder

Bipolar I is manifested by typical periods of mania and major depression (see figure 1.1). But the frequency and intensity of the periods of mania and depression vary among people and are difficult to track. For example, a child may have a period of depression followed by an episode of mania, or depression followed by a long period of normal mood and then mania, or several periods of depression and rarely mania, or several manic episodes followed by a long period of normal mood, or many other combinations.

Subtypes of Typical Bipolar Disorder[2]

- **Bipolar I:** periods of mania and major depression
- **Bipolar II:** periods of hypomania and major depression
- **Bipolar mixed:** simultaneous symptoms of mania and depression
- **Bipolar rapid cycling:** many periods of mania and depression per year (according to the American Psychiatric Association, at least four bipolar episodes per year)
- **Bipolar with psychotic features:** mood symptoms together with hallucinations or delusions (false beliefs)
- **Cyclothymic disorder:** periods of hypomania and mild depression

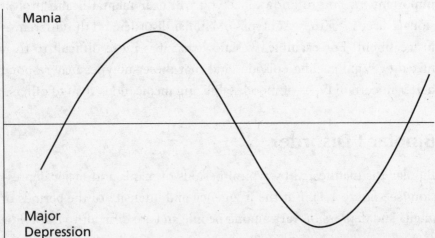

Figure 1.1—Bipolar I Disorder

Mania

Major
Depression

Tanisha, a 12-year-old girl who was referred to our clinic for assessment of her mood swings, wrote the following letter to describe her problems: "There are days that I feel very tired. I am a couch potato and lay down most of the day like a beanie baby. I feel very lonely. I want to be hugged but when my parents come around me, I become an alligator and bite them. It is strange that I want to be cuddled, but then I get mad easily at them. There are days that I am the opposite. I feel like a butterfly. I fly all around, talk too much, laugh and get in trouble at school because I cannot sit still and I bother my friends." Tanisha was describing symptoms of depression (low energy, tiredness, isolation, irritability) and periods of mania (elevated mood, high energy, talkativeness). When she was successfully treated with medication to stabilize her mood, the "beanie baby/alligator and butterfly periods" disappeared.

George is a 15-year-old boy who began to experience periods of depression, severe irritability, and temper tantrums at the age of 7. Such periods occurred every 7 to 8 months and affected his relationships with family, friends, and teachers. His academic performance was also affected. At age 12, he had serious thoughts of shooting himself with his mother's gun and needed to be hospitalized. He was very quiet during his hospital stay. Feelings of hopelessness, sleeping disorders, and the inability to concentrate for long periods of time isolated George from other patients. However, he responded well to antidepressant therapy and 4 weeks later was released from the hospital. Within 6 months, George began to feel depressed again but this time manifested symptoms of mania. Agitation caused rapid speech patterns and grandiose thoughts. He felt invincible. He began to partake in minor thievery, stealing small items from the local supermarket. He also felt superior to his friends. When he was down to only 3 hours of sleep per night, he was readmitted to the hospital and treated with lithium. Although he responded well to lithium, he stopped the medication 6 months later and suffered another manic episode. George has typical symptoms of bipolar I, but it is important to note that the symptoms of your child may vary in severity and duration.

Bipolar II Disorder

Bipolar II is characterized by periods of major depression and episodes of hypomania (see figure 1.2). Remember, the symptoms of hypomania are similar to the ones described for mania but are less intense. In the case of Helene, her hypomanic periods usually last 4 to 5 days and occur every other month. The rest of the time, Helene's mood is stable, but once or twice a year, particularly during the winter when daylight is short, she develops major depression. She feels very sad, cries often, eats without any self-control, and sleeps many hours.

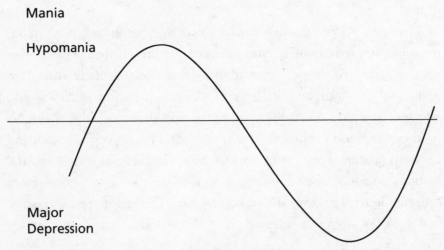

Figure 1.2—Bipolar II Disorder

Mania

Hypomania

Major
Depression

It is common to feel great while hypomanic and refuse treatment, but hypomanic episodes should not be ignored because they can lead to full-blown mania. In adults, about 20 percent of patients with hypomania eventually develop mania.[3,4] While it appears that young people go from hypomania to mania more readily, such speculation cannot be confirmed until additional studies are completed. Following any hypomanic episode is the risk of becoming depressed.

A child may have any combination or frequency of hypomanic and depressive episodes. For example, children and teens may have two hypomanic episodes in a row, then a prolonged time of normal mood, followed by a depressive episode. Another person may have more frequent hypomanic periods and depressions. The duration and severity of the episodes also varies greatly among different children.

> *It is common to feel great while hypomanic and refuse treatment, but hypomanic episodes should not be ignored because they can lead to full-blown mania.*

Bipolar Disorder—Mixed Type

Bipolar mixed type is manifested by a mixture of depressive and manic symptoms (see figure 1.3). The person experiences manic symptoms and at the same time can feel miserable, confused, anxious, and suicidal. During such mixed episodes, Liz looked happy and agitated and sometimes laughed excessively. However, her depression was internal, and she had suicidal thoughts and felt confused. This subtype of bipolar disorder frequently occurs in children and teens. Unfortunately, mixed episodes are difficult to treat (as explained in chapter 8).

Figure 1.3—Bipolar Disorder—Mixed

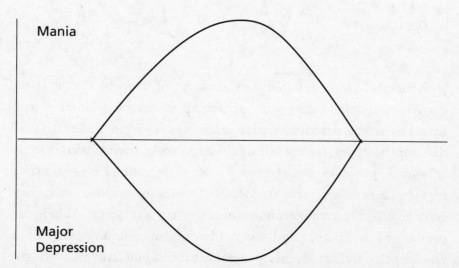

Bipolar Disorder—Rapid Cycling Type

Children and teens with rapid cycling go through many cycles of depression or mania throughout the year (see figure 1.4). According to the American Psychiatric Association,[2] to be classified as a rapid cycler, a person needs to have at least four episodes of depression or mania in the span of 1 year, but children and teens seem to cycle more often within the same 1-year time frame.[3,6,7] Similar to the mixed subtype, it is difficult to diagnose, treat, and prevent this subtype of bipolar disorder.

Figure 1.4—Bipolar Disorder—Rapid Cycling

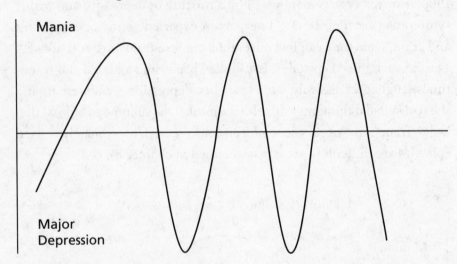

Kenneth is an 8-year-old with episodes of depression that last 7 days, speedily alternating with periods of mania for another 4 to 6 days. His parents describe these mood swings as a rapid "roller coaster" that constantly interfere with his ability to make friends and to study at school. He does not have any friends because during a manic episode he becomes very "intense" (talkative, hyperactive, and over-controlling). He cannot follow the rules for any game. When depressed, he is irritable and feisty. He does not attend school on a regular basis, and his parents are unable to send him away to overnight camp with other boys and girls. Neither can they take him to religious services or restaurants because he misbehaves and becomes disrespectful.

Another child, Steven, has rapid mood cycles every 24 hours. During these periods, he exhibits rapid speech and thoughts, fidgetiness, high activity, and mild silliness. He has brief (but frightening) temper explosions, and the smallest problems send him into fits of crying spells. After these periods, his mood returns to normal, or he has "meltdowns" triggered by minor frustrations such as being unable to perform a skateboard stunt or to find the game he wants to play. Following treatment with mood stabilizers, Steven stopped cycling multiple times within a 24-hour period but continued to experience depression or mild mania two to three times each year. Kenneth and Steven have typical symptoms of children with rapid cycling, but the frequency of the cycles and the intensity of the symptoms may change from child to child. Therefore, it is important to carefully observe your child's symptoms because the cycles can be so rapid that they can be easily missed.

Bipolar Disorder with Psychotic Features

Some children and teens may experience psychotic symptoms such as hallucinations (voices that nobody else can hear) or delusions (unreal thoughts such as "people are out to get me") while they are in a depressed or manic state. When depressed, Danielle becomes extremely anxious, cannot be alone, cannot eat, and becomes constipated. She believes that she's a sinner and sees and hears the devil telling her that she is bad. Conversely, when she is manic, she dances around the room, feels most energetic, wants to save the world, and "sees and hears" her deceased great-grandmother telling her how important she is.

The experience of psychosis is very frightening for any person, particularly children. Fortunately, most youth with bipolar disorder do not experience these symptoms.

Cyclothymic Disorder

This type of bipolar disorder is characterized by periods of hypomania and mild symptoms of major depression (see figure 1.5). To diagnose this condition, children and teens need to have experienced the symptoms for a minimum of 1 year, and symptoms cannot be accounted for by another psychiatric disorder or medical condition. Although symptoms are mild, they may still interfere with the child's functioning.

Figure 1.5—Cyclothymic Disorder

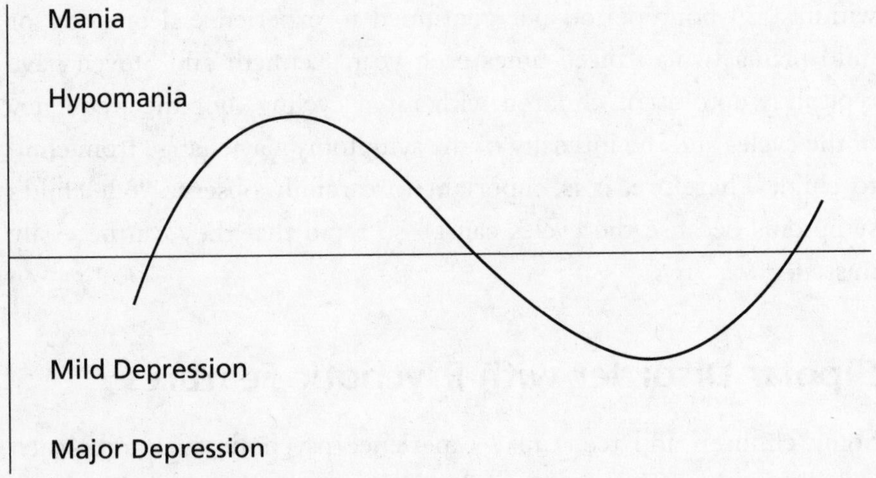

Francine has periodic episodes during which she feels down, lazy, and mildly irritable; has low frustration tolerance; and lacks the motivation to socialize with friends. She performs well at school but must force herself to study. Periods of mild depression alternate with periods of great energy when she feels active, outgoing, and social. Her self-esteem is then elevated, and she needs a minimum of 5 to 6 hours of sleep per night. While hypomanic, Francine is more productive at school and can quickly finish assignments. It's interesting to note that a hypomanic state can sometimes be beneficial, allowing a child to function at a higher than normal level.

Symptoms of Bipolar Disorder in Young Children

As figure 1.6 illustrates, the subtypes of rapid cyclic, mixed, and the presence of psychotic symptoms appear to be very common in children. This figure shows a study of the occurrence of these symptoms in children younger than 12 years.[6]

Figure 1.6—Symptoms of Bipolar Disorder in Young Children

Legend:
- Mixed Mania
- Rapid Cycling
- Psychosis
- Suicidal (plan and intent)

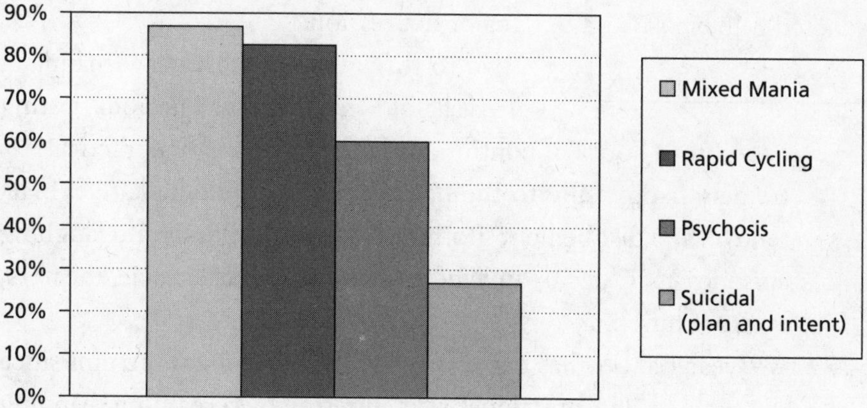

Source: Geller and colleagues, 2000[5]

CHILDREN WITH SHORT-DURATION TYPICAL SYMPTOMS

This category includes children and teens with classic symptoms of bipolar disorder who do not fit exactly into the standard classification criteria currently accepted by the American Psychiatric Association[2] for diagnosis. Instead, because their classic symptoms of mania, hypomania, depression, or subtypes do not last for the duration required in

Bipolar NOS

Children with bipolar symptoms who do not fulfill the criteria for bipolar I or II disorder, because of the short duration of symptoms, receive the diagnosis of *bipolar NOS* (not otherwise specified). It is important for parents to be aware of this diagnosis since many children and teens are currently diagnosed with bipolar NOS.

order to be classified as bipolar I, II, or any of the subtypes of bipolar disorder, they usually are classified with *bipolar disorder not otherwise specified (NOS)*.

Here are a few examples of how bipolar NOS shows itself in children.

- A 14-year-old boy had clear symptoms of mania, but the symptoms appeared for only 3 days and occurred just once each month.
- A girl, age 13, has frequent bouts of hypomania but never exhibits symptoms of major depression.
- Two to three times each week Amanda, a 14-year-old girl, exhibits periods lasting only 2 to 4 hours of continuous laughter and is hyperactive, extremely happy, silly to the point of being giddy, talkative, inattentive, and disobedient. Both her temper outbursts and laughing episodes may occur anywhere—supermarkets, movie theaters, even at church.
- A 9-year-old boy has had severe recurrent temper tantrums since the age of 2. His tantrums are manifested by screaming, banging his head against the wall, kicking, destroying objects, and biting anyone within close range. Such temper tantrums are triggered by minor frustrations and can last from 30 minutes up to 6 hours per day. These temper outbursts are intermingled with periods where he is exceptionally giggly and funny or sad for a few hours.

Children with bipolar disorder NOS have as many problems as children with other types of bipolar disorders. However, child psychiatrists disagree about how to diagnose this subtype of bipolar disorder. Ongoing studies across the country will help clarify this diagnosis and its treatment in the future.

CHILDREN WITH SEVERE MOOD LABILITY

Children with severe mood lability show symptoms of·extreme irritability, mood swings, temper tantrums, impulsivity, and hyperactivity. Most of the children currently consulting bipolar clinics for assessment of bipolar disorder belong to the severe mood group. *However, professionals cannot agree as to whether these children have bipolar disorder or another disorder that closely mimics bipolar.*[3,7] My own experience indicates that while some children referred to our clinic for severe mood lability have bipolar disorder, others have nonbipolar psychiatric disorders such as oppositional, anxiety, recurrent depression (without mania or hypomania), attention deficit hyperactivity, and Asperger's (mild autism) disorders. For example, an 11-year-old girl consulted our clinic due to severe temper outbursts and rage attacks. Her mood was very labile, and her frustration tolerance was low. Sometimes she became depressed, even hopeless, and experienced suicidal tendencies, particularly when she was frustrated or got into trouble. Her ability to concentrate was poor, and she was hyperactive and defiant at home and at school. Her rages were so extreme that her parents found themselves phoning the police as a means to help control her behavior. She has only somewhat responded to psychotherapy and medication therapy for bipolar disorder. At our clinic, she was treated with antidepressants and medications to manage her attention deficit hyperactive disorder with good response. She was followed several years without any indication of bipolar disorder. In contrast, Jane was brought to the clinic because of severe attention problems, hyperactivity, impulsivity, and mood lability. I thought she had only attention deficit hyperactive disorders, but one year after following her, it was clear that in addition to her attention problems she also had bipolar disorder.

Ongoing course and outcome (follow-up) studies will help clarify whether children who belong to this group actually have bipolar disorder and will offer the most cutting-edge treatment to manage these youths. (See Appendix II for clinics performing investigations of bipolar children.)

SUMMARY

The diagnosis of bipolar disorder in children and teens may be challenging because it presents in multiple forms, intensity, and duration. The fact that bipolar disorder in children cycles very rapidly or presents as a mixed episode, and is usually accompanied by other psychiatric disorders, makes its recognition and diagnosis even more difficult. The following list will help you separate out the most common symptoms of this very complex disorder.

For mania or hypomania, look for *periodic episodes* of the following signs:

- Significant decreased need for sleep
- Exaggerated or inappropriate happiness, silliness, or giddiness
- Inappropriate grandiose ideations, exaggerated self-esteem, or unrealistic beliefs in one's own abilities or powers
- High energy levels that are much more than what is typical for the child
- Exaggerated talkativeness
- Racing thoughts
- Hypersexuality

For depression, look for *periodic episodes* of the following:

- Exaggerated sadness, tearfulness
- Lack or significant decrease in the ability to enjoy things
- Lack of desire to be with friends and family members, withdrawn, isolated
- Lack of motivation to do things that the child enjoyed before
- Tiredness, low energy, quietness, or periodic poor performance at school
- Wishing they were dead, thoughts of suicide, or suicide attempts

For both mania and depression, watch for *periodic episodes* of these signs:

- Marked changes in sleep patterns
- Marked changes in school performance
- Anxiety, worries, or panic attacks
- Agitation
- Poor concentration
- Excessive and inappropriate irritability
- Hallucinations (hearing voices or seeing things that are not real) or having delusions (false beliefs that are unusual for the child)
- Aggressive behaviors against others or self

The risk of bipolar disorder is high if there is a family history of bipolar disorder and if many of these noted symptoms occur together, cannot be explained by the presence of other psychiatric or medical conditions or by environmental factors, and affect the child's functioning.

Fortunately, the awareness that bipolar disorder exists in children and teens has fostered a rapid increase in investigations that will clarify the diagnosis of this severe psychiatric disorder, particularly in youth with bipolar disorder NOS and severe mood lability. As you start to unravel the complex set of symptoms of bipolar disorder, chapter 2 will help you better distinguish bipolar disorder from other disorders with similar symptoms.

Bipolar Disorder Versus Healthy Behaviors, Other Psychiatric Disorders, and Medical Illnesses

৶৹

ALL CHILDREN OFTEN GET very silly, giddy, fidgety, and impulsive. We have all seen small children singing, jumping, laughing, talking to themselves, and giggling in places where they otherwise should be quiet, such as in school or places of worship. These same children also can have a low frustration tolerance and short attention spans. Usually, these moods and behaviors are completely normal for the children's ages and stages of development.

However, a recent study reported that approximately 10 years before bipolar disorder was diagnosed in a group of adults, these individuals had long been experiencing mood and behavior symptoms.[1] As children they performed erratically and often poorly at school; were moody, sometimes very irritable and sad; and had occasional insomnia. Everyone in this group cycled from periods of quietness and isolation from peers or family to times of high energy and gregariousness.

So, if children and teens can normally experience mood swings, irritability, and other problems that cause them to act out, yet these very same behaviors can indicate bipolar disorder, you might ask, "How can I tell the difference between normal childhood and adolescent behaviors and abnormal behaviors that signal possible bipolar disorder?"

Although it would require a complete book to describe normal child development, this chapter will help you become familiar with the similarities and differences between bipolar disorder and a child's normal moodiness and misbehavior, as well as the symptoms of other psychiatric and medical disorders.

WARNING SIGNS IN MOOD AND BEHAVIOR

There's no doubt that the moods and behaviors of all children and teens are unpredictable! They swing from loud laughing one moment to angry foot stomping the next. In some instances, their periods of extreme happiness or sadness, as well as their determination to confront authority, are annoying but perfectly normal. In other cases, these actions are cause for concern. This section will help you distinguish between the two.

Extremely Happy

The periods of extreme happiness found in normal children are usually related to specific events. They may be sparked by something that is happening in their environment if, for example, they are participating in exciting activities such as sports or going to an amusement park, or even if they are experiencing joy in their imagination. Certainly, their actions are sometimes viewed as inappropriate. If, for example, young children are in a formal setting such as school or a place of worship and are called forward to participate, they may laugh, talk among themselves, dance, cry, interrupt, pick their noses, and so on. Still, usually these behaviors are normal.

How worrisome a child's behaviors are depends on the age of the child, the severity, and persistence of the behaviors, the ability to control themselves, the context in which these moods and behaviors occur, cultural and ethnic background, as well as the parents' and society's level of tolerance for children's moods and behaviors. For example, if a child goes

How worrisome a child's behaviors are depends on the age of the child, the severity, and persistence of the behaviors, the ability to control themselves, the context in which these moods and behaviors occur, cultural and ethnic background, as well as the parents' and society's level of tolerance for children's moods and behaviors.

to the stage by herself and interrupts the ceremony, destroys objects, laughs, swears, and is uncontrollable, and if these behaviors are repetitive and occur in more than one setting (such as at school, home, or other public places), it is advisable to seek professional advice and counseling. Also, some cultural or ethnic groups tolerate more of children's normal behaviors than others, such as fidgetiness, interrupting, and making noises.

Consider these typical situations that point out the contrasts between "normal" and worrisome behaviors:

- You have seen teens at the mall walking around, making noises, calling each other names, and having fun. However, these behaviors are usually short-lived and occur in specific situations.

Teens with mania may continue to be loud, silly, impulsive, hyperactive, and talkative. Even their friends may notice that there is a problem and ask them to be quiet. If these teens have persistent problems controlling themselves and these problems occur at home, school, and other settings, it is a warning sign that something is wrong.

- Normal children can get very happy and have periods when they feel more confident about themselves. For example, after successfully playing a game or performing well in an exam, she or he may be content, happy, and confident. In contrast, a hypomanic or manic child may get overly confident or have exaggerated feelings of self-esteem that are disproportionate for the occasion. A hypomanic or manic child may become agitated, hyperactive, and irritable and have other symptoms that will affect her or his functioning at school and home.

Children and teens may be silly, extra happy, or goofy without having bipolar disorder.

Feeling "In the Sky"

When Allen, age 16, was asked to explain the difference between feeling manic and happy, he said, "When I feel happy, I feel content. However, when I am manic, I am exaggeratedly happy, silly, talkative, and overconfident. My self-esteem is 'in the sky,' and I laugh a lot. Even my friends notice the difference in my mood, and they keep asking me if I am drugged."

Extremely Sad

It is also normal for children and teens to be sad sometimes, especially when something bad has happened or when they get frustrated. During these periods of sadness, your child may be irritable, quiet, or tearful, and she or he may want to be alone. These normal periods of sadness are usually short-lived, are usually attributable to whatever is happening, and do not significantly affect your child's functioning.

On the other hand, the symptoms of depression can be out of proportion to a situation if they last more than a few days, recur, affect your child's functioning in multiple areas (such as academic and social), and are accompanied by suicidal thoughts or behaviors. If you suspect your child's bouts with "sadness" are beyond the range of normal, look back in chapter 1 at the sidebar summarizing the symptoms of major depression. If your child's behaviors match these warning signs, you should take him or her for a professional consultation. After a death or loss of a relative, friend, or a pet, a child can be expected to undergo a longer period of grief or bereavement and display symptoms of depression similar to those described for major depression, without sounding the warning alarm. The bereavement or grief period usually lasts for 6 to 12 months; during this time, the child gradually returns to his or her normal life, begins to enjoy things as before, is able to concentrate, and copes with the loss. The child may feel sad, particularly during the anniversary of the death of the person or during special times, such as holidays or the birthday of the deceased person. These are typical and healthy coping strategies. But if your child is struggling through a period of prolonged bereavement, and if his or her behavior matches the warning signs described in the accompanying sidebar, you should be concerned and seek professional consultation.

Warning Signs During Bereavement or After a Stressful Situation

- Severe depressive symptoms that are impairing the child's functioning
- Symptoms of mania or hypomania
- Severe and persistent behavior problems
- Suicidal thoughts or behaviors
- Delusions or hallucinations
- No gradual improvement in the symptoms of bereavement

Challenging Authority

If your child shows significant mood and/or behavior problems or exaggerated and recurrent rebellious behaviors that are affecting her or his functioning and judgment, your child needs to be assessed for the presence of psychiatric, medical, or other kinds of problems.

In addition to the fluctuations in happy and sad periods during childhood and adolescence, part of the normal psychological development in children, especially during their teen years, entails questioning or challenging parental opinion. As you are aware, children and teens are constantly testing boundaries. This is their way of asserting some independence and proving to themselves and to others that they have their own ideas and plans. These "rebellious behaviors," however, are not necessarily extreme. On the contrary, research has shown that most teenagers do not have extreme mood swings, irritability, or behavior problems and that most teens will end up following the values of their parents and communities.

However, if your child shows significant mood and/or behavior problems or exaggerated and recurrent rebellious behaviors that are affecting her or his functioning and judgment, your child needs to be assessed for the presence of psychiatric, medical, or other kinds of problems.

WARNING SIGNS IN THINKING AND PERCEPTION

A strong imagination is a sign of a healthy and intelligent child. Young children love to pretend by dressing up, play acting, and telling stories. Teens, too, use their rich imaginations to solve problems and create their future lives. But there is a rather firm distinction between normal ways of thinking and perceiving the world and abnormal ways that cause parents concern and require professional evaluation. In this section, we'll take a look at that distinction in the areas of fantasy, paranoia, and hallucinations.

Fantasy Versus Reality

All children fantasize. They may imagine that they are "the best" at sports or that they possess special superpowers. However, normal children know the difference between fantasy and reality. Even small children can separate illusions from real situations. When evaluating a child's fantasy life for possible abnormalities, it is important to consider his or her age and developmental stage. Children may have grandiose ideas, fantasies, and strange behaviors without having psychiatric problems. For example, when a normal 4-year-old who likes to be Superman and pretends to have superpowers is asked to show how he can fly or melt objects with his X-ray vision, he will say, "I was only kidding!" On the other hand, while in a manic phase, children may really believe their fantasies and act on their unreal beliefs. A manic child who believes he is Superman, for example, might actually try to fly from a high place.

Children may have grandiose ideas, fantasies, and strange behaviors without having psychiatric problems.

Healthy teens also have fantasies, but they know better than to act on them. A teen with bipolar disorder, however, does not know better. Once, while in a manic episode, a young man called the police asking questions about robberies, assaults, weapons, and so on. When the police came to his house, he asked them to meet at his father's office because he was an undercover agent and had special information to share with them. This teen really believed he was a spy.

If you or your child's teachers think that your child cannot differentiate between fantasy and reality, or if your child is persistently acting on fantasies without considering that it may be dangerous to self or others, you should consult a mental health professional.

Careful or Paranoid?

It is normal for children to sometimes be suspicious of others, especially when they are angry, in trouble, or anxious. For example, anxious children may be afraid of people in the shopping mall because they fear that something bad will happen to them or their parents. This is particularly true if the child has been exposed to stressful situations like violence and abuse, or if the child has been watching or reading scary, violent movies or books.

However, if your child is persistently or episodically suspicious ("paranoid"), acts strangely, or avoids going places because of her or his suspiciousness, and these ideas are not shared by you, your relatives, or cultural/religious group, you should take your child for a consultation with a professional.

Hallucinations

Healthy children and teens sometimes complain about occasional hallucinations. They may hear a voice calling them, hear noises, or see things or persons others cannot see or hear. While children are falling asleep or waking up in the morning, they may experience a few halluci-nations. (These types of hallucinations are called *hypnagogic* or *hypnopom-pic*, respectively.) But they are aware that this is an unusual experience and it is not real. This is no cause for concern.

It is also not uncommon or abnormal for children to have *"illusions."* When a child has an illusion, he or she and others see the same object or hear the same noise, but the child distorts what is seen or heard. An example of an illusion would be if your child sees a shadow in his room at night and thinks that it is a monster or a ghost. Once you turn on the light, the child will calm down because he sees that the "monster" was really only his toy or a chair.

However, if your child is having *recurrent hallucinations*, particularly if they occur during both day and night, if the voices (or whatever your child is seeing) are telling him or her to do inappropriate things (such as hurt others or themselves), or *if your child really believes and acts on the hallucinations* (such as running out of his room screaming because a per-son or animal was there, or avoiding going to places because she hears a "real" voice), you should promptly seek professional help.

Persistent and Repetitive Problems

Proper assessment is mandatory if your child:
- Has *persistent* or episodic behavior, academic, or emotional problems *that are affecting* her or his social, academic, and family relations
- Talks about wishing to be dead or to commit suicide
- Describes hurting or killing others
- Talks about hearing voices or seeing things that other people cannot hear or see
- Behaves in a very strange way or being very agitated
- Is having strange beliefs
- Uses illicit drugs or alcohol
- Has significant academic or behavior problems at school (e.g., frequent suspensions or any expulsion)

In general, any child or teen with persistent or repetitive exaggerated mood problems (such as depression, euphoria, silliness, irritability), behavior problems (odd, impulsive, agitated), or cognitive problems (slowed or rapid thoughts, lack of judgment) must be evaluated to rule out the presence of psychiatric and/or medical illnesses. If the changes in a child's behavior are episodic, then a mood disorder (bipolar or unipolar depression) is a possible diagnosis. This is especially true if other people in your family have mood disorders.

BIPOLAR DISORDER VERSUS OTHER PSYCHIATRIC DISORDERS

Knowing which symptoms belong to bipolar versus other psychiatric disorders is not an easy task. An accurate diagnosis requires a solid understanding of normal child development and knowledge of the symptoms of various psychiatric disorders. In this section, we will first look at the psychiatric conditions that can be confused with bipolar disorder and cause misdiagnosis. Then we will discuss psychiatric disorders that can coexist along with bipolar disorder.

Psychiatric Conditions That Can Be Confused with Bipolar Disorder

Just because your child has a fever does not necessarily mean he or she has the flu. The fever might be a sign of an infection, or an immunological problem, or even cancer. That's why your physician would not make a diagnosis of flu based on the symptom of fever alone. In the same way, although your child may have symptoms associated with bipolar disorder, those symptoms may in fact be caused by a variety of other psychiatric conditions. Differentiating bipolar disorder from other psychiatric conditions has important implications for treatment of the child. That's why it's important not to jump to conclusions without ruling out other possibilities.

Some of the disorders[2-9] that are commonly confused with bipolar disorder in children and teens include the following:

- Schizophrenia
- Unipolar major depression
- Attention deficit hyperactivity disorder (ADHD)
- Oppositional defiant disorder and conduct disorder
- Anxiety disorders
- Asperger's disorder
- Borderline personality disorder
- Substance abuse disorders

Differentiating bipolar disorder from other psychiatric conditions has important implications for treatment of the child.

Schizophrenia

Until recently, it was common to misdiagnose children and teens with bipolar disorder as schizophrenics.[8] The reason for this misdiagnosis

Symptoms of Schizophrenia

According to the *DSM-IV,* of the American Psychiatric Association, the following symptoms should be *persistent* for at least 6 months to diagnose a person with schizophrenia:[10]

- Delusions (false beliefs)
- Hallucinations (mainly auditory and visual)
- Disorganized speech
- Grossly disorganized behaviors
- Lack of motivation
- Flat or inappropriate affect

These symptoms are not due to other psychiatric and medical conditions or the use of illicit drugs, alcohol, or prescribed medicines.

was the belief that bipolar disorder was rare in youth and that any child or teen with hallucinations or delusions (common symptoms of both bipolar disorder and schizophrenia) was schizophrenic or had the beginnings of schizophrenia. But schizophrenia is very rare in children, usually beginning during the teen years. It is chronic (unless treated) without the obvious ups and downs seen in bipolar disorder, and it causes a slow deterioration in the person's functioning across all aspects of his or her life. Schizophrenia is manifested by problems in mood, thinking, and behavior, as listed in the sidebar.

In schizophrenia, the mood is usually "flat" (no expression, blunt) or not appropriate. For example, the person may be laughing and at the same time talking about something very sad. People with schizophrenia often do not relate well to others and avoid social contact. Their thoughts are not logical, and it is difficult to understand what they are trying to communicate because the sentences do not connect with each other (this is called *loose associations*). Sometimes the person's sentence structure is so confused and disorganized that it is called *"word salad."* For example, during an acute episode of schizophrenia, a 16-year-old boy with schizophrenia said, "The movie is about to start, is about . . . my dad has a do, tomorrow is my birthday, the weather is bad. . . ."

Thought content is also affected. People with schizophrenia may have *grandiose or paranoid delusions*. Unlike people with bipolar disorder, while schizophrenics are thinking that they are very important or that they have a special mission, they do not have the typical euphoria that accompanies mania. A 17-year-old girl thought that people were watching her, talking, and planning to hurt her. She could not go anywhere even if family members went along and reassured her that nobody was after her. When her illness got worse, she was convinced that microphones were hidden in her house taping her conversations. She began to be suspicious about her family, very agitated, and aggressive and needed to be hospitalized.

The hallucinations experienced by schizophrenics are usually more complex (such as several people talking about the person) than those found in individuals with bipolar disorder, and they are not related to their mood. For example, a schizophrenic may be feeling sad or "flat" even though a voice is telling him that he is the Messiah. Schizophrenia is also accompanied by bizarre, strange, or disorganized behaviors and a lack of motivation (such as eating garbage, talking alone, dressing with unusual things).

Before the onset of the schizophrenia, children and teens may have what is called *prodromal* symptoms (symptoms that appear before the full-blown illness). Children may be isolative, quiet, and not very social and have "weird" ideas; however, since these symptoms are not very specific, it is hard to predict who will develop schizophrenia. Jack, for example, was a quiet, introverted child but did not have any particular problems until he was 12 years old. He then withdrew

> ### Negative and Positive Symptoms in Schizophrenia
>
> Symptoms such as agitation, hallucinations, and delusions are usually called *positive symptoms* of schizophrenia, while a lack of motivation, withdrawal from others, and flat affect are called *negative symptoms*.

from others, stayed in his room playing video games, did not keep up with his hygiene, and could not concentrate. If interrupted, he became angry and sometimes aggressive. Initially his psychiatrist thought that he was depressed and treated him with antidepressants without any change in his symptoms. Slowly, Jack became suspicious; he thought people were out to get him, and he could not go to the mall or to any social activities because he was sure that people were talking about him. He became more agitated and heard voices talking among themselves about him, saying that he was a bad person or that he was important. He talked to himself, and it was difficult to understand what he was saying. He was admitted to the hospital, diagnosed with bipolar disorder, and treated with mood stabilizers without any improvement in his symptoms. Jack improved only after receiving antipsychotic medications, and he was then able to return to school. (See chapter 6 for a detailed description of medication used for psychotic symptoms.)

A similar initial misdiagnosis happened in the case of Sarah. After her first menstruation, she became agitated, irritable, energetic, happy, and hypersexual. She ran away from home several times and had sex with strangers. She was extremely talkative, and she heard a voice that told her that she was the most beautiful girl at her school. Despite these symptoms and a family history of bipolar disorder, she was diagnosed with schizophrenia and treated only with antipsychotics, with partial response. After several of these episodes and a period of severe depression, Sarah was finally diagnosed with bipolar disorder and treated with appropriate mood-stabilizing medications, and she improved dramatically. Sarah married, had two normal children, and did well as long as she continued to take her mood stabilizers.

Schizoaffective Disorder

Sometimes people with schizophrenia have symptoms of mania or major depression, or the person with bipolar disorder has symptoms of schizophrenia when he or she is not depressed or manic. In these situations, the diagnosis of *schizoaffective disorder* may be reasonable.

As these case studies show, it is very difficult to differentiate bipolar disorder from schizophrenia, particularly in youth. It is important to keep careful track of all symptoms and tell your child's doctors all the details of the child's development and family history in order to obtain a correct diagnosis.

Unipolar Major Depression

In contrast to those with bipolar disorder, children and teens with unipolar major depression have *episodes of major depression only, without mania or hypomania*. When these episodes happen more than once, they are called *recurrent unipolar depressions* to differentiate them from the depression(s) experienced by youth with bipolar disorder. Most of the symptoms of unipolar and bipolar depression are the same, but it appears that the symptoms of bipolar depression are more severe. The main difference between these two disorders is the periodic occurrence of manic or hypomanic symptoms in people with bipolar disorder.

Shaniqua is a 13-year-old girl diagnosed with unipolar depression. She has had three periods of major depression in the previous 4 years, each lasting between 3 and 6 months. During these periods, she is very sad and irritable, does not enjoy activities as much as usual, does poorly at school, feels tired, and sometimes wishes that she were dead. When she is not depressed, she is happier but never hypomanic or manic.

An important issue is that most of the children and teens seen at our psychiatric clinics are experiencing their first episode of depression. Some of these young people may develop bipolar disorder (periods of depression and mania or hypomania) in the future, but it is almost impossible to know who will develop bipolar and who will not at the time of first assessment. However, youth with the following signs have up to a 40 percent increased risk to develop bipolar disorder in a period of 5 years:[11,12]

- Depressed children with psychosis (delusions or hallucinations)
- Depressed children with a family history of bipolar disorder
- Depressed children who develop symptoms of mania while taking antidepressants

> *It is very important to make the distinction between unipolar and bipolar depressions because the treatment is different. Antidepressants (medications that treat depression) may trigger an episode of mania or hypomania in patients with bipolar disorder.*

It is very important to make the distinction between unipolar and bipolar depressions because the treatment is different. Antidepressants (medications that treat depression) may trigger an episode of mania or hypomania in patients with bipolar disorder.

Attention Deficit Hyperactivity Disorder (ADHD)

The core symptoms of ADHD are hyperactivity or fidgetiness, impulsivity, and inattention (see the sidebar on page 44). Appearing early in childhood, ADHD's symptoms are usually constant over time. There may be some fluctuations in the severity of symptoms depending on whether the child is in a structured environment or is highly motivated to do certain tasks. For example, children with ADHD can behave better when they are doing activities that they enjoy, such as watching cartoons or playing video games, or behave worse when they are tired or excited. A highly motivated child with ADHD may concentrate, but often he or she loses interest quickly when a task is too difficult.

> *A highly motivated child with ADHD may concentrate, but often he or she loses interest quickly when a task is too difficult.*

Symptoms of ADHD

The *DSM-IV* indicates that a person should have *persistent* problems in the following areas for at least 6 months to be diagnosed with ADHD:[10]

- Inattention
    - Makes careless mistakes
    - Has difficulty sustaining attention in tasks or play
    - Does not seem to listen
    - Does not follow instructions or fails to finish what he or she starts
    - Has problems with organization (e.g., homework)
    - Avoids tasks that require mental effort
    - Is easily distracted
    - Is forgetful
    - High activity level
    - Fidgets ("ants in the pants")
    - Has difficulty remaining seated
    - Runs or climbs in excess
    - Is often "on the go" as though "driven by a motor"
    - Talks too much
- Impulsivity (does not think about the consequences before he or she acts or talks)
    - Blurts out answers before questions have been completed
    - Has difficulty awaiting his or her turn
    - Interrupts

These symptoms also began before the child was 7 years old, affect her or his functioning, are not mainly due to other psychiatric or medical conditions, and are inconsistent with the child's age or developmental level.

Parents of children with ADHD know that it is difficult to take their children to a restaurant, a place of worship, or other public places because the child is unable to sit quietly and will usually misbehave. It is difficult for a child with ADHD to do his or her homework, and assignments that should only take a short time to complete can often take hours. Teachers usually observe that the child is easily distracted, daydreams, talks too much and out of turn, interrupts, makes careless mistakes and is impulsive (blurts out answers without waiting for his or her turn, cuts lines), and loses or misplaces things often (e.g., pencils, erasers, flyers, money). These symptoms may be easily confused with some of the symptoms of bipolar disorder.

Common Reasons for Not Diagnosing ADHD

There are many reasons that the symptoms of ADHD may be overlooked. Here are three you should be alert for:

- Very intelligent children with ADHD often go misdiagnosed because they do not need to concentrate very long at school to understand what the teachers are explaining.
- Girls with ADHD are often underdiagnosed because some clinicians think that ADHD occurs only in boys.
- Some parents may "overfunction" for their children and help them with their homework. Once the children become teens and refuse their parents' help, the symptoms of ADHD begin to affect the child's performance at school.
- Since symptoms such as hyperactivity improve with age, teens who were ADHD during childhood may not get the diagnosis of ADHD.

COMPARISON STUDIES

Several researchers have compared the symptoms seen in children with ADHD and in children with bipolar disorder. Here are a few highlights:

- One of the first investigators who published a study comparing the symptoms of bipolar and ADHD in children was Dr. Mary Fristad and colleagues.[13] She found that children with bipolar disorder had significantly more frequent elevated mood, high energy, thought problems, flight of ideas, rapid speech, and irritability compared to children with ADHD. There were no differences in inattention and hyperactivity.

- Dr. Joseph Biederman and colleagues compared the symptoms in children with bipolar disorder, others with ADHD, and a group of healthy children using a questionnaire that evaluates overall psychiatric problems in youth.[14] They found that in comparison to healthy children, the children with bipolar had problems in all the areas assessed, including thought problems, inattention, anxiety, depression, social problems, somatic complaints (headaches, stomachaches), withdrawal from others, aggression, and delinquency. Compared to the children with ADHD, the group with bipolar disorder had more thought problems, anxiety, depression, aggression, and delinquent behaviors.

- Dr. Barbara Geller and colleagues compared the symptoms between children with ADHD and children with bipolar disorder.[15] To participate in the study, the children diagnosed with bipolar disorder were required to have grandiose ideas and/or euphoria. As expected, children with bipolar disorder had more euphoria and grandiose ideations than the children with ADHD. They also had more racing thoughts and decreased sleep than children with ADHD, but there were no differences in problems with judgment, irritability, distractibility, and energy levels.

- Drs. David Axelson and Boris Birmaher and colleagues compared a large group of children and teens with bipolar disorder to a large group of patients with depression, anxiety, ADHD, and behavior disorders.[16] They found that euphoria and high levels of energy distinguished the youth with bipolar disorder from those with other psychiatric disorders. There were no differences in inattention, irritability, and other symptoms, but the groups with bipolar and depression both had more suicidal thoughts, attempts, and psychotic symptoms than the others.

OVERLAPPING SYMPTOMS OF BIPOLAR DISORDER AND ADHD

There is substantial overlap in the symptoms between bipolar and ADHD, sometimes making it difficult to diagnose bipolar disorder in children. However, as figure 2.1 shows, some symptoms occur only in children with bipolar disorder and may help differentiate between this condition and ADHD. For example, no need for sleep during the night, elevated mood (superhappiness, euphoria, and elation), grandiose delusions, and hallucinations are found only in people with bipolar disorder. Some of the symptoms shared between individuals with bipolar disorder and those with ADHD, such as irritability, are much more severe in people with bipolar disorder.

It is not uncommon for children with ADHD to become demoral-

Figure 2.1—Overlap Between the Symptoms of Bipolar and ADHD

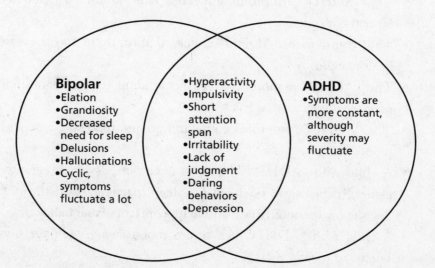

ized and sad and have low self-esteem, especially when they perform poorly academically and socially. Youth with ADHD can also develop episodes of major depressive disorder. These children with ADHD and depression can easily be misdiagnosed as bipolar.

Another source of confusion comes from the short effect of the stimulants (see chapter 9 for a description of the medications used to treat ADHD). While these medications are exerting their effect (the new medications can last up to 10 hours), children usually do relatively well. However, early morning, before the medication begins to work, and late afternoon, when the effects of the medication wear off, the child will show symptoms of ADHD. Thus, for a person with limited diagnostic experience, the child may be thought to have "mood swings" (normal behavior during the day and very hyperactive and impulsive early morning and during the evening and night) and be misdiagnosed as bipolar. Moreover, the stimulants may cause irritability or sadness, and these side effects together with the symptoms of ADHD can again lead to a misdiagnosis of bipolar disorder.

TIPS FOR DISTINGUISHING BETWEEN BIPOLAR DISORDER AND ADHD

Suspect the presence bipolar disorder instead of ADHD if:

- The "ADHD" symptoms appeared later in life (e.g., at age 10 years or older).
- The symptoms of "ADHD" appeared abruptly in an otherwise healthy child.
- The "ADHD" symptoms were responding to stimulants and now are not.
- The "ADHD" symptoms come and go and tend to occur with mood changes.
- A child with "ADHD" begins to have periods of exaggerated elation, depression, no need for sleep (particularly if the next day she or he is not tired), and inappropriate sexual behaviors.
- A child with "ADHD" has severe mood swings, temper outbursts, or rages.

- A child with "ADHD" has hallucinations or delusions.
- A child with "ADHD" has a strong family history of bipolar disorder in his or her family, particularly if the child is not responding to appropriate treatments.

Also, take into account that these warning signs can also be due to other psychiatric disorders (e.g., unipolar depressions, abuse of illicit drugs), *medical problems* (e.g., thyroid problems; brain illnesses such as seizures, tumors, etc.; use of medications such as prednisone), and *environmental stressors* (e.g., family conflict, chaotic environment, sexual or physical abuse) that may coexist with ADHD. Also remember, as explained later in this chapter, that a child may have both ADHD and bipolar disorder.

> *It is not uncommon for children with ADHD to become demoralized and sad and have low self-esteem, especially when they perform poorly academically and socially. Youth with ADHD can also develop episodes of major depressive disorder. These children with ADHD and depression can easily be misdiagnosed as bipolar.*

Oppositional Defiant Disorder and Conduct Disorder

Children with *oppositional defiant disorder* (ODD) are frequently stubborn, defiant, and irritable; frequently lie; and get in minor fights at home and school (see the sidebar "Symptoms of Oppositional Defiant Disorder"). When these behaviors are more severe and the child has persistent problems such as stealing, running away, fights, and abusing others, the diagnosis of *conduct disorder* is made (see the sidebar, "Symptoms of Conduct Disorder"). Many of these children and teens also have ADHD, and a significant percentage abuse drugs or alcohol as teenagers. Because children and teens with bipolar disorder can be very irritable, stubborn, aggressive, and defiant, when they are manic or depressed, they can be misdiagnosed as having oppositional or conduct disorder.

An example of the misdiagnosis of bipolar disorder is found in Lisa, a 12-year-old with persistent severe defiance against teachers and her parents. She disobeys, lies, and has temper outbursts when things do not go her way. During these outbursts, she swears, destroys objects, and sometimes threatens to hurt others. Since early childhood she has been forgetful, impulsive, and fidgety. Lisa was diagnosed as bipolar and treated with medications to stabilize her mood, but her behavior did not improve. A second consultation revealed that she does not have bipolar disorder at all but rather oppositional defiant disorder and ADHD. Individual and family psychotherapy and medication treatment for her ADHD symptoms improved her behavior significantly.

Symptoms of Oppositional Defiant Disorder

According to the *DSM-IV,* to be diagnosed with ODD a person must show, for at least 6 months, *persistent* problems such as the following:[10]

- Argumentative
- Defiant, noncompliant
- Loses temper easily; tantrums
- Deliberately annoys others
- Angry, irritable, easily annoyed
- Resentful
- Vindictive
- Blames others for his or her misbehavior

These behaviors are not mainly due to other psychiatric or medical conditions, cause significant problems with the child's functioning, and are inconsistent with the child's age or developmental level.

Certain behavioral signs may help determine whether a child has bipolar disorder and/or oppositional defiant or conduct disorders:

- If the behavior problems only occur while the child is in the midst of an episode of mania or depression, and if the behavior problems disappear when the mood symptoms improve, the diagnoses of oppositional or conduct disorder should not be made.

Symptoms of Conduct Disorder

The *DSM-IV* indicates a diagnosis of conduct disorder when a person, for at least 12 months, has *persistent* problems such as these:[10]

- Aggressive to people or animals
    - Bullies or threatens others
    - Initiates physical fights
    - Uses weapons to harm others
    - Is physically cruel to people or animals
    - Steals and usually physically confronts the victim
    - Forces others to have sex
- Destroys property
    - Destroys others' property
    - Sets fires
- Theft or dishonesty
    - Breaks into other people's houses, cars, and other property
    - Lies to obtain goods, favors, or to avoid obligations
    - Steals items of value
- Serious and recurrent violations of the rules
    - Stays out late at night without permission
    - Runs away
    - Truant from school

Note: These behaviors are not due mainly to other psychiatric or medical conditions; they do not cause significant problems with the child's functioning, and they are inconsistent with the child's age or developmental level.

- If a child has "off and on" oppositional or conduct symptoms, or if these symptoms only appear when the child has mood problems, the diagnosis of bipolar (or other disorders such as unipolar depression or substance abuse) should be considered.

- If the child had oppositional behaviors before the onset of the mood disorders, both diagnoses may be given.
- If a child has severe behavior problems that are not responding to treatment, consider the possibility of a mood disorder (bipolar and nonbipolar depressions) or the possibility of ADHD or substance abuse.
- If a child has behavior problems and a family history of bipolar disorder, consider the possibility that the child has a mood disorder (unipolar major depression or bipolar disorder).
- If a child has behavior problems and she/he is only sleeping a few hours during the night and the next day she/he is not tired, consider bipolar disorder. Also consider it if the child is exaggeratedly happy, high-energy, or grandiose.
- If a child has behavior problems and is having hallucinations and delusions, consider the possibility of bipolar disorder. Also consider the possibility of schizophrenia, use of illicit drugs/alcohol, or a medical/neurological condition.

Anxiety Disorders

There are several types of anxiety disorders. Children with *separation anxiety disorder* have problems separating from their parents, sleeping alone, going to school, and doing other activities because they are afraid that something bad will happen to them or to their parents. Children with *social phobia* are too shy and overly afraid of being embarrassed. They avoid social situations and any situation in which they may be exposed to the scrutiny of other people, such as reading in front of class or dancing. Youth with *general anxiety disorder* worry too much about minor things. Their worries affect their concentration and sleep, and they usually complain of headaches, stomachaches, and tiredness. Youth with *panic disorder* have periods that occur "out of the blue" of high anxiety, characterized by shortness of breath, heart palpitations, chest pressure, and the feeling that something "bad" is going to happen without knowing what. Youth with *obsessive compulsive disorder* (OCD) have recurrent, undesirable thoughts that they cannot stop or control and/or do repetitive actions and activities without been able to stop. Finally, children and teens with *posttraumatic stress disorder* (PTSD) have anxiety symptoms, physical symptoms, nightmares, and persistent recollections or "flashbacks" of a traumatic experience such as physical or sexual abuse, neglect, or exposure to violence in or outside their home. They usually avoid places related to the event.

Youth with anxiety disorders can be misdiagnosed as having bipolar disorder, especially if they develop depression and have temper outbursts, have coexisting ADHD, or are acting out. For example, Bobby, a 10-year-old boy with social phobia and separation anxiety, has difficulties staying at school without his parents. When his parents forced him to go to school, he had severe temper tantrums and on several occasions mentioned that he wanted to die. Bobby slowly became very depressed, and due to his irritability and temper tantrums, he was diagnosed as having bipolar disorder. Specific treatments for bipolar disorder did not help. When Bobby was then treated with medications for anxiety and with cognitive behavior therapy for anxiety, he showed dramatic improvement.

> **Hypersexuality**
>
> Because children with bipolar disorder may get hypersexual, it is sometimes difficult to differentiate whether these behaviors are due to a bipolar disorder, sexual abuse, or exposure to sexually explicit materials.

Asperger's Disorder

Children and teens with this disorder have problems socializing with other children and adults, are not personable, lack social skills, and have poor eye contact. They are inflexible with their routines; become upset when interrupted; usually ask questions that are out of context; have odd behaviors; and grow obsessed with objects, activities, or hobbies. They are often ostracized and rejected by peers and called "weird." Children with Asperger's disorder may be irritable and have mood swings and severe temper tantrums (see the sidebar "Symptoms of Asperger's Disorder"). These symptoms may be confused with the mood swings and irritability seen in youth with bipolar disorder.

Symptoms of Asperger's Disorder

The *DSM-IV* suggests a diagnosis of Asperger's disorder when a pattern of the following symptoms exists:[10]

- Problems with social interactions
  - Poor or no use of nonverbal behaviors (eye-to-eye-contact, body posture, facial expression) to interact with others
  - Failure to develop peer relationships appropriate for the age and developmental stage
  - No spontaneous seeking or diminished interest of others
  - Lack of social or emotional reciprocity (the child does not share or "return" to others their emotions), not personable
- Restrictive and repetitive behaviors, interests, and/or activities
  - Inflexible adherence to routines or rituals
  - Excessive preoccupation or "obsession" with objects, parts of objects, or activities
  - Repetitive motor movements (hand or finger flapping, odd body movements)
- No delays in language development
- No delays in cognitive (thinking) development

These behaviors are not mainly due to other psychiatric (e.g., autism) or medical conditions, cause significant problems with the child's functioning, and are inconsistent with the child's age or developmental level.

Marty is a 10-year-old who likes to play by himself, has several routines before bedtime (such as arranging his books in a certain order in his backpack), and gets upset when anyone moves anything in his backpack or interferes with his routines. He is fascinated with famous people's addresses—he collects the addresses and has memorized most of them. When he talks to other children his age or an adult, he does not look them in the eye, does not pay attention to what they are saying, and asks questions that are completely out of context. Other children make fun of him and never invite him to parties or any other social activities. Marty also has severe temper tantrums and mood swings and sometimes looks depressed. He was diagnosed with bipolar disorder and treated with medications without response. His parents consulted with a second child psychiatrist, who diagnosed him with Asperger's disorder and treated him with one of the new antipsychotics and family therapy. Although Marty continues to have symptoms of Asperger's disorder, his mood swings and temper tantrums have improved significantly.

Borderline Personality Disorder

Although there is controversy around the validity of this disorder, particularly in youth, it is important to describe this condition because people with bipolar disorder, in particular bipolar II disorder, may be misdiagnosed as having borderline personality disorder.

Borderline personality disorder is manifested by mood lability (rapid and unpredictable changes in mood), irritability, anger, depression, anxiety, low self-esteem, poor frustration tolerance, and suicidal ideation and attempts. People with this disorder often see everything in black and white, without shades of gray; overidealize or exaggeratedly dislike a person; and are very sensitive to imagined or real rejections by others. They are usually manipulative and impulsive, get involved in risky behaviors, and often have self-injurious behaviors (e.g., superficially cutting their skin). They cannot control their anger, and they have either an exaggerated love or hate for their treating clinicians, making treatment difficult. (See the sidebar, "Symptoms of Borderline Personality Disorder.")

In my experience, many of the teens diagnosed with borderline personality disorder have chronic depressions or bipolar II. With appropriate treatment for their mood disorder, the borderline characteristics of their personality also improve or disappear. For example, Francine, age 16, had recurrent depressions since early age. She did not respond to any treatments and was sent to a mental health state hospital due to her continuing suicidal attempts. At the hospital, she continued to cut her arms, and she manipulated and argued with the staff and her friends.

Symptoms of Borderline Personality Disorder

The American Psychiatric Association's *DSM-IV* describes the symptoms of borderline personality disorder as follows:[10]

- Frantic efforts to avoid real or imagined abandonment
- Persistent unstable and intense interpersonal relationships characterized by alternating between extremes of idealization and devaluation
- Identity problems characterized by a persistent unstable self-image or sense of self
- Persistent impulsive behaviors (spending too much money, promiscuity, abuse of drugs, binge eating, reckless driving)
- Recurrent suicidal or self-damaging behaviors (e.g., cutting themselves)
- Mood lability; a marked reactivity of mood and low frustration tolerance
- Inappropriate and intense anger; difficulty controlling anger
- Transient periods of suspiciousness or paranoid thinking triggered by stress

All the symptoms of borderline personality disorder may be present in youth with mood disorders, in particular when the mood problems have been present for a long time and have not responded to treatment.

Francine was diagnosed with borderline personality disorder and treated with psychotherapy and antidepressants without any response.

Upon closer observation, it became clear that she was also experiencing periods of 3 to 6 days during which she was euphoric, more agitated, very silly, and talkative. During these periods, she was very extroverted, less manipulative, needed few hours of sleep, and did not injure herself. These episodes were followed by depression, irritability, self-injurious behaviors, and poor motivation. Francine was diagnosed with bipolar disorder and treated with mood stabilizers with good response, and her typical "borderline" symptoms disappeared.

Substance Abuse

Teenagers and, more rarely, children may experiment with illicit drugs or alcohol. Unfortunately, some of them continue to use drugs in such a way that it affects their social, family, and academic functioning and increases the risk for suicide, aggressive behaviors, legal problems, and development of other psychiatric disorders (such as depression and behavior problems). When the use of these substances affects the teen's functioning, the diagnosis of *substance abuse disorder* is made.

> ### Other Personality Disorders
> It is beyond the scope of this chapter to describe all the personality disorders. However, it is important to note that other personality disorders (such as histrionic personality disorder) may also be confused with the symptoms of bipolar disorder.

The diagnosis of *substance dependence* is warranted when the teen needs to keep increasing the quantity of the drug or alcohol to obtain the same effect, and she or he experiences psychological and physical symptoms (such as tremor anxiety and diarrhea) when the drug or alcohol is not available.

The diagnosis of bipolar or depressive disorders in youth who are abusing drugs or alcohol may be difficult because youth with substance abuse or dependence frequently have mood and behavior problems. At the same time, youth with mood disorders are at higher risk for using illicit drugs or alcohol as a way to deal with their mood and daily problems. In these cases the only way to determine whether a child has bipolar disorder (or another psychiatric disorder) is to "clean" the child of illicit drugs or alcohol. Because some teens cannot or will not stop using drugs by themselves, they need to be admitted to the hospital or rehabilitation center and carefully observed free of drugs and alcohol for several days.

The diagnosis of bipolar or depressive disorders in youth who are abusing drugs or alcohol may be difficult because youth with substance abuse or dependence frequently have mood and behavior problems.

In general, if the mood symptoms are present only while the person is using illicit drugs or alcohol, the diagnosis of bipolar disorder is not appropriate. However, if, after a child has stopped using illicit drugs, he or she continues to show episodes of depression or mania, such a diagnosis may be warranted.

Consider Rob, who could have been incorrectly diagnosed based on symptoms that appeared to be bipolar disorder. Rob was a 16-year-old having periods of agitation and euphoria. Sometimes he did not sleep for several nights in a row, and his parents observed that he was getting "paranoid," irritable, and aggressive. They thought that he had bipolar disorder and consulted a child psychiatrist. After several sessions, Rob admitted that he was using cocaine. As soon as he stopped using this drug, his mood and behavior improved.

Ellen, on the other hand, was a 17-year-old with bipolar disorder who presented a difficult case because her symptoms were masked by her drinking problem. She went to a party with friends and had several beers. While under the effects of the alcohol, she felt temporary relief of her depressive symptoms. She tried alcohol several times and occasionally tried marijuana, finding that these drugs somewhat eased her despair. She began drinking alcoholic beverages to "treat" her mood problems. After several months of this self-treatment, her depressive symptoms got worse, but she could not stop the alcohol abuse because every time she tried, she craved it and became shaky and nauseated. She had become dependent and addicted to alcohol. After a run-in with the police for theft (to support her addiction), Ellen was admitted to a residential facility, where she was detoxified and her mood disorder was properly treated.

Psychiatric Conditions Coexisting with Bipolar Disorder

The diagnosis and treatment of bipolar disorder is easier if it is the child's only diagnosis and can be separated from other psychiatric conditions. However, it is very common that children and teens with bipolar disorder have other psychiatric disorders *along with* bipolar disorder.[2-9] Approximately 50 to 80 percent of children and teens with bipolar disorder also have ADHD, 20 to 60 percent have oppositional or conduct disorders, and 30 to 70 percent have anxiety disorders.[2-9] These coexisting disorders are usually referred to as *comorbid psychiatric conditions*. The coexistence of various illnesses is also commonly seen in children and teens with medical problems. For example, a person with diabetes may also have high blood pressure and kidney problems.

The recognition of coexisting disorders is of crucial importance because *each* disorder must be treated adequately in order to help your child. The conditions most commonly found to coexist with bipolar are the following:

- ADHD
- Oppositional defiant disorder and conduct disorder
- Anxiety disorders (social phobia, general anxiety, separation anxiety, panic, obsessive compulsive disorder, and posttraumatic stress disorders)
- Substance abuse (nicotine, alcohol, marijuana, and other illicit drugs)
- Eating disorders
- Learning and language disabilities
- Family and environmental stressors (e.g., frequent conflicts, violent neighborhood)

These coexisting conditions are demonstrated in each of the following case examples.

> ## Risk of Sexual Abuse
>
> Children and teens with bipolar disorder and other psychiatric disorders (e.g., ADHD, oppositional and conduct disorder, depression, and substance abuse) are at risk to be physically or sexually abused.

ADHD

Abraham is a 10-year-old child with bipolar disorder. His mood swings improved substantially with mood stabilizers and psychotherapy, but he continued to have problems at school due to his lack of concentration, careless mistakes, and impulsivity. When his symptoms of ADHD were treated with stimulant medications, Abraham finally began to excel and behave well at school.

Oppositional Defiant Disorder and Conduct Disorder

Fourteen-year-old Matt has periods where he gets very oppositional, agitated, and energetic. During these times he steals, lies, disobeys his parents, answers back to his teachers, and gets drunk. On one occasion, he stole three cars and wrecked them. He was sent to a juvenile detention center and was diagnosed with conduct disorder. The nurse from the detention center observed that he was very talkative, energetic, and only needed to sleep a few hours at night. He was then diagnosed with bipolar disorder as well and treated with medications and improved significantly. While he took his medications, Matt did well, and the conduct symptoms were not a problem. However, since he did not take them consistently, he had recurrent episodes of mania and depression and problems with the law.

Anxiety Disorder

Yolanda, a 16-year-old girl, was diagnosed with general anxiety, social phobia, and major depressive disorder. During the initial evaluation, her short hypomanic episodes and her family history of bipolar disorder were overlooked. Her anxiety and depression were successfully treated with medication. However, 4 weeks after she started treatment, she developed mania. (The medications used to treat anxiety disorders can exacerbate or trigger an episode of mania in anxious children predisposed to bipolar disorder.) The anxiety medication was stopped, but she continued to have manic symptoms for several weeks. Yolanda was then given medication to control her agitation and insomnia, and these helped control the bipolar disorder. Her anxiety symptoms improved with cognitive behavior therapy.

Illicit Drug Use

George is a 14-year-old boy with bipolar disorder. Despite appropriate treatment with medications and psychotherapy, he did not respond to the treatment because of his continuous use of marijuana and alcohol. George was admitted to a detoxification program. After he stopped using illicit drugs, his mood and functioning improved significantly.

Eating Disorders

Kelly is a teen with anorexia (a disorder manifested by chronic restriction of food and the belief of being obese despite being underweight), and Renee is a 17-year-old girl with bipolar disorder and bulimia (a disorder characterized by frequent vomiting and binging). Both of them have bipolar disorder, but they could not be treated appropriately with medications because they were throwing up frequently. Kelly was usually tired and unable to concentrate because of her malnutrition. These symptoms (fatigue and difficulty concentrating) were difficult to differentiate from the symptoms of depression. Renee became dehydrated from her frequent vomiting.

Learning and Language Disabilities

Twelve-year-old Ben has bipolar disorder. His problems with reading and math are causing severe problems with his self-esteem. He feels that he is "stupid," and the stress caused by his learning problems is aggravating his mood symptoms. Ben also has language problems. He cannot express himself well, which increases his frustration and acting-out behaviors. It is often difficult to know if Ben's depressed mood is due to his bipolar disorder or to his learning difficulties.

Family and Environmental Stressors

Pedro is a 12-year-old boy with bipolar disorder who lives in a family where his parents argue and fight frequently. It is difficult to know whether his depressive symptoms, irritability, and acting out are due to his bipolar disorder or the environment where he lives. Stress caused by family conflict and environmental factors complicate the treatment of bipolar disorder. After his parents attended marital therapy and there was less conflict in their home, Pedro's symptoms improved considerably.

Making Things Worse

Some conditions such as learning problems are not difficult to differentiate from bipolar disorder, but their presence may worsen and may change the way that the symptoms of bipolar disorder manifest.

As you have read, the diagnosis of bipolar disorder can be very challenging because some psychiatric disorders, particularly ADHD, have symptoms in common, and many other disorders may coexist with bipolar disorder. Therefore, your child needs careful and ongoing assessments by a mental health professional trained to diagnose bipolar *as well as* other psychiatric disorders.

BIPOLAR DISORDER VERSUS MEDICAL ILLNESSES

Several medical conditions have symptoms similar to those found in depression and sometimes observed in mania or hypomania. This makes it difficult to always distinguish between the medical problem and various psychiatric conditions. For example, a girl may experience periodic irritability, sadness, low frustration tolerance, and other symptoms similar to major depression only before her menstruation (*premenstrual syndrome, or PMS*). Children with symptoms of depression may in fact merely have a common viral infection or mononucleosis. They feel tired, irritable, and unmotivated and are unable to concentrate. Their appetite can be disrupted, and they may sleep too much. The main differences between these symptoms in medically ill children and in children with major depression is that the symptoms related to the medical illness will be short-lived, the children do not complain about being severely depressed or wanting to die or commit suicide, and they may not have a history of major depression in their families.

However, bipolar disorder, depression, and medical illnesses are not necessarily always entirely separate. It is important to know that a child with a medical illness can also develop a mood disorder, or a child with mood disorder may get physically ill. Children with chronic illness, particularly those with very incapacitating or incurable illnesses such as cancer, may become hopeless, develop suicidal thoughts, and even try to commit suicide. In such cases, if these children and teens have the symptoms of mania or major depression, the diagnosis of bipolar or major depressive disorder, respectively, may be appropriate. If the child is depressed, he or she does not have the criteria for major depressive disorder, and the illness is directly responsible for the low mood, the diagnosis of a *mood disorder caused by a medical illness* is warranted.

When I was a resident in general psychiatry, I treated a 17-year-old girl who had a tumor in her pelvis that had invaded her lower spine. She was paralyzed from her waist down and could not urinate without a tube connected into her bladder. She was also severely constipated and could not have bowel movements without help. Every time the surgeons took out the tumor, it grew again, and, little by little, they had to remove more and more of her spinal column. When I saw this young woman, she was very depressed, hopeless, without appetite, unmotivated, and suicidal. She used to play the violin beautifully and sing, but she refused to do these activities then. She

> ## Behavior Changes Due to Medications
>
> In certain children, the use of medications such as the corticosteroids (e.g., prednisone), antihistamines (for allergies), antidepressants, and benzodiazepines (e.g., lorazepam, clonazepan) can also cause mood swings, irritability, agitation, or silliness.

could not sleep due to pain and the despair of knowing that she was going to die. She had dreams of being in a boat in the "dead sea" with her boyfriend and relatives. Suddenly, in the middle of the sea, a ladder would appear from heaven, and only she would climb it. She would look down and see all her loved ones saying good-bye. I remember thinking, "Of course, she is depressed because she has a terminal illness," and gave her all my support and care, pain killers, and sometimes pills to help her sleep.

When I went on vacation, I asked a friend to cover for me while I was away. Fortunately, my friend saw that in addition to her medical problems this young woman also had major depression and treated her with antidepressants. When I came back, she still had a fatal illness, but she was happier. She was playing the violin, eating and sleeping better, not constipated, and coping much better with her sad destiny.

I also remember an 18-year-old girl who was in the medical ward for a checkup of chronic nonspecific body complaints (feeling tired and unable to concentrate). As a consultant on the medical unit, I was called because she did not follow through with her doctor's recommendations. When I saw her, she was irritable and uncooperative. After I brought this behavior to her attention, she cried and told me that she was feeling very tired and cranky and could not concentrate; her thinking was slow, and her legs were getting swollen without any obvious reason. She never had depression or other psychiatric disorders in the past, and there were no family members with depression, anxiety, or bipolar disorder. A thyroid test showed that she had a low-functioning thyroid gland. Treatment with thyroid hormone solved her symptoms, and she began cooperating with the medical treatment.

These cases have taught me always to be aware of the possibility of psychiatric disorders in patients whom I expect to be sad due to their medical conditions and vice versa—to look for medical illness in patients with a psychiatric diagnosis. I believe that it is important to treat mood disorders in youth with a medical or neurological illness, even if the illness does not have a cure, because the mood disorder diminishes their quality of life, and it may worsen their medical problem.

Many psychiatric, medical, and neurological conditions (e.g., multiple sclerosis, cancer, low thyroid function, brain tumors, and seizures) can be confused with major depression and more rarely with bipolar disorder, indicating the importance of a good psychiatric and medical/neurological examination by a professional acquainted with the diagnosis of psychiatric and medical disorders.

A Predisposition

I continue to learn that some people are predisposed to developing major depression or bipolar disorder while others are not. I have met adults who spent most of their teen years in concentration camps and, despite this terrible experience, were happy and coping well with life. In contrast, others developed recurrent depressions and needed psychiatric help.

SUMMARY

Bipolar disorder is a psychiatric condition manifested by recurrent periods of mania or elevated mood and depression or sadness. It is now known that children and teens may have bipolar disorder. However, since they are growing and developing, the way that bipolar disorder presents in children and teens may look somewhat different than it does in adults. The difficulty in getting an accurate diagnosis is compounded by the fact that bipolar disorder is commonly misdiagnosed because of the presence of coexisting psychiatric conditions and the fact that some of the bipolar disorder symptoms, such as defiance, hyperactivity, inattention, and irritability, overlap with the symptoms of other psychiatric disorders.

Knowing the symptoms of various psychiatric disorders will help you be alert to the possibility of a misdiagnosis or an overlapping condition. This consideration is absolutely vital in the current medical climate in which doctors have such limited time to observe and follow the progress of all their patients. This information will also help you as you move on to chapter 3, where you will explore what you can expect over time from bipolar disorder.

CHAPTER 3

Course and Outcome of Bipolar Disorder in Children and Teens

O NCE YOUR CHILD HAS been diagnosed with bipolar disorder, you may wonder, "Now what? How long will this last?
Will he ever be 'normal'?" The answers to these questions may not always be what you are hoping for. Unfortunately, bipolar disorder is not
yet curable. Unless promptly and successfully treated, it may disrupt
your child's normal emotional, cognitive (way of thinking), and social
development, and it may increase the risk of his or her developing behavior problems, using illicit drugs or alcohol, and attempting suicide.
But on the positive side, like other lifelong illnesses such as diabetes
or epilepsy, bipolar disorder can be medically managed to ensure your
child's well-being.

In this chapter, we will explore the course and complications of
bipolar disorder, as well as the value of proper treatment and the possible positive consequences of this complex psychiatric disorder.

BIPOLAR DISORDER OVER TIME

The few studies that have followed children and teens with bipolar disorder over time have shown that this disorder is a recurrent illness that

may considerably affect your child's functioning.[1-4] It has also been found that as the illness progresses, the episodes of mania and depression tend to become more frequent. These facts stress the variable and unpredictable nature of this psychiatric disorder that make it so important for you to seek prompt, effective treatments for your child.

Bipolar Disorder Adversely Affects High Schoolers Who Do Not Seek Treatment

Because most follow-up studies have been carried out with teens with bipolar disorder who had already sought treatment at psychiatric clinics, it is possible that these youth had the most severe illness and therefore showed a higher rate of recurrences and problems at school, at home, and with peers. However, a study that included high school students who were never referred for treatment showed similar results, indicating that regardless of severity, bipolar disorder can adversely affect a youth's functioning and that prompt, effective treatment is critical.[2]

The Variable Course of Bipolar Disorder

Some children and teens with bipolar disorder may experience only one episode of depression and then after several years of feeling well go through an episode of mania. Others may have several episodes of depression, followed by one period of mania, while others experience several consecutive episodes of depression and mania. In fact, your child may experience various subtypes of bipolar disorder over his or her lifetime. As your child's illness changes, so will his or her diagnosis and, perhaps, treatment.

As described in chapter 1, children in particular appear to have multiple episodes of depression and mania over their lifetimes, and some have fast cycles, switching between symptoms of mania and depression during the same week or the same day. Youth who have mixed depression and mania or rapid cycling are more difficult to treat and have more bipolar episodes in comparison to children with other types of bipolar disorder.

The course of this disorder is unpredictable because your child may exhibit different symptoms over time. The following are some examples of the variable course of bipolar disorder in children and teens:

- Martha, a 16-year-old girl, was diagnosed with bipolar disorder when she was 12. Since then, she has experienced three episodes of major depression, each lasting 3 to 4 months, and two episodes of mania.
- Ed, age 8, has frequent, brief periods of depression and mania each week.
- Allen, a 17-year-old boy, had one episode of severe depression that lasted 4 months. During the same time, he also experienced panic attacks, hallucinations, and delusions (psychotic symptoms). One year later he had an episode of mania and needed to be admitted to the hospital for treatment. Now 25 years old, Allen has not experienced any more episodes of mania or depression, which may be due, at least partially, to his cooperation with treatment.
- Suzy had an episode of mania followed by an episode of major depression when she was 14 years old. Since then, she has experienced one or two episodes of depression per year and then one episode of mania when she was 23.
- Helene, an 11-year-old, had a severe episode of depression after her father committed suicide. Three years later, she developed a second episode of depression, followed by a manic episode with psychotic features (delusions).

Changing Subtypes

A child may experience different subtypes of bipolar disorder during his or her lifetime.

As your child's illness progresses, his or her diagnoses of bipolar subtypes may also change. For example, 15-year-old Monica consulted our clinic because she had symptoms of bipolar II (periods of depression and hypomania). Approximately 18 weeks after she started treatment, she developed mania and major depression. In light of these developments (as illustrated in figure 3.1), her diagnosis was changed from bipolar II to bipolar I.

Figure 3.1—A Child with Bipolar Disorder II
That Converted to Bipolar Disorder I

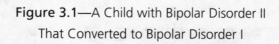

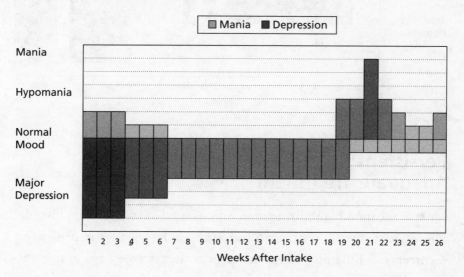

Another example of how bipolar disorder changes course over time can be seen in the case of Jamal, a 10-year-old boy with brief symptoms of mania and mild depression. During the initial assessment at our bipolar clinic, he was diagnosed with bipolar disorder not otherwise specified (NOS). Approximately 19 weeks after his admission to our bipolar program, he showed typical periods of mania and major depression (as illustrated in figure 3.2), and his diagnosis was changed from bipolar NOS to bipolar I, mixed type.

Figure 3.2—A Child with Bipolar NOS
That Converted to Bipolar I, Mixed Disorder

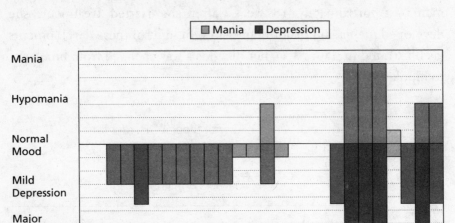

Weeks After Intake

Persistent Problems Despite Adequate Treatment

Most of the mood-stabilizing medications used to treat bipolar disorder (discussed further in chapters 6 and 8) are more effective in preventing recurrences of manic or hypomanic periods than they are in preventing episodes of depression. Thus, despite treatment, your child may continue to experience major depressions or to have mild periods of mania and depression. In fact, long follow-up studies in adults with bipolar disorder have shown that most people continue to experience short periods of depression and, less frequently, periods of hypomania.[5] If untreated, however, it is likely that these episodes would be much more severe, as seen in patients who do not adhere to treatment.

The following are some examples of the bipolar symptoms that might be evident periodically despite adequate treatment (all medications are discussed in chapter 6):

- Maria is a 15-year-old girl who was successfully treated with lithium for her bipolar disorder. However, every 3 to 4 months, she continues to have mild depressive episodes that last 1 to 2 weeks.

- Larry is a 12-year-old who responded well to treatment with valproate (Depakote), but he still gets depressed every fall and winter.

- Ten-year-old Rachel responded to a combination of valproate and lithium, but two to three times a year, she gets hypomanic for a period of approximately 4 weeks and sometimes feels depressed without any obvious reason.

It is more the rule than the exception to see a variable course in bipolar disorder. However, this variability may be reduced and sometimes eliminated with appropriate medication and psychotherapy.

Adherence to Treatment Is Essential

Although bipolar disorder is complex and unpredictable, your child's adherence to medication treatment is one of the most important factors to determine how she or he will do over time. Adequate treatment increases the chance that your child will develop normally and have a happy and successful life. In one study, a group of teens admitted to the hospital because of severe symptoms of bipolar disorder were successfully treated with lithium and discharged from the hospital.[6] They were followed for 18 months. Approximately 70 percent of those who stopped the lithium had new episodes of depression or mania and needed to be hospitalized again.

But even when properly treated, the episodes of depression and/or mania and hypomania will probably continue to occur intermittently. Children and teens with bipolar disorder can also undergo periods in which they have psychosis (delusions or hallucinations), rapid cycles, or mixed episodes. How frequently these episodes occur depends on many factors. These include the severity of the illness; the type

*A*dequate treatment increases the chance that your child will develop normally and have a happy and successful life.

of bipolar disorder (mixed, rapid cycling); the presence of coexisting psychiatric disorders (such as ADHD); abuse of alcohol or other illicit drugs; the use of medications that affect mood and can worsen the course of bipolar disorder (such as antidepressants, asthma medications); medical illnesses; the degree of adherence to treatment; and environmental factors such as stress, lack of sleep, or conflicts at home. (These factors are discussed in detail in chapter 8.)

COMPLICATIONS OF BIPOLAR DISORDER

If you or I develop bipolar disorder during our adult years, the negative consequences may be serious. In the same way, children and adolescents with bipolar disorder are likely also to have negative consequences (as summarized in table 3.1). However, because your child is in the process of maturing, if bipolar disorder is not treated appropriately, he or she may have additional problems because this disorder can affect a child's ability to develop normally.

TABLE 3.1—COMPLICATIONS OF BIPOLAR DISORDER

- Interference with normal emotional, cognitive, and social development
- Interpersonal difficulties with family, friends, teachers, and others
- Increased behavior problems, causing disciplinary and legal problems
- Poor academic functioning
- Increased hospitalizations
- Heavier emotional and economic burden to the family (parents, siblings, and other relatives)
- Greater use of tobacco, alcohol, and illicit drugs, such as marijuana
- Increased risk for suicide attempts and suicide

This section will help you understand the common problems with mood, behavior, thinking, physical functions (e.g., sleep, appetite), and family relationships that may occur as a consequence of bipolar disorder. It will also emphasize the importance of appropriate treatments to avoid the serious problems associated with *psychological "scars"* that remain after a bipolar episode, alcohol and drug abuse, and suicide.

Common Problems

The problems commonly associated with bipolar disorder are many and varied, with far-reaching consequences for your child's personal and social development. While depressed or manic, children with bipolar disorder can have serious problems with their mood, behavior, thinking, and physical functions (sleep, appetite, energy level). These problems can make them very irritable and impatient, causing conflicts with people around them. With every episode of bipolar disorder, the child is at risk for acting out; having temper tantrums; fighting with peers, siblings, and parents; and getting into trouble at school and at home.

> ### "Gaps or Parentheses in My Life"
> Mary, a 16-year-old who has had bipolar disorder since she was 10, described her experience this way: "The bipolar disorder caused many gaps or parentheses in my life." Every time she had a period of mania or depression that lasted for several months, she lost her friends, got behind at school, and had frequent arguments with her parents and siblings, which damaged her relationships with them.

The symptoms of mania or depression are also likely to interfere with school performance, household chores, and other responsibilities (athletics, jobs, clubs, etc.) and cause arguments with parents, siblings, grandparents, teachers, and friends. Children with bipolar disorder may isolate or withdraw from social activities or act and talk strangely, causing other people to reject or make fun of them. Some teens may steal, spend too much money, destroy property, and threaten or injure others. They may act impulsively and without judgment, getting into trouble with the law.

Bipolar disorder may also be accompanied by symptoms of psychosis, including delusions (false beliefs and/or hallucinations). If a child becomes psychotic, he or she may behave bizarrely and do inappropriate or dangerous things, such as talk aloud to him- or herself, touch people, run into traffic, dance naked in a public area, talk nonsense, or even become violent. A child who thinks that others are persecuting or want to harm him or her may try to "protect" or "defend" him- or herself, without meaning to hurt others, or get into trouble with the law. These behaviors can also lead to rejection by his or her friends and a worsening of the stigma of the illness.

Like so many other teens with bipolar disorder, 17-year-old Daniel suffers the consequences of his high and low periods. Daniel usually gets depressed during the fall and winter months. He hides in his house, stays in his room for many hours with the light off, rarely takes a shower, does not return calls, and does not study. In the summer, on the other hand, he usually gets manic and becomes active and extroverted. He calls his friends very late at night, cleans the house repeatedly, and sings and dances uncontrollably. During one such episode, he stole a car, used his parents' credit cards to buy expensive clothes, and was stopped by the police for driving 70 miles per hour in an area where the speed limit was 45 miles per hour. He was detained by the police for several hours until he was transferred to an emergency room because he was yelling, singing, talking very fast, and telling the police that he was an FBI agent. Fortunately, Daniel was treated successfully with mood stabilizers and psychotherapy, and as long as he takes his medications, he is better able to function socially.

Family Strain

The ongoing problems with acting out, temper tantrums, mood swings, problems at school, disobedience, and so forth, may create constant conflicts and arguments at home. This adds stress to your child's condition, as well as to your own mental and physical health. You and other family members may have angry feelings toward your child that make you feel depressed and guilty for being a "bad parent"; family members can also blame you for your child's problems. Moreover, due to the episodic nature of bipolar disorder, problems come and go, making it very difficult to have a consistent parenting strategy to raise and educate a child with bipolar disorder.

Often, instead of being able to enjoy your child, you may spend most of your time supervising, policing, and "putting out fires." For example, John is a 12-year-old with both bipolar disorder and attention deficit hyperactive disorder (ADHD) whose behavior is a constant strain on his family. His parents say that he was always hyperactive, impulsive, and inattentive, but then around the age of 8, he began to show symptoms of depression and a periodic worsening of his ADHD. His parents blamed his problems on themselves, and this feeling was reinforced by family comments such as, "He is spoiled," "You don't know how to manage him," "He needs more consistent punishment," and "You need to send him away." John's parents thought that they were "bad" parents, and they argued and blamed each other for their son's problems. The family could not go on vacation or to a house of worship or restaurants because John would touch everything, run, scream, and have temper tantrums. Moreover, they were unable to spend much time with John's siblings because John needed constant supervision, leaving John's brother and sister feeling lonely and resentful.

John's parents gradually became frustrated with him and even expressed regret for having had him. On one occasion, John had a severe tamper tantrum. He destroyed objects at home, kicked furniture and walls, and threatened his parents and siblings. His parents did not know what else to do, and, in a moment of hopelessness, his father hit him with a belt, leaving marks on his legs. A teacher saw these marks and appropriately called the child protection office and reported the case. While the case was being investigated, John's parents felt remorseful, ashamed, and depressed. John and his parents were referred for a psychiatric evaluation, and John was not taken away from home. John was diagnosed with bipolar disorder and was treated with medications to stabilize his mood. Six weeks later, John's mood and behavior had improved, and his relationships with his parents and siblings steadily got better as well. The extended family began finally to understand that John's problems were due to his illness and that his parents were doing all they could to help their son.

Just as you are not a "bad" parent when you can't control your child's bipolar symptoms, your child is not trying to be "bad" when he or she is having an acute bipolar episode. Knowing the symptoms and common complications of bipolar disorder will allow you to fully understand your child's behavior and seek appropriate treatment so that the entire family can better deal with this disorder.

The Economic Burden

The episodic and ongoing problems caused by bipolar disorder may place a significant economic burden on the family. The cost of frequent hospitalizations and the use of medications may not be covered completely by insurance companies (as explained in chapter 13). A study found that families with children diagnosed with bipolar disorder reported an increased economic burden, with 40 percent of the families having increased expenses, 70 percent needing to use their savings, and 94 percent incurring debts.[4]

Psychological Scars

Some of the complications of bipolar disorder continue even after the acute periods of mania or depression have resolved. These acute episodes can leave *psychological scars* on your child. For example, if your child acted very strangely while in an episode of mania or depression, she or he will have to face questions and sometimes rejection from peers. Your child will have to make up missed schoolwork, renew or rebuild friendships, deal with the misunderstanding of others, and explain and cope with his or her prior suicidal or psychotic experiences.

For example, while experiencing mania, all of the following children appeared extremely abnormal to others: Fourteen-year-old Allen talked to plants, thought he was the expected Messiah, and tried to baptize his friends at school. Eight-year-old Tanisha believed she was "Barbie" and acted like the doll. George, age 15, went from class to class teaching "real math" and got so upset that he broke a door when confronted with his behavior. Sixteen-year-old Leroy heard a voice telling him that he was the best basketball player in the world and spent all night writing game plans. Rachel, 10 years old, saw a ghost that told her that she was a princess and that all her friends needed to obey and listen to her.

> **Take Time to Rebuild**
>
> Not only do people with bipolar disorder need to recuperate from an acute episode, but family members and friends will also need time to rebuild trust and cope with their anger, disappointment, or guilt. As a parent, you may need to grieve over the loss of your child's health and begin to accept that he or she has a lifelong illness.

All of these children's friends laughed at them and avoided their company, even after the acute bipolar episode improved. The children with bipolar disorder were embarrassed about their prior bizarre behavior. They felt sad and worried that they were "crazy." Many of them refused to return to school. Like these children, your child will have to make peace with parents, siblings, other relatives, and teachers after having been irritable and disrespectful to them. He or she may also have to confront people who may have taken advantage of his or her bipolar-related hypersexuality, poor judgment, or impulsivity.

This situation can be very difficult for young people to address because illnesses that affect a child's mind are not well understood by most of society. It often seems that society understands and supports children and families with medical illness because clear physical signs are present, such as fever, difficulty breathing, seizures, and objective findings in laboratory tests.

But people often react to psychiatric disorders by avoiding or ostracizing the person or by blaming their families. In this way, society may also inadvertently increase the suffering and isolation the person diagnosed with bipolar disorder and his or her family experience.

People often react to psychiatric disorders by avoiding or ostracizing the person or by blaming their families. In this way, society may also inadvertently increase the suffering and isolation the person diagnosed with bipolar disorder and his or her family experience.

Alcohol and Illicit Drugs

Children and teens with bipolar disorder are especially likely to abuse alcohol and drugs for several reasons. For example, during mania, teens or children may be tempted to use alcohol and drugs because they are unable to think about the consequences; youth with bipolar disorder may find that drugs like alcohol or marijuana temporarily "help" them forget about problems and "enjoy" things again, and youth with bipolar disorder may hang around with other teens who are in trouble and who are using alcohol or illicit drugs.

The consequences of alcohol and drug abuse are in themselves dangerous for young people, but for the child with bipolar disorder, they are especially risky, because once a person gets hooked on illicit drugs or alcohol, treatment of the bipolar disorder becomes more complicated; these substances affect the child's mood and behavior and interfere with the medications used to treat bipolar disorder, increase the chance that the teen will not follow through with treatment, and heighten the risk for suicide. Both the bipolar disorder and the use of alcohol and drugs will require intensive treatment (as explained in chapter 9).

For example, Giovanna, a 16-year-old girl with frequent episodes of depression and hypomania, used marijuana and sometimes cocaine with her friends for temporary relief of her sadness. She was unable to stop using drugs because she was afraid that her friends would reject her and that her depression would worsen. After several months, her mood problems got worse; she attempted to commit suicide and was admitted into a psychiatric hospital. While in the hospital, she revealed her use of drugs and was treated with psychotherapy and mood stabilizers with good response. After her discharge from the hospital, under the pressure of her old

Youth with bipolar disorder may find that drugs like alcohol or marijuana temporarily "help" them forget about problems and "enjoy" things again.

"friends," she stopped the treatment and began to use illicit drugs again. Only after several hospitalizations did Giovanna realize the destructiveness of her drug use and nonadherence to treatment. She was then able to follow through with treatment and manage her bipolar disorder.

Suicide

> *Suicide is the most severe complication of bipolar disorder.*

Suicide is the most severe complication of bipolar disorder. Death wishes or suicidal thoughts are commonly seen in a young person with bipolar disorder, particularly when he or she is depressed or is in an episode of mania (especially during a mixed or psychotic state). In fact, as shown in figure 3.3, high school students with bipolar disorder have more suicidal thoughts and poorer functioning than youth with major depression (without mania or hypomania) or healthy teens.[3] We found similar results in a group of individuals referred to our clinic for treatment.

Depressed children may see themselves, their surroundings, and their future negatively. Some describe depression as "wearing dark

Figure 3.3—Suicide Attempts and Functioning in High School Students with Bipolar Disorder

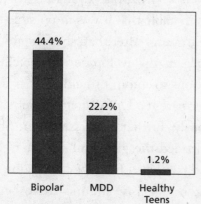

Suicide Attempts

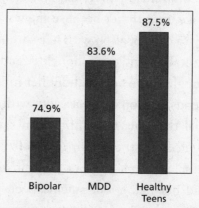

Overall Functioning

Lewinsohn PM, Klein DN, Seely JR (1995), Bipolar disorders in a community sample of older adolescents: prevalence, phenomenology, comorbidity, and course. *J Am Acad Child Adolesc Psychiatry* 34(4):454–63.

glasses," a state in which everything is seen pessimistically. A depressed person may feel hopeless and wish to be dead. As illustrated in figure 3.4, a sequence of events and factors may trigger or protect against a suicidal attempt: A child with a mood disorder (1 in the figure) may experience a negative event(s) (2) such as abuse; a fight with a friend; the death of a friend, relative, or pet; or exposure to violence. This negative event may cause this child's mood to worsen, and he or she may become very hopeless (3). If the child does not have the skills to cope with the stress and/or does not have support (4), he or she may consider suicide (5) as a solution for the problem. If the person who is considering suicide becomes desperate and has an available method, like a gun or drugs at home (4), he or she may use the gun, overdose, or try to commit suicide with other methods. As shown in item 4 in figure 3.4, the use of alcohol and drugs; the presence of impulsivity, ADHD, or conduct disorders; or a family history of suicidal behaviors in a depressed person increases the risk of suicide. On the other hand, good coping skills, support, spirituality, consideration of others' reactions to the suicide, and no access to a method of suicide diminishes the risk for suicide.

Consider the case of 14-year-old Pamela. Pamela developed bipolar disorder after her first menstruation. She had suicidal thoughts every time she became depressed, but she never attempted or planned to commit suicide. Once, while she was very depressed, her boyfriend broke up with her because she was so irritable that it was impossible to have a conversation with her without arguing. After that, she felt guilty, miserable, and very hopeless and began to develop serious suicidal thoughts. She talked about her intentions to commit suicide with some friends and, on one occasion, with her parents. Unfortunately, her suicidal thoughts were not taken seriously, further depressing her. She found her father's gun and bullets, loaded the gun, and shot herself. Pamela did not die, but she remained paralyzed from her waist down. Had her talk about suicide been taken seriously, she may have been evaluated and treated promptly, preventing this serious suicide attempt.

More information regarding suicidal behaviors in children and teens, assessment, and management are described in chapter 10.

Figure 3.4—Factors That May Trigger or
Protect Against Suicide in a Child with Bipolar Disorder

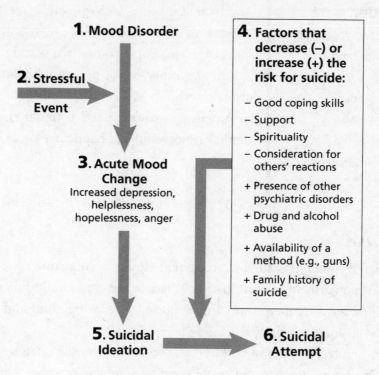

POSITIVE CONSEQUENCES

The consequences of bipolar disorder are not always negative. During
an episode of hypomania, your child can be very productive, social, and
intuitive. He or she may take the initiative to do great projects, work
hard and fast, and have great ideas. The problem is that the hypomania
does not last forever, and it can switch to a full manic or depressive
episode.

People with bipolar disorder may also be very creative and productive.[7] In fact, many famous poets, writers, painters, businesspeople, ath-
letes, and politicians have succeeded despite having bipolar disorder.
Famous people with bipolar disorder include Victor Hugo, Edgar Allan
Poe, Walt Whitman, Pyotr Tchaikovsky, Irving Berlin, Kurt Cobain,[8]

Famous People with Bipolar Disorder

For more information regarding famous people with bipolar or depressive disorders, you can do a search online for "bipolar + famous people." Be aware, however, that not all the information you find may be reliable!

Ernest Hemingway, J. C. Penney, Barrett Robins (from the Oakland Raiders), and Abraham Lincoln. Unfortunately, perhaps because of absent or ineffective treatment, some of these people committed suicide.

On the other hand, people with bipolar disorder who have followed through with treatment and whose mood is under control can have successful and happy lives.

SUMMARY

Bipolar disorder is a lifelong recurrent illness accompanied by substantial impairment in a child's social, academic, and family functioning. The most frequent outcomes reported in existing child and teen follow-up studies include the following:[1-4]

- Bipolar disorder in children and teens is a chronic (lifelong) and recurrent (comes and goes) condition similar to other chronic medical illnesses, such as epilepsy, asthma, or diabetes.
- If untreated, bipolar disorder can severely affect the child's normal development; cause behavior, academic, and family problems; and greatly increase the risk for substance abuse and suicide.
- A substantial number (30 to 70 percent) of children and teens may recover from an acute episode, but most continue to have mild periods of mania or depression, and up to 70 percent will experience full-blown recurrences.
- Youth with bipolar disorder, mixed type and rapid cycling, have more recurrences and respond less fully to treatment.
- Children with few or mild bipolar symptoms have levels of impairment comparable to those of children with the full bipolar disorder and therefore also need prompt, adequate treatment.

- The effective treatment of bipolar disorder in children usually requires multiple medications and psychosocial interventions.
- Youth with bipolar disorder usually require several admissions to psychiatric hospitals for the management of severe episodes.
- Most families do not seek treatment for their children with bipolar disorder, and those who do seek treatment do not usually follow through with it.
- Bipolar disorder severely impacts family relationships and may cause significant economic burdens.

All the complications discussed in this chapter may sound very discouraging. But the situation is not entirely bleak. These problems may be avoided or at the very least diminished with the treatments explained in chapters 6 to 9. But first, to help you better answer the question "Why?" chapter 4 will explore the causes of bipolar disorder.

CHAPTER 4

Causes of Bipolar Disorder

Although we do have some ideas, we have yet to find the responsible brain mechanism for bipolar disorder.[1,2] However, recent technological developments in brain imaging have allowed us to see the brain functioning live and even note how medications that are specific for the treatment of bipolar disorder work inside the human brain. These advances in brain imaging, together with studies investigating the genetic, biological, psychological, and environmental factors that are associated with bipolar disorder (as illustrated in figure 4.1), will eventually lead to better understanding and treatment and, hopefully one day, the prevention of this illness.

As you read through this chapter, it's important to note that these factors overlap with each other but are presented here separately for clarity and basic discussion.

FAMILY FACTORS

Bipolar disorder runs in families.[3,4] Thus, if there is a person with bipolar disorder in a family, the chance is greater of finding another family member with this disorder in comparison with families in which no one

Figure 4.1—Factors Associated with Bipolar Disorder

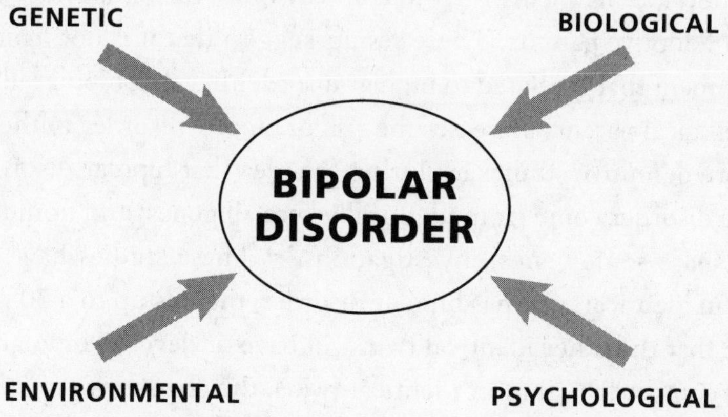

GENETIC   BIOLOGICAL

BIPOLAR DISORDER

ENVIRONMENTAL   PSYCHOLOGICAL

has bipolar disorder. This has been proven in investigations that enroll parents who have bipolar disorder and then evaluate whether their children and other relatives also have the disorder. It has also been researched in studies that involve children who have bipolar disorder and then evaluate whether their parents and other relatives (siblings, uncles, aunts, and grandparents) also have this disorder. In both types of studies, the connection is clear. In general, approximately 1 percent of the population in the world is at risk for bipolar disorder.[2–4] If one parent has bipolar disorder, the risk for their children increases to approximately 10 percent. If both parents have bipolar disorder, the risk rises up to 60 percent. As researchers continue to examine the link between family factors and bipolar disease, they are looking closely at the role of genetics as well as other family influences.

Genetic Factors

The fact that bipolar disorder runs in families suggests that it is transmitted through genes. To evaluate whether this is indeed the case, adoption and twin studies have been carried out.[3,4] In the adoption studies, the rate of bipolar disorder is compared between children born of parents with bipolar disorder who have been adopted and raised by parents without bipolar disorder and the rate of bipolar disorder in their stepsiblings. The adoption studies have found that adopted children whose biological parents have bipolar disorder have an increased risk of developing the disorder in comparison to the biological children of their adoptive parents. These results suggest that it is not mainly the environment that is related to bipolar disorder but that bipolar illness in the biological parents increases the risk of bipolar disorder in the child.

More definitive studies exploring the idea that bipolar disorder is a genetic disorder come from identical (share all genes) and nonidentical twins (share some genes) investigations.[2-4] These studies have shown that if an identical twin has bipolar disorder, there is up to a 70 percent chance that the other identical twin will have or develop bipolar disorder. In comparison, in non-identical twins, the chance of one twin developing bipolar disorder if the other nonidentical twin has bipolar is around 10 to 20 percent.[2-4]

> These studies have shown that if an identical twin has bipolar disorder, there is up to a 70 percent chance that the other identical twin will have or develop bipolar disorder.

Researchers have been trying to delineate the specific genes associated with the transmission of bipolar disorder. However, similar to illnesses that are caused by several genes (such as diabetes and blood hypertension), it has been difficult to find which combination of genes may cause bipolar disorder. Some genes for bipolar disorder have been identified, but the results have been inconsistent.[2,4]

The Human Genome Project has been very encouraging to researchers in this field. This project identified *all* the human genes and it is currently evaluating their functions. The results will no doubt provide new insights into the genetic causes of bipolar disorder. It will also allow the development of more specific medications and preventative interventions for better treatment of this illness.

BIOLOGICAL FACTORS

The roots of bipolar disorder may lie in the way the brain works. If the brain mechanisms that control mood are in some way dysfunctional, this may explain why a child with bipolar disorder cannot, no matter how hard he or she tries, stop those disruptive highs and lows. The studies exploring this possibility are still in their infancy, but the findings at this point make it likely that an understanding of neurotransmitters, brain structure, and brain networks or circuits will give you a fuller picture of the difficulties your child faces.

Neurotransmitters

Neurotransmitters are substances that act like "messengers," enabling neurons to communicate among themselves. There are many types of neurotransmitters in the brain. Some, such as dopamine, norepinephrine, and serotonin, may be familiar to you because they are related to the effects of commonly used antidepressants such as fluoxetine (Prozac) and sertraline (Zoloft). To understand the role of biological factors in bipolar disorder, it is helpful to see how neurotransmitters function in the brain.

Figure 4.2 shows, in a simplistic way, the communication between two neurons separated by a gap, called the *synaptic space* (1). Stimulated by an electrical impulse (2), the presynaptic (located before the synapse) neuron (3) secretes several messengers called *neurotransmitters* into the synaptic space (4). These messengers are substances such as dopamine, serotonin, and norepinephrine. The neurotransmitters transmit the message from the presynaptic neuron to the postsynaptic neuron (located after the synapse) (5) by attaching themselves to specific locations, called *receptors* (6). When they attach to the receptor, they stimulate other messengers (7) inside the postsynaptic neuron. These internal messengers stimulate the postsynaptic neuron, which in turn will transmit the electrical impulse to many other neurons (8). The messengers in the synaptic space can also attach themselves to receptors on the presynaptic neuron (3) and in this way control how much neurotransmitter is secreted into the synaptic space. Medications such as the antidepressants fluoxetine (Prozac), sertraline (Zoloft), and others block the presynaptic receptors, increasing the amount of neurotransmitter (in this case serotonin) that is available to stimulate the postsynaptic neuron. It is believed that the increase in the levels of serotonin is the mechanism by which these medications improve the symptoms of depression.

Figure 4.2—Schematic Diagram Showing the Communication
Between Two Neurons

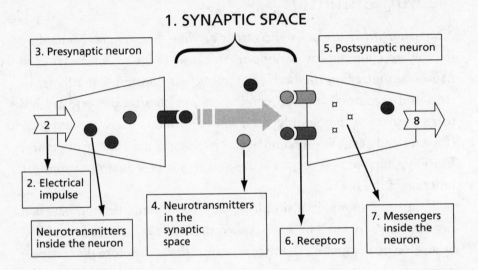

Numerous studies have been carried out to investigate whether the neurotransmitters and the receptors that are located on the neurons are involved in bipolar disorder.[1-3] However, results have not been consistent, and we do not know whether the changes in these neurotransmitters and receptors existed before the illness started or whether they may be a cause of the illness. We also do not know whether the changes in these substances are close to or far away from the primary cause of bipolar disorder.

This uncertainty about the location of the changes in neurotransmitters can be illustrated by imagining a large chain. The first link in the chain is the primary cause of the illness, and changes in this link affect the other links. The changes we are observing could be in a link quite far away from the first one, obscuring or only giving a vague idea of the primary cause of the illness.

Currently, we believe that the molecules or substances produced or released inside the neurons (number 7 in figure 4.2) in response to the stimulation by a neurotransmitter are more closely related to the causes of bipolar disorder.[1,2] Ongoing studies will help clarify the role of these molecules, and the results will help develop more specific treatments that we hope will cause fewer side effects than the current medications.

> ## The Effect of Medication on Mood
>
> Several studies have shown that several neurotransmitters—including dopamine, norepinephrine, and serotonin, among others—influence the person's mood and are affected by the medications used to stabilize mood in patients with bipolar disorder, such as lithium and valproate (Depakote).[3,4]

Brain Imaging

We can study the human brain after a person has died, and we can study the brains of animals, but these laboratory situations are not ideal for studying the human brain's neurotransmitters and receptors. Death can change the chemistry of the brain, and an animal's brain is not identical to that of a human. Fortunately, the following advances in technology are allowing us to study the brain functioning after treatment with medications specific for the treatment of bipolar disorder. The new techniques in brain imaging explained in this section are positron emission tomography (PET), functional magnetic resonance imaging (fMRI), and magnetic encephalography (MEG) of the brain. *At the present time, these brain imaging techniques are being used only as research tools and are not available for making the diagnosis of bipolar or other psychiatric disorders.*

Positron Emission Tomography (PET)

PET scans are limited to older teens and adults because they involve the administration of a radioactive substance. This substance allows investigators to track how much blood is flowing through various regions of the brain and how much glucose is being utilized by the neurons. These are indicators of how active the neurons are.

Functional Magnetic Resonance Imaging (fMRI)

This technique measures brain function without the need of radioactive substances. It measures the brain activity by monitoring how much oxygen the neurons are consuming. That serves as an indicator of how much blood is flowing through several brain regions, which in turn shows how active the neurons are.

Magnetic Encephalography (MEG)

The newest technique, MEG, directly measures the electricity generated by neurons by detecting changes in very small magnetic signals produced by active neurons. With MEG, investigators can observe the order and pattern of various brain regions when a person performs certain tasks. For example, using this brain imaging technique, we can evaluate different parts and circuits of the brain function while the child is performing certain tasks (such as math exercises) or being emotionally challenged (e.g., seeing scary, sad, and happy faces).

Recent brain imaging studies of adults with bipolar disorder and of others with recurrent unipolar depressions (depressions without mania or hypomania) have given researchers interesting insights. As illustrated in figures 4.3 and 4.4, they have shown that parts of the brain including the frontal cortex, hippocampus, and basal ganglia were decreased in size.[1,2] The brain cells of these regions were not functioning well, but in contrast with illnesses like Alzheimer's (an illness that produces severe memory problems and irreversible damage of the brain), the cells are not dead. Interestingly, lithium and perhaps valproate (Depakote) (medications presently used to treat bipolar disorder) may reverse the shrinking, helping to stimulate growth factors inside the neurons.

Brain Networks or Circuits

The brain has millions of neurons that are connected and constantly communicating among themselves. The neurons do not work alone. To perform their functions, they need to communicate with each other in a precise manner, creating many specialized centers and circuits throughout

Figure 4.3—Schematic Diagram of the Human Brain

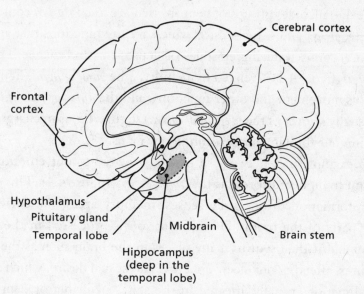

the brain. We are born with many of these connections; others develop or are transformed during the course of our lives by our daily experiences.

Changing Brain Circuits

The brain circuits and the way they communicate among themselves are not written in stone. They undergo changes during our life span. These changes may be part of the way the development of the brain has been programmed by the genes, or they may occur because of the constant positive and negative events that we experience.

These centers and networks or circuits of neurons work together like the instruments of an orchestra and are responsible for our cognition, fantasies, emotions, and the regulation of several bodily functions. For example, as illustrated in figure 4.4, the *amygdala* seems to be associated with emotions, in particular fear reactions. The *hypothalamus* (figure 4.4) includes groups of neurons that are in charge of controlling appetite, sleep, and sexual desire, which are the functions that are usually compromised during episodes of depression and mania. The *hippocampus* (figure 4.3) is related to memory. The *basal ganglia* (figure 4.4) controls movement and other functions, and the *anterior part of the cortex* (usually known as the *prefrontal cortex*) (figure 4.3) is in charge of organizing our thinking and executing our plans.

An example of a network of neurons related to our emotions and relevant to bipolar disorder is the *limbic system* (figure 4.4). This system gets information through the senses, memory areas, the cortex, and other parts of the brain. The information is processed in the limbic system and is then sent to many places in the brain such as the hypothalamus, affecting our sleep, appetite, and sexual desire, which are the body functions usually affected in the states of mania or depression. The limbic system also communicates with the *brain stem* (figure 4.3), an area that has special groups of neurons that send messages to the muscles, skin, eyes, and many other parts of the body, telling them how

Figure 4.4—Schematic Diagram of the Limbic System and the Basal Ganglia

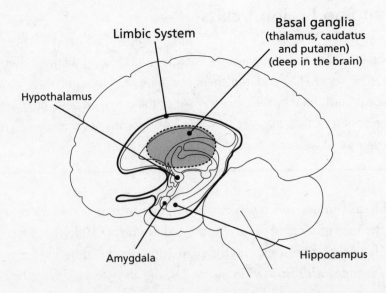

to act (e.g., run, stay put, look toward the left). Thus, when a person is too anxious, manic, or depressed, he or she may pace around, run, or stay immobile. The brain stem also has many neurons that belong to the *autonomic nervous system.* These neurons regulate many of the involuntary actions of the body, including heart rate, the movement of the lungs, blood pressure, and the movements of the intestine. Thus, when we experience an emotion such as depression or anxiety, we may feel that our heart is racing fast and have shortness of breath, nausea, stomachaches, loose stools, or frequent urination.

Illness such as bipolar disorder can be caused by a malfunctioning of these networks. In fact, fMRI and PET studies comparing the brains of youth and adults with bipolar disorder with those of healthy controls have suggested that people with bipolar disorder have problems in the circuits in charge of modulating emotions, particularly the frontal lobes, amygdala, and the limbic system.[1,2] These studies are in their infancy, and their findings require replication, but they provide hope that we may find the biological causes of bipolar disorder and better treatments.

PSYCHOLOGICAL AND ENVIRONMENTAL FACTORS

Because the genetic effect accounts for only up to 70 percent of the causes of bipolar disorder, other nongenetic influences must be responsible for the other 30 percent. Psychological factors such as mood dysregulation and environmental factors that are shared or not shared by a family, such as stressors, toxic substances, infections, or exposure to substances or infections while the child is in the mother's womb, may also play a role in the development of this disorder.

Mood Dysregulation

Several investigators have suggested that people with bipolar disorder have difficulties regulating or controlling their mood, in particular dur-

Antidepressant Medication May Trigger Mania

Medications to treat depression do not cause bipolar disorder, but they may trigger or unmask a manic episode in a child with a predisposition for bipolar disorder.

ing periods of stress, and this may be one the reasons why their mood fluctuates widely.[1,2,5] Investigators usually refer to a mood regulation problem as *mood dysregulation*. It is important to emphasize that although mood dysregulation is discussed here in the psychological/environmental section, mood regulation also is strongly determined by biological and genetic factors.

Problems with the regulation of mood can be modeled in a simplistic way by comparing it with the malfunction of a thermostat of an aquarium. The thermostat maintains or regulates the temperature of the water at a certain predetermined level. If the temperature is too low, the thermostat turns on and raises the temperature of the water. If the temperature gets too high, the thermostat turns off, and the water gets cooler. If the thermostat does not function well, the water can become too hot or too cold. Suppose that people have a network of neurons in their brains that regulates their emotional state, and let me call this network of neurons the "thymostat" (*thymo* = mood) or the mood regulatory system. (*Note*: Although we know that certain centers in the brain regulate mood, no such system has yet been found.) When healthy children experience frustration, they will get cranky, and their mood will naturally go down. When these children get excited, their mood may skyrocket up. This is not a problem, however, because the thymostat, in conjunction with other areas of the brain (e.g., the prefrontal cortex), then balances the mood by slowly bringing the mood back to an appropriate level.

Children with bipolar disorder, however, seem to have a problem with their thymostat. During periods of mania, their mood may increase (whether spontaneously or triggered by an internal or external stressor), and they cannot bring it back down. The same dysfunction occurs during periods of depression when the mood drops down dramatically, and the child cannot bring it back up again.

This dysfunction in mood regulation leaves the child with bipolar disorder "stuck" in the highs and lows that he or she may not be able to control.

Lifestyle and Environmental Factors

The interaction between genes and environment in bipolar disorder may be similar to what has been observed in other medical illnesses such as diabetes and high blood pressure. Like bipolar disorder, these illnesses also run in families and have a strong genetic component, but the manifestations are influenced by the child's environment and lifestyle. For example, a child may be at risk of developing diabetes or high blood pressure because one or more family members have one of these illnesses. However, if this child exercises, eats a healthy diet, and follows a healthy lifestyle, he or she may prevent the development of diabetes or high blood pressure. The same may happen to youth with bipolar disorder.

Few studies have been done to evaluate the effects of lifestyle and environmental factors on bipolar disorder.[2,5] However, you well know that factors such as sleep deprivation (e.g., going to bed late, jet lag), hunger, and the weather may change your child's mood and behavior and, in fact, sleep deprivation may trigger an episode of mania.[5] Also, illicit drugs, alcohol, stressful situations, caffeine, and sometimes medications can alter your child's ability to control mood and may trigger an episode of mania. You yourself may have experienced the high mood induced by alcohol and understand the difficulties you encountered while trying to control your mood and behavior—even when you notice that you are doing or saying inappropriate things. The same may be true for a person with bipolar disorder during a manic, hypomanic, or depressive episode.

Stress may also affect bipolar episodes. The few studies published have reported that adults with bipolar disorder who live in very stressful environments where there are high levels of criticism and hostility have more recurrence of mania and depressions than those who live in environments that are less hostile. Other factors such as the person's coping skills, intelligence, temperament, and support from others also contribute to the modulation of the person's mood.[2]

Future studies regarding the familial and nonfamilial factors associated with the triggering of bipolar disorder, particularly in youth, will shed light on this highly likely relationship.

Certainly, much more research is needed into the effects of mood dysfunction and lifestyle and environmental factors on bipolar disorder. For now, keep in mind that along with genetic and biological factors, they, too, may play a role.

The Role of Internal Conflicts

In the past, several theories assumed that certain internal conflicts such as "anger directed toward the self" may produce depression and that "psychological defenses against depression" produce mania. These theories, although interesting, have not been proven. But like other human beings, youth with bipolar disorder have internal conflicts and problems that need to be resolved.

SUMMARY

Bipolar disorder is a genetic illness that runs in families. Like many genetic illnesses, bipolar disorder is also influenced by biological and psychological factors as well as the child's environment, family situation, stress, moods, and lifestyle. Whatever the exact reason for your child's bipolar episodes, it is important to emphasize that neither you nor your child is to blame. Poor parental skills and persistent family conflicts may aggravate the bipolar disorder or make the child more oppositional, sad, and irritable, but none of these factors *cause* bipolar disorder. Hopefully, this chapter has helped you better understand why, because the reasons for bipolar disorder are so uncertain, it is so difficult to control the highs and lows of a bipolar episode, yet how, with professional help, your child may learn how it can be done.

In the future, new and exciting techniques to observe brain functioning along with molecular and genetic studies may help clarify the causes of bipolar disorder and help develop new treatments. But until these breakthroughs occur, chapter 5 will help you understand the present methods of assessing bipolar disorder.

> *Whatever the exact reason for your child's bipolar episodes, it is important to emphasize that neither you nor your child is to blame. Poor parental skills and persistent family conflicts may aggravate the bipolar disorder or make the child more oppositional, sad, and irritable, but none of these factors* cause *bipolar disorder.*

CHAPTER 5

How to Assess Bipolar Disorder in Children

MEDICAL SCIENCE DOES NOT yet have any blood, radiological, or brain study tests to confirm the diagnosis of any psychiatric disorder. The only way of making and validating a diagnosis of bipolar disorder is by obtaining *ongoing* information from the child as well as from parents, teachers, and other individuals who know the child well. As subjective as this method is, a correct diagnosis is critical to the success of any prescribed treatment your child may receive. So your input in the assessment of your child's symptoms is vitally important to your child's future well-being.

This chapter focuses on the process of diagnosis, from the initial assessment through the various steps clinicians and families must undertake to establish an accurate diagnosis. It will also give you the information you need to facilitate the initial and follow-up evaluations, understand diagnostic instruments and tests, and evaluate the proposed methods of treatment.

THE CLINICIAN

In addition to communication on the part of parents and child, the psychiatric diagnosis also depends on the clinician's awareness of how bipolar and other psychiatric disorders manifest in childhood. The clinician should also be familiar with normal child development as well as with the cultural and ethnic background of the child. (The word *clinician* here includes psychiatrists, psychologists, and other mental health-care workers, unless otherwise specified.)

> ## A Well-Prepared Clinician
> A well-prepared clinician needs to take into account the cognitive, social, and emotional development of the child as well as the parents' own problems, the family's ideas about the child's psychiatric disorder(s), and the cultural and ethnic background of the family.

It is most important that the clinician not "suggest" the answers. For example, asking a child, "It is true that you have mood swings, right?" or "I am sure that there are times when you are superhappy and silly," may induce the child (or the parent) to answer affirmatively in order to please the interviewer. Rephrasing the questions to be more open-ended, such as "Do you ever have mood swings?" or "Are there any times when you are superhappy and silly?" allows the interviewee to answer more honestly and in an unbiased way.

The clinician must inform the child or teen that most of the information he or she communicates to the clinician is confidential, with the exception of ideas or behaviors that may be dangerous to the child or others.

THE INITIAL APPOINTMENT

During the initial appointment, a preliminary diagnosis of your child's disorder is made. At this time it is essential to give the clinician baseline information about your child's psychiatric and medical symptoms (temper tantrums, oppositional behaviors, headaches, stomachaches, etc.) in order for him or her to make an accurate diagnosis and later to evaluate your child's response to any prescribed treatment.

Information Needed

A psychiatric diagnosis depends on how well the child, parents, and others communicate the child's symptoms to the person who is making the diagnosis. In preparation for the initial appointment, you should carefully observe, collect, and report the following information to your child's clinician. I realize that this list is long and exhaustive. Do not feel as though you must have all of this information before your first appointment! Go to the appointment with the information you feel is most relevant, and discuss with the clinician what additional information might be important to your child's case.

Information About the Child

CURRENT PSYCHIATRIC PROBLEMS

- A description of the child's current psychiatric symptoms or problems
- When the symptoms started (1 year ago, 2 months ago, 5 years ago, or when your child was in fifth grade or sixth grade, etc.)
- How often the symptoms occur (once a week, twice a month)
- Duration of symptoms. Because it is difficult to remember how long the symptoms last, it is better to inform the clinician of a range of time. For example, the manic or depressive symptoms last between 2 hours and 2 days, between 1 day and 1 week, and so forth.
- How the symptoms are affecting the child's functioning at home, at school, with peers, and with the family
- A summary of any current psychotherapy treatments and medications, including the dosages, blood levels, any side effects, and how long the medications have been administered

PAST PSYCHIATRIC HISTORY

- A description of any past psychiatric problems
- A summary of any prior psychiatric medications, including the dosages, blood levels, any side effects, and how long the medications were administered. (This information can be obtained from the clinician who treated your child or the pharmacies where you filled the prescriptions.)
- A description of any prior psychotherapy and how long the therapy lasted
- The results of any other prior psychiatric evaluation
- The results of any prior psychological testing

DEVELOPMENTAL AND MEDICAL HISTORY

- A review of the child's developmental history, including any problems with growing (a height and weight growth chart is helpful), walking, talking, controlling bladder or bowel movements, expressing emotions, relating to others, puberty, and menses
- A summary of any medical or neurological problems (including problems with hearing or vision) and their treatments
- A description of any problems during the mother's pregnancy and labor and use of any medications, cigarettes, alcohol, or illicit drugs during pregnancy
- Any use of caffeine, alcohol, cigarettes, or illicit drugs by child

SCHOOL HISTORY

- A summary of current and past academic or behavior problems (poor grades, learning disabilities, capacity to understand subjects at school, retentions, absenteeism, suspensions, expulsions)
- If available, school records since first grade or kindergarten
- If available, teacher reports describing your child's problems at school

PSYCHOSOCIAL HISTORY

- A description of your child's strengths and degree of creativity ("What is your child good at?")
- A description of how your child thinks or copes with problems and his or her self-esteem
- A depiction of your child's social skills and any problems relating to other children and adults
- A report of any problems with daily routines and activities (e.g., sleeping, eating, studying, playing sports, sex)

NAMES, ADDRESSES, AND TELEPHONE NUMBERS

- Prior psychiatrists and clinicians
- Pediatrician or family doctor
- Teachers who know the child well
  (*Note*: These people will not be contacted without the permission of parents and children. Also, you need to give permission to your pediatrician or prior psychiatrist to talk with your current clinician.)

Information About the Family

- Provide a family history of any significant psychiatric disorders in parents, siblings, uncles, aunts, cousins, grandparents, and other relatives
- Report parents' and siblings' psychiatric treatments and response to these treatments, if any
- Summarize any significant medical and neurological problems in the family
- Explain the parents' or family's attitude and ideas about your child's psychiatric problems

Information About the Environment

- A description of the environment in which your child lives (home, school, and neighborhood)

- Information about any ethnic, cultural, or religious issue relevant for your child's diagnosis, evaluation, and treatment
- A list of possible stressors that may have triggered or worsened your child's psychiatric disorder (e.g., parental separation or divorce, death or illness in the family, family conflicts, moving to another city)

(Do not forget to highlight your child's *strengths* in all of these noted areas as well.)

A List of Problems

To create a working a diagnosis and treatment plan, list your child's problems in order of their severity during the initial appointment. This is important because beyond treatment of the child's psychiatric disorder(s), certain behaviors may require specific treatments, such as family or behavior therapy. The list of problems can also be used to monitor the child's response to treatment.

For example, 8-year-old Moses has bipolar disorder and ADHD. His parents complained that his main problems included (1) having temper tantrums, (2) stealing, (3) lying, (4) fighting with his siblings, and (4) not doing his homework. While his symptoms of bipolar disorder and ADHD responded well to treatment with valproate (Depakote) and stimulants, he continued to have problems with stealing, lying, and fighting with his siblings. With family and behavior therapy targeting these specific problems, his relationships with his siblings improved, he stopped stealing, and his lying diminished.

A Working Diagnosis

As detailed in chapters 1 and 2, clinicians often use a predetermined set of criteria to diagnose bipolar disorder. However, criteria for the diagnosis of bipolar disorder, particularly those for children, are not fixed and will keep changing in accordance with new developments and discoveries in the field. Presently, in the United States diagnosis is usually based on the *Diagnostic and Statistical Manual (DSM)* criteria created by the American Psychiatric Association,[1] but in other parts of the world clinicians use different types of criteria, such as the *International Statistical Classification of Diseases and Related Health Problems (ICD-10).*[2]

But whatever method your child's clinician uses, the initial diagnosis of your child is extremely important. You do not want him or her to be misdiagnosed and given treatment for the wrong disorder. With improper treatment, your child may not only fail to improve but could even experience a worsening of symptoms. Thus, the main goal of the initial appointment is to make a working diagnosis of your child's psychiatric disorder(s) and to create a preliminary treatment plan. A working diagnosis and preliminary treatment plan are "rough drafts" that will be edited and refined as more information is gathered.

> Criteria for the diagnosis of bipolar disorder, particularly those for children, are not fixed and will keep changing in accordance with new developments and discoveries in the field.

It cannot be overemphasized that, especially for *disorders that fluctuate over time such as bipolar disorder, one initial evaluation is not sufficient.* It is necessary to arrange a series of assessments during which the clinician becomes familiar with the child, the parent(s), and the environment (home, school, neighborhood, friends, etc.) in which the child is being raised. The clinician may also need to see the results of a series of tests he or she may order before the initial diagnosis can be made with any degree of certainty.

FURTHER TESTING

In addition to the initial evaluation, the clinician may request further assessments. Many different instruments are currently used to assess psychiatric symptoms, the level of functioning at home and at school, family relationships, the response to treatment, side effects of medications, and other issues (such as family conflicts and peer problems). While the description of these instruments is beyond the scope of this chapter, it is important for you to be familiar with their existence and use.

In general, instruments used for the assessment of the symptoms of bipolar disorder can be divided into four categories: psychological tests, psychiatric interviews, questionnaires, and medical and neurological evaluations.

Psychological Tests

Overall, psychological tests are helpful to identify learning (e.g., reading, writing, and mathematics) and language problems, attention difficulties, and whether the child has any cognitive (thinking processes) deficits or strengths. Some people believe that psychological tests will provide the diagnosis of bipolar disorder or other psychiatric disorders. However, with the exception of mental retardation and learning disabilities, available psychological tests do not make a psychiatric diagnosis. As stated in this chapter, the diagnosis is made by good history and careful observation of the child over time at different settings.

> *Psychological tests are helpful to identify learning (e.g., reading, writing, and mathematics) and language problems, attention difficulties, and whether the child has any cognitive (thinking processes) deficits or strengths.*

Psychiatric Interviews

Psychiatric interviews are used for both clinical and research purposes and include, among many others, the Schedule for Affective Disorders and Schizophrenia in School-Aged Children—Present and Lifetime Version (K-SADS-PL)[3] and the Diagnostic Interview Schedule (DISC).[4] These interviews include many questions based on the manual of the American Psychiatric Association or other criteria for the diagnosis of psychiatric disorders.[1] It is important to emphasize that these interviews require special training for their administration, are lengthy, and are not required to make a psychiatric diagnosis. A clinician with a good knowledge of psychiatric symptoms and normal child development, as well as experience, can do an excellent psychiatric evaluation without the need of sophisticated interviews. (When conducting research, however, these interviews are necessary.)

Questionnaires

Questionnaires that evaluate for psychiatric symptoms can be completed by the clinician, parent, or child. Clinicians usually administer questionnaires to assess the severity of the child's symptoms (such as depression, mania, and ADHD) and the child's response to treatment. Parent questionnaires typically ask the parent to answer questions about the child, and some questionnaires ask questions about the parent's own problems. Children and teens usually answer questions about themselves (self-reports).

All of these questionnaires are helpful because they give the clinician an idea of your child's main strengths and weaknesses from the perspective of the parent as well as that of the child. These instruments are also useful in measuring your child's response to treatment and the development of side effects from prescribed medications. Moreover, a child may sometimes deny certain symptoms (such as suicidal ideation) during the face-to-face psychiatric interview, but then indicate the presence of these symptoms in self-questionnaires.

A few of these questionnaires that may be used during a psychiatric evaluation are briefly discussed here. Samples and further instructions are included in Appendix I.

> *All of these questionnaires are helpful because they give the clinician an idea of your child's main strengths and weaknesses from the perspective of the parent as well as that of the child.*

Mood and Feelings Questionnaire (MFQ)[5]

This questionnaire is used to screen for the presence of depressive symptoms. There is a parent and a child version. Total values equal or above 40 suggest that the child has significant depressive symptoms and that a complete evaluation is warranted.

Screen for Child Anxiety Related Disorders (SCARED)[6]

This questionnaire has a parent and a child version, and total scores equaling or above 25 suggest that the child has significant anxiety symptoms. However, given that there are several types of anxiety disorders, such as separation anxiety, social phobia, general anxiety, and panic disorder, a child may have a low total score that it is high for a specific anxiety disorder.

Disruptive Behavior Disorder (DBD)[7]

This scale assesses symptoms of ADHD and oppositional and conduct disorders.

Child Global Assessment Scale (CGAS)[8]

This is one of several instruments useful in evaluating a child's general functioning. Scores below 70 denote that the child has poor functioning in several areas such as academics and peer and family relationships.

Child Mania Rating Scale, Parent Version (CMRS-P)

Ongoing studies are evaluating several parental and child self-reports to screen for manic and hypomanic symptoms in children and teens. For example, recently Dr. Mani Pulvuri developed a parent questionnaire called CMRS-P to screen for mania in children and teens. Although this questionnaire is in the process of being studied, with Dr. Pulvuri's permission it has been included in Appendix I. In the near future, we will have more information regarding how to score it. In the meantime, if your child scores many 3s or 4s, particularly in items such as "superhappy," "grandiose ideas," and "no need for sleep," consult with his or her doctor. Also, it appears that scores ≥ 35 are significant.

As you look over the questionnaires in Appendix I, *remember that questionnaires do* not

> **Sample Questionnaires**
>
> Some questionnaires utilized for the assessment of depression, anxiety, ADHD, and behavior problems, as well as questionnaires to measure general functioning, can be found in Appendix I. Only self-reports that are reliable and not under copyright are included.

make a diagnosis. While they are helpful tools for the screening of psychiatric disorders, the actual diagnosis is made by careful interviews of the child and parent(s) in conjunction with ongoing observations of the child at various settings over time.

Medical and Neurological Evaluations

Medical and neurological evaluations may be necessary to find out whether your child has any conditions that may explain his or her current psychiatric symptoms. While there are currently no laboratory tests that can be used to reliably diagnose a psychiatric disorder or predict response to treatment, certain cases may suggest a medical or neurological illness for which tests are available:

- **Clinical presentation.** Acute or rapid onset, presence of confusion, uncommon or rare symptoms, progressive decline in the ability to think, and no response to treatment
- **Family history.** Congenital brain illnesses, genetic conditions, and medical or neurological problems such as thyroid problems, seizures, and immune illnesses
- **Physical exam.** Abnormal neurological signs such as tremors and lack of strength in an arm can suggest an underlying medical or neurological cause for the current psychiatric symptoms.

Laboratory tests such as chromosomal studies, thyroid function tests, screens for toxic substances (such as drugs, poor metabolism of copper in the body), liver function tests, brain imaging (MRI), electrocardiogram (ECG), electroencephalogram (EEG), and other tests may be necessary to determine whether a medical or neurological illness is the cause of the present symptoms. Laboratory tests may also be administered before starting a child on medications that can affect his or her bodily functions (as discussed later in this chapter).

MONITORING MOOD CHANGES AT HOME

Because the symptoms of bipolar disorder fluctuate often, you can best keep track of your child's symptoms during and after the diagnosis period with a *mood diary*. Both you and your child should keep separate diaries in order to present different perspectives of what is going on and to allow your child to express his or her feelings and other things that may be private.

There are many types of mood diaries. After trying several diaries at our clinic, the mood diary included in Appendix I, although not perfect, is the one that most of our patients have been able to complete with the fewest problems. The diary consists of a line with 0 at one extreme and 10 at the other. The child and parent(s) each rate the mood of the child daily, with 0 being very sad (or very irritable), 5 in the middle, and 10 being superhappy and silly beyond what is expected for the child's age and the situation. For example, it is normal that a child will be extremely happy when he has been taken to a special event or she has received a special present. Also, it is common to see groups of teens in the mall screaming, having fun, and being silly. This may be normal, but a manic or hypomanic person will not be able to stop. The reaction will be exaggerated, out of context, and often annoying, and even friends will notice the problem.

Before bedtime each night, the parent and child each mark on the line how the child's mood was during the day. If the child's mood is changing frequently, it is possible to make a mark for the morning (marking it with the letters AM) and a mark for the afternoon or evening (marking it with the letters PM). For example, a child might mark a 2 for the morning and 7 in the evening. There is also space to add some comments. This will help identify whether the child's mood was consistent with the situation or out of context. For example, you can note in the diary that your child was 2 when you did not buy the toy she was requesting (low score in response to an upsetting situation), or your child may note that he was a 1 without any specific reason. Girls can also include the day they menstruate in order to observe whether their mood is related to the patterns in their menstrual cycle.

If possible, it is helpful to complete the mood diary for 2 to 4 weeks before any treatment starts. This baseline information will be helpful in measuring response to treatment. For example, a child might score 1 to 3 during most of the baseline period, and, several weeks after treatment started, his or her mood might be on a 6 or 7. Because the child's mood went up after treatment started, this is an indication that treatment is working well. Once treatment begins, parents are encouraged to include in the diary the dose of medication or any changes in medications to keep track of the child's responsiveness to changes in treatment.

FOLLOW-UP APPOINTMENTS

The goals of the follow-up appointments are to confirm the diagnosis of bipolar or other psychiatric disorders and to monitor the treatment plan. This is accomplished by collecting more information; your child's clinician will want to talk more about family or peer problems that were mentioned during the initial evaluation. He or she will ask more questions about the child's daily routines and any stressors. This is also a time for additional laboratory or psychological tests if the clinician feels they are necessary for further clarification. It is also when your child will begin treatment, and later visits will allow the clinician to monitor the response and side effects of that treatment.

The frequency of follow-ups depends on the severity of the symptoms (the presence of agitation, psychotic symptoms, aggression, and suicidal ideations). Appointments are typically once a week (or more) initially until the child improves and thereafter once a month or as needed. Follow-ups are usually held in an outpatient setting or clinic, but it is sometimes necessary to admit the child into the hospital or a partial program (as explained in chapter 8).

EVALUATION OF TREATMENT

In a perfect world, a clinician could say, "Your child has bipolar disorder, and these pills will cure him." But as you know, this is not a perfect world. Bipolar disorder is a very difficult diagnosis to make and often takes time and many reevaluations. When the diagnosis is finally determined, no cure exists. The treatment plan your child's psychiatrist will recommend is designed to reduce the severity of symptoms and help him or her lead a more normal life. But you must remember that there is still no pill that will make this go away.

Your child's psychiatrist will closely monitor the safe administration of the prescribed medication, the treatment response, and the possible side effects.

Medication Monitoring

It is important to measure vital signs before and during treatment with some medications. For example, your child may need to have his or her lying-down and standing blood pressure and pulse taken for medications that can produce high blood pressure, hypotension (low blood pressure), and pulse changes. Cell blood count is necessary before administering medications that may affect the red and white blood cells or the platelets (essential for the body to form blood clots). An electrocardiogram (ECG) should be given before administering medications that affect the heart's electrical activity, and lipids and glucose in blood should be tested before administering medication that may elevate these substances.

During treatment with certain medications, laboratory tests may also be needed (such as liver function tests for valproate, and kidney and thyroid function for lithium), and monitoring of the medication blood levels can be important in certain cases. (For further information about laboratory tests for each of the medications used for children and teens with bipolar disorder, see chapters 6 and 9.)

Making Lab Tests a Little Easier

Several of the medications used for bipolar disorder require baseline and on-going blood tests to check for side effects as well as medication blood levels. Many children, particularly those who are obese or anxious, have great difficulty submitting to these tests. Use of a topical anesthetic (such as Emla cream) can be extremely helpful in minimizing the child's discomfort. Also, some medication blood levels can now be measured with very small amounts of blood from a "finger stick." A few laboratories can now measure lithium in saliva. Ask your child's clinician for more information about these helpful advances and to teach your child behavioral techniques that can diminish his or her fear of blood tests.

Treatment Response

In psychiatry, treatment response has traditionally been determined by the absence of all but one or two symptoms for any particular psychiatric disorder. Response to treatment has also been defined as a significant reduction (e.g., a 50 percent reduction) in symptom severity as determined by using self-report questionnaires or some of the clinician-based instruments (such as the K-SADS Mania Rating Scale[9] or the Child's Depression Rating Scale[10]).

Using these criteria, children considered "improved" may still have considerable symptoms. For example, 16-year-old Allen showed a 50 percent reduction in his depressive symptoms with treatment. However, he was still cranky, had problems concentrating at school, and could not sleep well. Therefore, instead of a 50 percent reduction in the total score, a better reflection of satisfactory response may be a persistent (for several weeks) low score on a questionnaire, together with consistent improvement in his functioning in several areas, such as with family and peers and at school.

Side Effects

In addition to the desired effects of medications, almost all have undesirable side effects. The child psychiatrist will ask you to keep track of your child's physical and emotional health (good and bad) both before and after treatment begins. Any changes in your child's condition will be discussed at the follow-up appointments.

Having a clear record of before and after symptoms is very important to treatment evaluation. Children and teens may have headaches, stomachaches, or skin problems, for example, before medication is started. If these symptoms were not noted beforehand, the child, parents, or child psychiatrist may believe that the medication is causing these symptoms and therefore unnecessarily discontinue that treatment. When Maria began to take lithium for her bipolar disorder, she complained about headaches. Maria and her parents thought that the lithium was causing the headaches and wanted to discontinue the medication. However, after carefully reviewing her medical records, Maria's child psychiatrist found that she had been complaining of headaches before she started lithium, thus eliminating the possibility that lithium was the cause of her headaches. Maria continued taking lithium, and she and her child psychiatrist then sought other causes for her headaches.

> ## Pre- and Posttreatment Evaluations
>
> The measurement of any symptoms before starting treatment is important because the child may have physical and emotional symptoms before the initiation of the treatment that can be confused with side effects of the medication.

Once treatment has begun, it is vitally important to measure the medication side effects consistently to ensure the child is not experiencing any unwanted negative effects. Your child's psychiatrist will be alert to known and unknown side effects, in particular when using a new medication and for children needing pharmacological treatment for long periods of time. Although questionnaires are available to evaluate medication side effects, such effects are usually assessed by directly asking the parent(s) and child about specific problems for each of the most important systems in the body. For example, for the neurological system, we ask for the presence of headaches, tremors (shakes), or seizures. For the gastrointestinal system, we ask for the presence of nausea, vomiting, diarrhea, or stomachaches. The most common side effects for each of the medications used in the treatment of bipolar disorder and other psychiatric disorders are described in chapters 6 and 9.

SUMMARY

The assessment of a child with bipolar disorder requires careful examination of his or her past and current psychiatric, medical, and developmental history as well as ongoing evaluations of his or her symptoms, response to treatment, and medication side effects. It is a complex process but an absolutely necessary one to assure that your child is correctly diagnosed and treated.

The next chapter presents detailed information about the medications and other biological treatments that may be prescribed for your child following the assessment. This information will help you stay involved in every step of your child's recovery.

CHAPTER 6

Tools for Treating Bipolar Disorder: Biological Treatments

IT IS VERY IMPORTANT for you to be informed about the medication(s) prescribed to your child. That's the only way you can become partners with your child's doctor and health-care team and carefully monitor your child's response to treatments. To help you do this, this chapter includes an overview of the three types of medications currently used to treat bipolar disorder:[1-4] (1) mood stabilizers, (2) antidepressants, and (3) adjunctive or additional medications. For each category of drug, you will be given information about its use, presentations, dosage, precautions, management of specific side effects, and laboratory tests that will help you better understand and monitor the medications your child may be given to treat the symptoms of bipolar disorder. Also, at the end of this chapter is a summary of the general management of common side effects produced by medications often used for treating children with bipolar disorders. (Note: It is impossible to include all medications' side effects. Therefore, if you have a question regarding side effects, ask your child's doctor.)

In addition to these conventional medications, this chapter also discusses the role of other treatments, such as St. John's wort and the essential fatty acids, and other biological therapies, including bright light therapy, electroconvulsive treatment (ECT), and transcranial magnetic stimulation (TMS) for the treatment of bipolar disorder in youth.

Consult Your Child Psychiatrist

Because the pharmacological treatment of bipolar disorders is a rapidly expanding area, you should consult with your child's psychiatrist regarding new advances in treatment options.[1-4] You may also want to consult other resources, including books and the Internet (see Appendix II), but you should be cautious regarding the accuracy of the information presented. Any questions or conflicting information should be discussed with your child's doctor.

GENERAL INFORMATION ABOUT MEDICATIONS

As described in detail in chapter 5, before your child starts taking any medications, it is helpful to make a list, with your child's doctor or another member of the treating team, of the symptoms you and your child have observed. You should know which symptoms the medications are expected to help so that you can observe which symptoms are getting better, which are staying the same, or which are getting worse as treatment proceeds. In addition, record the emergence of any new symptoms, and discuss these with your child's doctor. The list of symptoms will also help you differentiate between the symptoms that existed before starting treatment and the symptoms that are side effects of the medications.

Once a medication has been prescribed, it's up to you to monitor its safe use. A prescribed treatment often needs to be adjusted or changed before the most effective plan is found. Your child's doctor cannot know how your child reacts to the treatment without your constant supervision and feedback. The following general tips will guide you as you work with your child's health-care team to find the right treatment program for your child.

- Before starting treatment with medications, inform your child's doctor if your child has a history of any significant medical problems (high or low blood pressure, allergies, seizures, heart problems, diabetes, asthma, etc.) and if he or she is taking any other medications.

- If your child has been on medications for psychiatric problems before, let your child's doctor know which medication(s), dosages, and the length of time your child took the medication(s).

- The medication dosage will depend on the specific medication being used, the child's response to the medication, the presence of side effects, and sometimes the medication blood levels and the child's weight. Most of these medications are started at very low dosages that are then slowly increased over several weeks until symptoms begin to improve. Some children may need higher or lower dosages in order to show progress in symptoms.

- Many psychiatric medications, including the medications used to treat bipolar disorder, take several weeks before a noticeable improvement in symptoms becomes evident. Discontinuing the medication prematurely may result in the loss of any improvements made, a significant delay in illness treatment, and a reemergence or worsening of symptoms. Don't be alarmed if you and your child don't notice improvement in symptoms right away.

- Do not change the dosage or schedule of medication without talking to your child's doctor. It is very important that your child take his or her medication every day as prescribed. Ask your doctor what to do if a dosage is missed. For most medications, if a dosage is missed, wait until the next dosage is due and resume the usual schedule. Do not give your child two dosages at once. If missing dosages becomes a regular problem, contact your child's doctor to discuss alternate treatment options.

- Do not stop a medication abruptly. Suddenly stopping a medication may result in unpleasant *withdrawal* symptoms (i.e., nausea, vomiting, upset stomach, headache, cold or flulike symptoms, confusion, and, in children with seizures, worsening of their seizures) and may lead to a relapse of your child's disorder. Most medications require a gradual reduction in dosage, which should be supervised by your child's doctor.

> *Suddenly stopping a medication may result in unpleasant withdrawal symptoms and may lead to a relapse of your child's disorder.*

- The potential for accidental or purposeful overdose is present with all medications. Medication use should be supervised by an adult, and medication should be kept out of reach of young children. If you suspect that your child had an overdose (e.g., unexplained nausea, vomiting, diarrhea, drowsiness, dizziness, or lack of consciousness), contact the poison control center, call your child's doctor or nurse, and if necessary take your child to a hospital emergency room immediately.

- If there is a chance that your child may be pregnant, inform your doctor immediately. Some of these medications have been associated with birth defects if taken in the first trimester of pregnancy, and many of these medications are secreted in breast milk. If there is any possibility of your child becoming pregnant while receiving treatment, speak to your child's doctor regarding pregnancy prevention and to ensure the safety of your child and her fetus.

- Consult with your child's doctor, nurse, or pharmacist to determine whether the prescribed medications need to be stored at room temperature or in the refrigerator, if the medications should be taken with food or on an empty stomach, and if the tablets can be broken in half or if the capsule's contents can be sprinkled on food.

MOOD STABILIZERS

Mood stabilizers are a group of medications used to stabilize the extreme mood fluctuations between mania and depression and to prevent recurrence of these mood swings. Mood stabilizers include lithium carbonate, the anticonvulsants, and the second generation of antipsychotics. These medications will be discussed in detail below.

Mood Stabilizer: Lithium Carbonate

Lithium is a very useful medication to treat bipolar disorder, particularly manic symptoms. It is also used to prevent further episodes of bipolar disorder. Lithium may also be used in conjunction with antidepressants to treat depression that has not responded to usual antidepressant treatment.

> ### Future Studies on Mood Stabilizers and Children
>
> Most of the studies using mood stabilizers for bipolar disorder were carried out in adults, but it appears that these medications are also useful for the management of bipolar symptoms in youth. Ongoing investigations using mood stabilizers will give us further information about the use and side effects of these medications in children and teens (see Appendix II).

Lithium: Presentation and Dosage

Lithium may be prescribed in several different preparations and is available in both short-acting (immediate-release) and long-acting (controlled or slow-release) formulations (table 6.1). The slow-release formulations result in more stable blood levels of lithium throughout the day and may therefore be associated with fewer side effects than the immediate-release formulations.

The dosage of lithium used will depend on the child's clinical response, lithium blood levels, and the presence of any side effects. Lithium is usually administered to obtain blood levels between 0.6 to 1.1 mEq/liter (milliequivalents per liter). Some children may need lower or higher blood levels to achieve improvement in symptoms. To reach these blood levels, dosages of 300 to 1,800 milligrams a day are generally required, but the dosage will vary from child to child.

TABLE 6.1—LITHIUM CARBONATE

Generic Name	Brand Name	Preparation	Dosage
Lithium carbonate (immediate-release)	Eskalith, Lithium	Capsules: 150, 300, and 600 mg	300–1,800 mg/day given 2–3 times a day
Lithium carbonate (immediate-release)	Lithotabs	Tablets: 300 mg	300–1,800 mg/day given 2–3 times a day
Lithium citrate	Lithium citrate	Liquid: 8 mEq/ in 1 tsp (5 ml)	300–1,800 mg/day given 2–3 times a day
Lithium carbonate controlled-release (CR)	Eskalith CR	Capsules: 450 mg	300–1,800 mg/day given twice daily
Lithium carbonate slow-release (SR)	Lithobid	Capsules: 300 mg	300–1,800 mg/day given twice daily

Lithium: Precautions

- Lithium should not be given to children with significant kidney problems.
- Lithium should be administered with caution to children with cardiac, thyroid, and seizure problems.
- Lithium may cause cardiac defects in the fetus if taken during the first 3 months of pregnancy and can be excreted in the breast milk of mothers who are taking this medication.
- Changes in the amount of salt and water in the body can affect blood levels of lithium. For example, eating a lot of salty foods can potentially lower lithium blood levels. On the other hand, cutting salt from the diet may lead to high lithium blood levels. These changes in salt intake must be quite dramatic in order to

affect your child. Of more practical concern is your child's body water. Decreases in body water may result from not drinking enough fluids or from perspiring excessively and can lead to dehydration, high blood lithium levels, and possible lithium toxicity. It is therefore important to ensure that your child drinks enough water, especially on hot days and while exercising.

- Be cautious when giving your child other prescription or over-the-counter medications while he or she is on lithium. Using lithium with nonsteroidal anti-inflammatory medications (i.e., ibuprofen, indomethacin, or naproxen), some blood pressure medications (i.e., Enapril, Captopril, and thiazide diuretics), the antibiotic metronidazole (brand name Flagyl), and some anti-seizure medications (i.e., carbamazepine, phenytoin, and divalproex) may increase blood lithium levels. Always ask your child's doctor or pharmacist for possible interactions between lithium and other medications, and always inform your child's doctor and dentist of the medications being taken.

Lithium: Common Side Effects

For responding to common side effects, including weight gain, nausea, vomiting, sedation, cognitive problems, dry mouth, and diarrhea, see the section on "Management of Common Side Effects" later in this chapter.

Other specific side effects your child may experience when taking lithium are as follows.

Lithium: Management of Specific Side Effects

- **Increased thirst.** Because lithium increases the amount of urine produced by the kidneys, it is common for children to experience an increase in the frequency of urination and an associated increased thirst. Your child may complain of dry mouth and drink large quantities of liquids. Good hydration is very important because dehydration can lead to elevated lithium levels and an accompanied increase in side effects and risk of toxicity. Therefore, ensure that your child drinks enough water especially on hot days or while exercising. For dry mouth and thirst, try to avoid sweets and high-calorie beverages, which may lead to increased weight and cause cavities. Instead, try sugarless gum and drink water, and be sure your child brushes his or her teeth regularly. Remember to send a note to your child's school requesting that your child be allowed to have bottles of water in the classroom.

- **Increased urination.** It is common for children to experience an increase in the frequency of urination as well as an increased urine volume while taking lithium. Inform teachers that your child may need to use the bathroom more frequently than most students. The increased urine volume may also result in bed-wetting, especially in children who are already predisposed to this problem. Bedwetting can be minimized by having your child cut down on liquids in the evening and use the bathroom before he or she goes to bed. Also take your child to the bathroom before you go to bed.

  If the increase in urination persists or gets worse, or the volume of urine increases and is associated with other symptoms (i.e., abdominal pain, pain when using the bathroom, foul-smelling urine, or a change in the color of urine), talk to your child's doctor as these symptoms may indicate a medical problem not related to lithium (i.e., kidney problems, diabetes, urinary tract infection).

- **Hand tremor.** Lithium may induce a mild hand tremor that generally does not affect your child's functioning. Check your child's handwriting and talk to your child's doctor if his or her writing is too "shaky." Lowering the dosage of lithium or sometimes adding a medication called a *beta-blocker* may help.

- **Skin and hair problems.** Lithium may cause acne or worsen acne that is already present. It may also exacerbate a skin condition called *psoriasis*. If your child has acne or psoriasis, consult with a dermatologist before starting treatment with lithium. If acne or psoriasis worsens despite appropriate treatment of these conditions, your doctor may consider switching to a different medication.

Hair thinning is usually transient. Although not proven, zinc and selenium supplements (e.g., Centrum) may help.

- **Thyroid problems.** Lithium can affect the functioning of the thyroid and parathyroid glands. The most common abnormality is *hypothyroidism.* This side effect is more common in women and usually develops within the first 2 years of therapy. In hypothyroidism, the thyroid gland does not produce enough thyroid hormone. Symptoms of this disorder include weakness, fatigue, constipation, slowed speech, dry skin, muscle cramps, and weight gain. Some of these symptoms, such as weakness, fatigue, slowed speech, weight gain, and low motivation, may be confused with other side effects of lithium or with depression. If your child is experiencing these symptoms, inform his or her doctor.

  Before your child starts lithium, your child's doctor will order blood tests to measure levels of thyroid hormone and will continue to measure these blood levels periodically thereafter. If your child develops symptoms of hypothyroidism, these blood tests will be repeated to determine whether the symptoms are due to a thyroid problem. If your child is found to have hypothyroidism related to lithium therapy, a decision will need to be made to either discontinue the lithium and switch to a different medication, or to continue the lithium and treat the hypothyroidism with thyroid hormone pills (i.e., Synthroid). This decision will depend on how well your child has responded to lithium therapy. If your child has done very well on lithium, remaining on this medication while treating the hypothyroidism is a reasonable option. On the other hand, if lithium has not been effective for your child, discontinuing the medication in favor of another medication may be a better choice.

- **Kidney problems.** Kidney problems caused by lithium therapy are rare but may be irreversible. Individuals with preexisting kidney problems or those who have experienced repeated lithium toxicity are at highest risk. Kidney problems are diagnosed by blood and urine tests, which will be ordered by your child's doctor periodically throughout the course of treatment. If your child develops kidney problems, you and your child's doctor will have to weigh the pros and cons of remaining on lithium therapy versus changing to a different medication.

- **Lithium toxicity.** One of the most serious side effects is the risk of developing lithium toxicity. Lithium toxicity generally occurs when lithium blood levels are above 1.5 mEq/liter, although symptoms of toxicity may occur with levels lower than this in some children. High blood lithium levels may result from taking more than the recommended dosage of lithium, interactions with other medications, a low-salt diet, or dehydration. Symptoms that could indicate high lithium levels include nausea, vomiting, diarrhea, dry mouth, dizziness, unsteadiness, weakness, and slurred speech.

High Blood Levels of Lithium

If your child appears "drunk" while taking lithium (nausea, vomiting, unsteady steps, slurred speech, and confusion), take your child to the emergency room because he or she may have very high blood levels of lithium. These symptoms may progress to abnormal muscle movements, inability to pass urine, seizures, and coma. If your child is experiencing symptoms of toxicity, stop the medication and take your child to the emergency room.

Lithium: Laboratory Tests Needed Before and During Treatment

- Before starting lithium, your child's doctor will order a urine test and blood tests to determine the number of white and red blood cells and the levels of electrolytes, thyroid hormones, and kidney function.

- Once the medication has been started, your child's doctor will order blood tests to measure lithium levels. Lithium blood levels *must* be measured 8 to 12 hours after the last dosage. Levels will be measured frequently at the beginning of treatment to ensure that the level of medication in the blood is within the recommended range (0.6–1.1 mEq/liter).

- Throughout the course of treatment, your child's doctor will repeat the urine test and blood tests to measure the number of white and red blood cells and the levels of electrolytes, thyroid hormones, and kidney function every 2 to 6 months depending on how your child is doing and the presence of side effects.

- Other laboratory tests such as electrocardiograms (ECG) and electroencephalograms (EEGs) are sometimes necessary.

Mood Stabilizer: Anticonvulsants

The anticonvulsants include valproate (Depakote), carbamazepine (Tegretol), oxcarbazepine (Trileptal), lamotrigine (Lamictal), and topiramate (Topamax). These medications were originally made to control convulsions or seizures and were therefore called *anticonvulsants*. However, it was discovered that these medications are also useful for the acute treatment and the prevention of further episodes of bipolar disorder, particularly manic and hypomanic episodes, with lamotrigine being used for depression. They are also helpful for treating migraine headaches, pain, and sometimes aggressive behaviors.

Newer anticonvulsants, such as tiagabine (Gabitril), may also be useful for the treatment of bipolar disorder, but studies to support their use for bipolar illness are still pending. Gabapentin (Neurontin) is not beneficial for the treatment of bipolar disorder, but it appears to be useful in treating anxiety symptoms.

Benzodiazepines (such as Ativan and Klonopin) are also anticonvulsants, but they do not work as mood stabilizers and are used as adjunctive treatments, as explained later in this chapter.

Anticonvulsants: Presentation and Dosage

The dosage of anticonvulsants depends on the child's clinical response and presence of side effects. For some anticonvulsants, such as valproate and carbamazepine, the response depends on appropriate blood levels (table 6.2). Dosages and presentations (table 6.2), precautions, and common side effects for valproate, carbamazepine, oxcarbazepine, lamotrigine, and topiramate are discussed here. More specific side effects and the management of these side effects are considered for each individual medication.

TABLE 6.2—ANTICONVULSANTS: PRESENTATIONS AND DOSAGES

Generic Name	Brand Name	Preparation	Dosage
Valproate sodium	Depakote— delayed-release	Tablets: 125, 250, and 500 mg Sprinkle capsules: 125 mg	250–1,500 mg/day given 2 times a day to obtain blood levels between 60 and 120 μg/ml
	Depakote— extended-release (ER)	Tablets: 250 and 500 mg	500–1,500 mg/day given 1 time a day to obtain blood levels between 60 and 120 μg/ml
Carbamazepine	Tegretol	Chewable tablets: 100 and 200 mg Liquid: 100 mg per tsp (5 ml)	400–1,600 mg, given 2–3 times per day to obtain levels between 4 and 12 μg/ml
	Carbatrol	200 and 300 mg	

Generic Name	Brand Name	Preparation	Dosage
Carbamazepine XR	Tegretol XR	Tablets: 100, 200, and 400 mg	400–1,600 mg, 2–3 times per day; blood levels are not necessary
Oxcarbazepine	Trileptal	Tablets: 150, 300, and 600 mg Syrup: 300 mg in 1 tsp (5 ml)	300–2,400 mg, divided into 2–3 dosages a day
Lamotrigine	Lamictal	Tablets: 25, 100, 150, and 200 mg Chewable tablets: 2, 5, and 25 mg	50–400 mg, divided into 2 dosages per day; blood levels are not necessary
Topiramate	Topamax	Tablets: 25, 100, and 200 mg Capsules: 15 and 25 mg Sprinkle capsules	200–400 mg/day given twice a day; blood levels are not necessary

Anticonvulsants: Precautions

- Anticonvulsants should be administered with caution to children with certain medical illnesses such as liver or kidney illnesses. Do not administer them to children with prior allergic reactions to a particular medication.
- Some anticonvulsant medications may cause birth defects if taken during pregnancy, particularly during the first 3 months of the pregnancy. For example, valproate may produce damage in the fetuses' brain system. *Note:* Be cautious when giving your child other medications while he or she is taking anticonvulsants. For exam-

ple, using anticonvulsants with antipsychotic medications (e.g., haloperidol and risperidone, discussed later) and other prescription or over-the-counter medications that cause drowsiness may lead to oversedation. Taking some anticonvulsants with lithium may result in increased side effects (i.e., tremor). Always ask your child's doctor or pharmacist about possible interactions between the anticonvulsants and other medications, and always inform your child's doctor and dentist of the medications being taken.

- Anticonvulsants should not be stopped abruptly unless otherwise indicated by your child's doctor. Sudden discontinuation may increase the risk of further depressive or manic episodes in patients with bipolar disorder. If your child has a seizure disorder, suddenly stopping the anticonvulsants may result in the return or worsening of seizures.

- The anticonvulsants, particularly carbamazepine, may interact with many medications. Always ask your child's doctor or pharmacist for possible interactions between lamotrigine and other medications, and always inform your child's doctor and dentist of the medications being taken.

Anticonvulsants: Common Side Effects

Most of the anticonvulsants can produce nausea, heartburn, vomiting, diarrhea, constipation, dry mouth, drowsiness, tiredness, dizziness, clumsiness, skin rashes, or cognitive (thinking) problems. The anticonvulsants may increase or decrease appetite and weight. For example, valproate increases weight, and topiramate decreases weight. The section on "Management of Common Side Effects" later in this chapter describes additional side effects.

Anticonvulsants: Management of Specific Side Effects and Laboratory Tests Needed Before and During Treatment

VALPROATE (DEPAKOTE): SPECIFIC SIDE EFFECTS

Although uncommon, valproate may produce the following specific side effects.

- **Liver problems.** Liver problems may occur within the first few months of treatment. Children younger than 2 years who have medical problems and are taking other medications are at highest risk of developing serious liver problems. Signs of liver problems include unusual bruising or bleeding, nausea, vomiting, stomach discomfort, loss of appetite, weakness, fever, flulike symptoms, yellow tinge or discoloration of the skin or whites of the eyes, and dark-colored urine. These symptoms should be reported to your doctor immediately. Your child's doctor will obtain periodic blood tests from your child to monitor liver function while this medication is being prescribed. If blood levels of liver enzymes are too high, valproate may need to be discontinued in favor of another medication.
- **Inflammation of the pancreas.** This side effect is rare but may present with severe abdominal pain, nausea, vomiting, fever, and fatigue. Stop the medication, and contact your child's doctor if these symptoms appear.
- **Platelets and coagulation problems.** These are also rare but may be associated with high valproate blood levels. Symptoms of clotting or coagulation problems include easy bruising or abnormal bleeding (e.g., heavy menstrual flow, nose bleeds, bleeding gums after your child brushes his or her teeth, or wounds that take a long time to stop bleeding). These symptoms should be reported to your doctor immediately. These disorders can be diagnosed by blood tests taken by your child's doctor before medication is started and periodically during treatment.
- **Hand tremor.** Valproate may induce mild hand tremor that does not usually affect the functioning of your child. Check your child's handwriting. If his or her writing is too "shaky," talk to your child's doctor.
- **Hair problems.** Hair thinning is usually transient. Although not proven, zinc and selenium supplements (found in multivitamins) may help.

- **Problems with the ovaries.** Although controversial, valproate also seems to be associated with irregularities in the menstrual cycle and the development of cysts in the ovaries, particularly in girls who gain too much weight. Therefore, it is important to have a good assessment of your daughter's menstrual cycle before and during treatment with valproate.

VALPROATE: LABORATORY TESTS NEEDED BEFORE AND DURING TREATMENT

- Before starting valproate, your child's doctor will obtain blood tests to determine the number of white blood cells, red blood cells, platelets, and liver enzymes.
- Once valproate has been started, your child's doctor will order blood tests to measure valproate levels. Valproate blood levels *must* be measured 8 to 12 hours after the last dosage. Levels will be measured frequently at the beginning of treatment (monthly) to be sure that the level of medication in the blood is within the recommended range (60–120 µg/ml [micrograms/milliliter]). Thereafter, levels may be measured every 2 to 6 months or more frequently, depending on how the child is doing and the presence of side effects.
- Throughout the course of treatment, blood tests to measure the number of white blood cells, red blood cells, platelets, and liver enzymes will be repeated periodically to ensure the absence of negative side effects. These tests are measured more frequently during the first 6 months of treatment (e.g., monthly) and every 3 to 4 months thereafter.
- Other laboratory tests, such as blood tests for coagulation and hormone levels and pelvic sonograms to check for the development of cysts in the ovaries, are requested if needed.

CARBAMAZEPINE (TEGRETOL): SPECIFIC SIDE EFFECTS

Although they are uncommon, carbamazepine may produce the following serious side effects.

- **Blood disorders.** Signs of a possible serious blood problem include fever, sore throat, rash, and easy bruising or bleeding (e.g., heavy menstrual flow, nose bleeds, bleeding gums after your child brushes his or her teeth, bruises that do not heal). These symptoms should be reported to your doctor immediately. These disorders can be diagnosed by the blood tests that will be done by your child's doctor periodically during the course of treatment.

- **Decreased blood components.** Carbamazepine decreases the number of white blood cells and, more rarely, the number of red blood cells and platelets (one of the blood components that help with clotting). Minor blood changes are generally not significant in terms of your child's health. However, large decreases in these blood components can cause serious problems. The most serious blood abnormality associated with carbamazepine is a dramatic reduction in granulocytes, one component of white blood cells. The resulting disorder, agranulocytosis, places individuals at high risk for an infection that the body is then unable to fight off. If your child develops a fever with sore throat, he or she should have blood tests done as a precaution to make sure white blood cell numbers are adequate.

- **Skin rash.** Some individuals, particularly children, treated with carbamazepine will develop a skin rash, often within the first few weeks of treatment. Although usually benign, in rare instances this rash may signal the development of a very serious and possibly fatal rash. Therefore, any rash your child develops on this medication should be reported to your physician immediately. As a precaution, development of a rash may result in discontinuation of the medication by your child's doctor.

- **Liver problems.** Rarely, carbamazepine may induce irreversible liver damage. Signs of liver problems include unusual bruising or bleeding, nausea, vomiting, stomach discomfort, loss of appetite, weakness, fever, flulike symptoms, yellow tinge or discoloration of the skin or whites of the eyes, and dark-colored urine. These symptoms should be reported to your child's doctor immediately. Your doctor will obtain periodic blood tests from your child to ensure proper liver function while this medication is being prescribed.

- **Hand tremor.** Carbamazepine may induce mild hand tremor, but this usually does not affect your child's functioning. Check your child's handwriting. If his or her writing is too "shaky," talk to your child's doctor.
- **Clumsiness/lack of coordination/dizziness/slurred speech.** Report these side effects to your doctor. Carbamazepine blood levels may be too high, and the dosage may need to be adjusted.

CARBAMAZEPINE: LABORATORY TESTS NEEDED BEFORE AND DURING TREATMENT

- Before starting carbamazepine, your doctor will order blood tests to evaluate the number of white blood cells, red blood cells, platelets, electrolytes, and liver functioning. An ECG is necessary for children with a history of heart problems.
- Once carbamazepine has been started, blood levels need to be measured frequently to monitor the levels of medication in the blood. Carbamazepine blood levels *must* be measured 8 to 12 hours after the last dosage. Blood levels should generally fall between 4 and 12 μg/ml for the medication to be most effective. If levels are too high, your child may experience more side effects. On the other hand, if the levels are too low, the medication may not be working optimally. Once the dosage and levels of carbamazepine have been stabilized, blood levels will be measured every 2 to 6 months depending on how the child is doing and the presence of side effects.
- During treatment with carbamazepine, your doctor will periodically order blood tests to evaluate the number of white blood cells, red blood cells, platelets, and liver and kidney function. These tests are measured more frequently during the first 6 months of treatment (i.e., monthly) and every 3 to 4 months thereafter or more frequently depending on each case.
- It is expected that the number of white cells will decrease with

carbamazepine. However, if the total white cells diminish to 3,000 or less, carbamazepine should be immediately stopped. Remind your child's doctor to order periodic blood tests for your child. Other laboratory tests, such as blood clotting tests, will be requested if needed.

- Dosage may need to be adjusted after your child has been taking carbamazepine for a while to maintain blood levels within 4 to 12 μg/ml. With time, carbamazepine increases its own metabolism (the rate at which it is broken down by the body), and blood levels may fall regardless of the fact that the child is taking the correct dosage regularly. Blood tests will reveal the blood levels of carbamazepine and determine whether the dosage needs to be increased to reach the desired blood concentration of medication.

OXCARBAZEPINE (TRILEPTAL)

Oxcarbazepine is closely related to carbamazepine and is believed to have similar clinical properties to carbamazepine but with fewer side effects, without the blood problems and some of the interactions with other medications.

Rarely oxcarbazepine may lower the levels of sodium salt in the blood. Signs of low sodium levels include nausea, headache, sluggishness, or confusion. If severe, it may lead to seizures or loss of consciousness. The symptoms of low sodium levels can be vague and may be due to other conditions such as physical illness (flu or infection). Inform your child's doctor of these symptoms so that your child can be given a blood test to measure blood electrolytes to ensure proper sodium levels.

In general, no laboratory tests or other evaluations are necessary before beginning treatment with oxcarbazepine.

LAMOTRIGINE (LAMICTAL)

Among all the anticonvulsants, lamotrigine seems to work best for the acute treatment and the prevention of acute bipolar depression, but no studies have been done in children.

Unfortunately, lamotrigine can produce serious skin rashes, especially in children. Therefore, until further studies of lamotrigine's safety in children are completed, its use should be limited to adolescents who present with recurrent episodes of depression that are not responsive to other medications. The risk of developing a serious skin problem can be minimized by starting lamotrigine at a very low dosage, increasing the dosage very slowly, and discontinuing the medication immediately if a rash develops. Also, be aware that lamotrigine can interact with other medications such as valproate (Depakote) and increase the chance of rash. If your child develops a rash, do not give the next dosage of medication, and seek medical attention immediately to determine whether the rash is a side effect of the medication.

No laboratory tests or other investigations are necessary before using lamotrigine.

TOPIRAMATE (TOPAMAX)

This medication has not been well studied for the treatment of bipolar disorder and is recommended for use as a last resort when other medications have failed.

Topiramate may increase the risk of developing kidney stones, glaucoma (increased pressure inside the eye), lack or diminished ability to sweat, and increase in temperature. It also may cause difficulties with memory, remembering words, and concentrating; confusion; difficulty sleeping; dizziness; reduced appetite; and weight loss. The memory problems appear to be more common in children.

In general, no laboratory tests are necessary before and during the treatment with this medication.

Mood Stabilizer: Second-Generation or Novel Antipsychotic Medications

Second-generation antipsychotic medications, also called the *atypical antipsychotics*, are a newer group of medications that are unique from their predecessors, the typical or conventional antipsychotics (described later), in the way they work in the brain as well as in their reduced propensity for unwanted side effects. Whereas the older conventional antipsychotics work primarily through a chemical in the brain called *dopamine*, these newer medications affect dopamine as well as another chemical in the brain called *serotonin*. The action of these medications on dopamine is believed to underlie their ability to control symptoms of psychosis such as delusions and hallucinations. And their action on serotonin is believed to give these medications their unique capacity to help with mood symptoms. Therefore, although the novel antipsychotics, like their conventional predecessors, were made for the treatment of psychotic disorders such as schizophrenia, recent studies have shown that they are also effective in treating bipolar disorder.

Second-generation antipsychotic medications are used alone or in combination with other mood stabilizers for the acute (immediate) treatment of mania, depression, and mixed symptoms. They also seem useful to prevent further episodes of mania and depression and to treat irritability and aggressive behaviors. These medications may be used in combination with antidepressants for the treatment of depressions that do not respond to regular treatment.

The most commonly prescribed novel antipsychotic medications currently in use include risperidone (Risperdal), olanzapine (Zyprexa), quetiapine (Seroquel), ziprasidone (Geodon), aripiprazol (Abilify), and clozapine (Clozaril) (table 6.3).

Novel Antipsychotics: Presentation and Dosage

The dosage of the antipsychotics depends on the child's clinical response and presence of side effects. The antipsychotics are often started at a low dosage and slowly increased over a number of weeks. Some children may require higher or lower dosages than those outlined here to achieve an optimal level of improvement.

Novel Antipsychotics: Precautions

- Second-generation antipsychotic medications should not be given to those who have experienced a severe allergic reaction to one of these agents in the past.

TABLE 6.3—SECOND-GENERATION OR NOVEL ANTIPSYCHOTICS

Generic Name	Brand Name	Preparation	Dosage
Risperidone	Risperdal Risperdal M-Tab	Tablets: 1, 2, 3, and 4 mg 1 mg/ml liquid Orally disintegrating tablets, 0.5, 1, and 2 mg	0.5–6 mg per day given once or twice daily
Olanzapine	Zyprexa Zydis	Tablets: 2.5, 5, 7.5, 10, 15, and 20 mg Dissolvable tablets (placed on tongue): 5 and 10 mg	2.5–20 mg per day given once daily
Quetiapine	Seroquel	Tablets: 25, 100, 200, and 300 mg	25–800 mg per day given 2–3 times daily
Ziprasidone	Geodon	Tablets: 20, 40, 60, and 80 mg Injection: 20 mg/ml	20–160 mg per day given 2–3 times daily
Aripiprazole	Abilify	Tablets: 10, 15, 20, and 30 mg	10–30 mg per day given once daily
Clozapine	Clozaril	Tablets: 25 and 100 mg	25–900 mg per day given 2–3 times daily

- These medications should be avoided or administered with caution to children with a serious cardiac, seizure, liver or kidney disorder, or tardive dyskinesia (TD—abnormal muscular movements). (For TD, see the later section on "First-Generation or Conventional Antipsychotics.")

- Be cautious when giving your child other medications while he or she is taking second-generation antipsychotics. Clozapine should not be taken with other medications that may cause blood disorders (i.e., carbamazepine, phenytoin, and captopril). Taking second-generation antipsychotics with antihypertensive medications (i.e., Aldomet, Procardia, Vasotec, and Lasix) may lead to a drastic fall in blood pressure. Cigarettes and caffeinated beverages can reduce the effectiveness of some of these medications. Using second-generation antipsychotics with over-the-counter medications including cold and allergy medications and muscle relaxants can increase the sedative effects of these medications. Always ask your child's doctor or pharmacist for possible interactions between the antipsychotic medication being taken and other medications. Always inform your child's doctor and dentist of the medications being taken.

- Due to the risk of serious side effects and the need for frequent blood tests, the use of clozapine should be reserved for cases that have not responded to other medications. Clozapine should not be prescribed to patients with blood or bone marrow disorders or to anyone who has experienced agranulocytosis (a disease characterized by a dramatic reduction in granulocytes, a component of white blood cells) related to clozapine therapy in the past.

Novel Antipsychotics: Common Side Effects

Although the second-generation antipsychotic medications work by a similar mechanism (affecting the dopamine and serotonin systems), each individual medication also has its own unique properties and capacity to cause side effects.

The most common side effects of the second-generation antipsychotics include increase in appetite, weight gain (except for ziprasidone and aripiprazol), tiredness, drowsiness, abnormal movements, tremor, low blood pressure, and dizziness when getting up from a lying or seated position quickly. Other possible side effects include nausea or heartburn, constipation, headaches, skin rash and/or itching, night terrors, increase in the hormone prolactin, and decreased sexual interest. While taking clozapine, some individuals may experience seizures (in high dosages), increased salivation or drooling (called *sialorrhea*), and fewer red and white blood cells.

Uncommon side effects include ECG changes or heart rhythm problems, especially with ziprasidone. Although controversial, eye problems (cataracts) could be associated with quetiapine, and clozapine might be associated with lung problems.

Many of these side effects decrease over several weeks as your child's body adapts to the medication, and several of the common side effects can be managed according to the discussion at the beginning of this chapter. But your child's physician will closely supervise the occurrence of the more serious side effects, so do not hesitate to call him or her if you have any concerns.

Novel Antipsychotics: Management of Specific Side Effects

- **Abnormal muscular movements (Parkinsonism/akathisia/dystonia/tardive dyskinesia).** Although occurring less frequently than with the conventional antipsychotics (discussed later), these medications (particularly at high dosages) may produce abnormal muscular movements called *extrapyramidal side effects* (EPS). The management of these side effects is described later under the first-generation or conventional antipsychotics.
- **Breast tenderness, nipple discharge or missed periods.** These signs are indicative of high blood prolactin levels. Contact your child's doctor.
- **Increased saliva (sialorrhea).** This side effect is mainly linked with clozapine and tends to be most troublesome at night. Try using plastic-covered pillows and a towel on the bed. Speak to your doctor about other options for management.
- **Elevated prolactin level.** Risperidone, ziprasidone, and to a lesser degree quetiapine can increase the blood levels of the hor-

mone prolactin. When this hormone is increased, it can produce breast enlargement, nipple discharge, menstrual abnormalities (missed periods), and sexual problems (e.g., lack of sexual desire). *We do not know the long-term consequences of having high levels of this hormone, especially in children.*

- **Blood problems.** Clozapine (Clozaril) may decrease the number of white blood cells and, more rarely, the number of red blood cells and platelets (one of the blood components that help with clotting). Minor blood changes are generally benign and not significant in terms of your child's health. However, large decreases in these blood components can cause serious problems. The most serious blood abnormality associated with clozapine is a dramatic reduction in one component of the blood's white cells called *granulocytes*. The resulting disorder, *agranulocytosis*, places individuals at high risk for an infection that the body is then unable to fight off. Symptoms of agranulocytosis may be vague (fever, chills, sore throat, and fatigue) or even absent early on. As such, this medication requires close monitoring with frequent blood tests to ensure that these blood cells remain within a normal range. If your child develops fever with sore throat, he or she should have blood tests done to ensure that this is not a symptom of agranulocytosis caused by the medication.

- **Fever and stiffness.** One of the most serious side effects of these medications is the development of a syndrome involving fever and muscle stiffness called *neuroleptic malignant syndrome* (NMS). NMS is very rare and is characterized by fever associated with stiffness or rigidity and may be associated with confusion or a change in behavior and alertness. Make sure your child drinks plenty of liquids if he or she is active in sports and on hot days. This is a medical emergency and requires immediate medical intervention.

- **Elevated glucose and lipid (fat) blood levels.** The new antipsychotics have been associated with increases in glucose and lipid levels (cholesterol and triglycerides), particularly in subjects who have gained too much weight or are predisposed to have these problems. Therefore, it is recommended to do baseline measurements and thereafter follow-up *fasting* glucose and lipid blood levels.

Antipsychotics: Laboratory Tests Needed Before and During Treatment

- Before starting your child on these medications, your doctor will measure your child's weight and blood pressure and pulse while lying down and standing up. Your child's doctor will also obtain blood tests to determine the number of white blood cells, red blood cells, platelets, as well as liver and kidney function tests and fasting glucose and lipid levels; order an ECG; and examine your child for any abnormal movements of the head, neck, tongue, trunk, hands, and feet.

- Throughout the course of treatment, the examination for abnormal movements will be repeated at least every 3 months throughout the course of taking this medication. Ongoing tests will also include periodic evaluation of weight, blood pressure, pulse, blood tests (e.g., glucose and lipids) and, for clozapine, if appropriate, ECGs.

- No blood level tests are needed for the second-generation of antipsychotics.

CLOZAPINE: LABORATORY TESTS NEEDED BEFORE AND DURING TREATMENT

- Frequent blood tests to closely monitor white blood cell counts are essential for the early detection and prevention of agranulocytosis. Blood tests will be performed weekly for the first 6 months of treatment and every 2 weeks thereafter. A small fall in the white blood cell count may require more frequent blood tests while the person continues taking clozapine. A large fall in the white blood cell count will result in immediate discontinuation of clozapine.

- Clozapine levels in the blood also need to be measured frequently at the beginning of treatment. Blood levels should generally fall between 4 and 12 μg/ml for the medication to be most effective. If levels are too high, your child may experience more side effects; if the levels are too low, the medication may not be working optimally. Once the dosage and levels of clozapine have been stabilized, blood levels will be measured every 2 to 6 months depending on how the child is doing and the presence of side effects.

ANTIDEPRESSANTS

There are several types of antidepressant medications. This chapter reviews only the selective serotonin reuptake inhibitors (SSRIs), venlafaxine (Effexor), and bupropion (Wellbutrin) because these medications are the most commonly used in the treatment of bipolar depression. Other antidepressants that are problematic to use in children such as the monoamine oxidase inhibitors (MAOIs) and medications that are not effective for the treatment of depression in youth such as the tricyclic antidepressants (TCAIs) (imipramine, nortriptiline, desipramine, etc.) are not discussed here.

The SSRIs and venlafaxine are effective in the treatment of major depressive episodes and anxiety disorders including panic, obsessive-compulsive, general anxiety, separation anxiety, social phobic, bulimia, premenstrual syndrome, and posttraumatic stress disorders. Bupropion is effective for treating major depression in adults and possibly in children and for mild to moderate cases of ADHD.

All antidepressants need to be used with caution. Using antidepressants for the treatment of depression in people with bipolar disorder has not been well studied. In addition, because these medications may induce mania, rapid cycling, and mixed episodes in bipolar patients, their use for treating bipolar depression in youth needs to be carefully monitored by a clinician.

> Using antidepressants for the treatment of depression in people with bipolar disorder has not been well studied.

Currently the most commonly used antidepressants for the treatment of depression in children and adolescents include the SSRIs, venlafaxine (Effexor), and bupropion (Wellbutrin) (table 6.4).

TABLE 6.4—ANTIDEPRESSANTS MOST COMMONLY USED IN CHILDREN AND ADOLESCENTS

Brand Name	Generic Name	Preparation	Dosage
Selective Serotonin Reuptake Inhibitors (SSRIs)			
Fluoxetine	Prozac Prozac Weekly	Capsules: 10 and 20 mg Tablets: 10 mg Liquid: 1 tsp, or 5 ml, is equal to 20 mg Tablet: 90 mg; very long acting; given once weekly	10–80 mg a day given once a day 90 mg once a week
Sertraline	Zoloft	Tablets: 25, 50, and 100 mg Liquid: 20 mg/ml	25–300 mg a day, given once to twice daily
Paroxetine	Paxil Paxil CR (slow-release)	Tablets: 10, 20, 30, and 40 mg Liquid: 1 tsp, or 5 ml, is equal to 10 mg Capsules: 12.5, 25, and 37.5 mg	10–60 mg a day, given once to twice daily
Citalopram	Celexa	Tablets: 20 and 40 mg Liquid: 1 tsp, or 5 ml, is equal to 10 mg	10–60 mg a day
Escitalopram	Lexapro	Tablets: 10 and 20 mg Liquid: 1 tsp (5 ml) is equal to 5 mg	10–40 mg a day

Brand Name	Generic Name	Preparation	Dosage
Fluvoxamine	Luvox	Tablets: 25, 50, and 100 mg	25–300 mg a day
Other Types of Antidepressants			
Venlafaxine XR	Effexor XR	Capsules: 37.5, 75, and 150 mg	75–300 mg per day, often given twice daily
Bupropion SR	Wellbutrin SR (Slow release)	Tablets: 100, 150, and 200 mg	100–400 mg per day, given once or twice daily
	Wellbutrin XL (extended)	Tablets: 150 and 300 mg	150–450 mg per day given once a day

Antidepressants: Presentation and Dosage

The dosage of the antidepressants depends on the child's clinical response and presence of side effects. Also, some children may metabolize the antidepressants slowly and thus require small dosages to achieve maximum results. The antidepressants are often started at a low dosage and slowly increased over a number of weeks. Some children may require higher or lower dosages than those outlined to achieve an optimal level of improvement.

With the exception of fluoxetine, when given low dosages of antidepressants it is better for them to be prescribed twice a day to avoid withdrawal side effects (dizziness, stomachache, headaches, irritability). Adults break down these medications much more slowly than children and are therefore often prescribed these medications once daily. The dosage of the antidepressants should not be changed without speaking with your treating physician.

Antidepressants: Precautions

- Children with a prior allergy to a specific antidepressant should not be given this specific antidepressant.

- Be cautious when giving your child other medications while he or she is taking an antidepressant. Ask your child's doctor for possible interactions between the antidepressants and other medications. For example, if the SSRIs or venlafaxine are combined with other medications that increase serotonin levels, such as the MAOIs (e.g., Parnate and Nardil), lithium, or tryptophan, there is a risk of serotonin toxicity, called *serotonin syndrome*. In addition, some antidepressants may increase the sedative effects of alcohol and other drugs.

- Serotonin syndrome may begin with diarrhea and restlessness, developing into extreme agitation, unstable heart rate and blood pressure, seizures, elevated temperature, stiffness, and confusion. Symptoms may progress further to coma and death if untreated. If you suspect that your child may be experiencing serotonin syndrome, stop the medication and seek medical attention immediately.

- Except for fluoxetine (Prozac), suddenly stopping the antidepressants may lead to a withdrawal syndrome that may result in dizziness, weakness, nausea, headache, depressed mood, anxiety or nervousness, difficulty sleeping, poor concentration, and tingling sensations. These symptoms may be confused with a worsening of the child's psychiatric disorder. If these symptoms occur, contact your doctor. Although these symptoms will resolve without treatment in several weeks, they may be extremely uncomfortable. They can be avoided by not missing dosages of medication, taking the medication at the prescribed time, and gradually reducing the dosage under the supervision of your child's doctor if the medication needs to be discontinued.

- Antidepressants should be administered with caution to children with bipolar disorder. If it is necessary to administer an antidepressant, your child needs to be on a mood stabilizer to avoid worsening of his or her bipolar symptoms. However, you need to be aware that even when a person is taking mood stabilizers, the antidepressants may trigger a manic, mixed, or rapid cycling episode.

- Venlafaxine should be administered with caution to those with high blood pressure.

- Bupropion should not be administered to children with a clear history of seizures or allergies to bupropion. Also, this medication needs to be administered with caution to children with a history of head trauma, brain disease, or bulimia as these individuals may be at higher risk for experiencing seizures with bupropion.

Antidepressants: Common Side Effects

All of the antidepressants seem to be generally equally effective, but each antidepressant may produce distinct side effects in different individuals. Also, the way these medications are broken down in the body may also differ, causing some patients to experience more side effects with one antidepressant than another.

The most common side effects experienced when taking antidepressants include nausea, vomiting, diarrhea or constipation, heartburn, loss of appetite, weight gain or weight loss, headache, decreased sex drive, anxiety or nervousness, difficulty falling asleep or drowsiness, vivid dreams and nightmares, increased sweating (especially at night), dry mouth, and, rarely, unusual bruising. Although controversial, it seems that some individuals may experience a loss in motivation, listlessness, and low energy after long-term use of SSRIs.

Antidepressants: Management of Specific Side Effects

For handling common side effects, see the section on "Management of Common Side Effects" later in this chapter. Some important or specific side effects related to the use of the antidepressants are as follows:

- **Change in mood to markedly irritable or euphoric—mania.** The development of manic symptoms is one of the main concerns when prescribing this type of medication to depressed children with bipolar disorder. Your child may experience a switch in mood from downcast and sad to silly, giddy, careless, or frustrated and irritable. His or her behavior may become bold or

Manic-like Symptoms

If your child gets restless, disinhibited, or silly while taking an antidepressant, it does not necessarily mean that your child has bipolar disorder. Contact your child's doctor to discuss any manic-like symptoms.

brazen and unusually animated. This switch in mood must be differentiated from the onset of mania. If these symptoms arise, contact your child's doctor to determine whether these symptoms are indicative of mania.

- **Restlessness/nervousness/anxiety.** Some patients experience these symptoms after starting an antidepressant or after a dosage increase. These symptoms may require a change in the dosing schedule or a reduction in the dosage of medication. Do not change the dosage or dosage schedule without speaking to your child's doctor.

- **Increase in suicidal tendencies.** Recently, there has been controversy regarding whether some antidepressants may increase suicidal behavior in children. Although this effect has not been substantiated, it is important to carefully monitor your child, especially if he or she had suicidal behaviors or ideas before starting the antidepressants or if your child gets agitated.

- **Sexual side effects.** A reduction in dosage may alleviate these symptoms. Alternatively, the antidepressant medication may be changed to a different class of antidepressant, such as bupropion or nefazodone, or another medication may be added to counteract this side effect.

- **Unusual bruising.** This might indicate a problem with blood clotting or with liver function. Contact your child's doctor to arrange for a blood test.

- **Although rare, bupropion may induce seizures.** This side effect may occur when the dosage is increased rapidly and when dosages above 400 milligrams per day are used. This side effect is more likely to occur when the dosage is increased rapidly and when the regular as opposed to the slow-release preparations of bupropion is used. People with a history of seizures, head injury, brain disease, perhaps bulimia, and those who use alcohol or have recently stopped certain medications, such as benzodiazepines (Ativan, Klonopin, and Valium), are at higher risk of developing seizures while taking bupropion. If you suspect that your child is developing any abnormal movements or seizures, contact your child's doctor immediately.

Antidepressants: Laboratory Tests Needed Before and During Treatment

No laboratory tests are necessary before starting an antidepressant. However, if your child develops unusual bruising, your child's doctor will take a blood test to look at liver and blood-clotting function. Specifically for venlafaxine: Ask your child's nurse or doctor to measure your child's blood pressure before and during treatment.

ADJUNCTIVE MEDICATIONS

Adjunctive (or additional) medications are not used to treat bipolar disorder specifically but may be helpful for managing symptoms such as agitation, insomnia, and psychosis. These medications include the first generation or conventional antipsychotics and the benzodiazepines. However, the use of these medications, especially the first generation of antipsychotics, is diminishing in favor of the second-generation or novel antipsychotics. The adjunctive medications are usually used for short-term periods during a crisis.

First-Generation or Conventional Antipsychotic Medications

First-generation or conventional antipsychotic medications, also called *neuroleptics*, were developed for the treatment of schizophrenia. In bipolar patients, they can be used to control agitation, aggression, and psychosis. They are also used in the treatment of pervasive developmental disorder (i.e., autism) and tic disorders (i.e., Tourette's disorder).

First-Generation or Conventional Antipsychotic Medications: Presentation and Dosage

The first-generation antipsychotic medications are divided into two groups: the high-potency and the low-potency antipsychotic medications (table 6.5). This division is determined by how strongly each medication acts on the dopamine system—the high-potency medications act more strongly on the dopamine system than the low-potency medications.

TABLE 6.5—HIGH- AND LOW-POTENCY FIRST-GENERATION OR CONVENTIONAL ANTIPSYCHOTICS

Generic Name	Brand Name	Preparation	Dosage
High-Potency			
Haloperidol	Haldol	Tablets: 0.5, 1, 2, 5, 10, and 20 mg Also available as an injection	0.5–2 mg per day given once or twice daily; not used in children and teens
Fluphenazine	Prolixin	Tablets: 1, 2, 5, and 10 mg Liquid: 2.5 mg in 1 tsp	1–5 mg per day given once or twice daily
Pimozide	Orap	Tablets: 2, 4, and 10 mg	2–8 mg per day given once or twice daily
Trifluoperazine	Stelazine	Tablets: 1, 2, 5, and 10 mg	1–20 mg per day given once or twice daily
Low-Potency			
Chlorpromazine	Thorazine	Tablets: 10, 25, 50, 100, and 200 mg	25–1,000 mg a day given once or twice daily

Generic Name	Brand Name	Preparation	Dosage
Chlorpromazine (*cont.*)	Thorazine (*cont.*)	Liquid: 10 mg/5 cc Also available as suppositories and injections	
Thioridazine	Mellaril	Tablets: 10, 15, 25, 50, 100, 150, and 200 mg	25–600 mg given once or twice daily

The dosage of first-generation antipsychotic depends on the specific medication being used, the child's clinical response, and the presence of side effects. Most of these medications are started at very low dosages, which are slowly increased over several weeks. Some children may need higher or lower dosages in order to experience improvement in symptoms.

Several antipsychotic medications, including haloperidol (Haldol LA) and fluphenazine (Modecate), are available in long-acting injectable forms. The long-acting preparations are administered by intramuscular injection and are given once every 1 to 4 weeks depending on the medication chosen. These injections are used mainly for patients who are unable or unwilling to take oral medications regularly, but they rarely are used for children.

Currently most of these medications are used for short periods of time. If your child needs long-term treatment, second-generation or novel antipsychotics are preferred.

First-Generation or Conventional Antipsychotic Medications: Precautions

- First-generation antipsychotic medications should not be given to those who have experienced a severe allergic reaction to one of these agents in the past and to those with tardive dyskinesia. These medications should also be avoided in children with prior allergic reactions to first-generation antipsychotics.

- These medications should be given with caution to those with cardiac or liver problems.
- Some first-generation antipsychotic medications (e.g., Thorazine) can make the skin very sensitive to the sun.
- Be cautious when giving your child other medications while he or she is taking first-generation antipsychotics. Cigarettes and caffeinated beverages can reduce the effectiveness of these medications. Using first-generation antipsychotics with over-the-counter medications, including cold and allergy medications and muscle relaxants, can increase the sedative effects of these medications. Always ask your child's doctor or pharmacist for possible interactions between the antipsychotic medication being taken and other medications. Always inform your child's doctor and dentist of the medications being taken.

First-Generation or Conventional Antipsychotic Medications: Common Side Effects

The high- and low-potency medications differ in their propensity to cause certain types of side effects. For example, the high-potency medications are more likely to cause abnormal movement disorders called *extrapyramidal side effects* (EPS) than are the low-potency medications. Conversely, low-potency medications are more likely to cause drowsiness, increased weight, dry mouth, and dizziness than are the high-potency medications.

Potential side effects for all conventional antipsychotics include nausea or heartburn, constipation, decreased sexual interest, change in sexual function, skin rash and/or itching, increased appetite, weight gain, breast fullness or tenderness, nipple discharge, menstrual abnormalities, constipation, increased heart rate, low blood pressure (especially when getting up from a lying or sitting position quickly—most common in the low-potency antipsychotics), and EPS. For the management of the common side effects, see the section on "Management of Common Side Effects" later in this chapter.

Less common side effects for all conventional antipsychotics include allergic skin rashes and itching; heart rhythm problems; increased skin sensitivity to the sun, with greater risk of sunburn and possible skin discoloration; and jaundice. Signs of jaundice include a yellow tinge in the eyes or skin, upper abdominal pain, nausea, vomiting, a flu-like syndrome, fever, rash, and dark-colored urine. Be sure to contact your child's doctor if you have any concerns about these side effects. Additional side effects and their management are as follows.

First-Generation or Conventional Antipsychotic Medications: Management of Specific Side Effects

- **Problems urinating.** Some people taking these medications can experience a difficulty in urinating that ranges from mild problems in starting urination to complete inability to urinate, a condition that requires prompt medical attention. These symptoms should be reported to your child's doctor immediately.
- **Vision.** Thioridazine (Mellaril) is rarely associated with irreversible pigmentation of the retina that may lead to blindness when very high dosages (above 800 milligrams per day) are used.
- **ECG changes.** ECG changes are most common for the low-potency antipsychotics, particularly thioridazine (Mellaril). If your child complains about palpitations or fainting, immediately consult his or her doctor. The only way to detect whether your child has ECG problems is to measure it before and during treatment. Depending on the ECG changes observed, your child's doctor may decide to discontinue the medication.
- **Extrapyramidal side effects (EPS).** The high-potency antipsychotics cause more EPS than the low-potency antipsychotics. EPS can be divided into those that occur early in the course of treatment (parkinsonism, akathisia, and dystonia) and those that occur after long-term treatment (tardive dyskinesia, or TD). TD is the least common but most serious of the EPS, is associated with long-term use of antipsychotic medication, and is potentially ir-

> *Development of any abnormal movements should be reported to your doctor immediately.*

reversible. Development of any abnormal movements should be reported to your doctor immediately.

Parkinsonism, akathisia, and dystonia often develop soon after starting the medication or after an increase in medication but may also develop after several months or longer. *Parkinsonism* manifests symptoms that closely resemble those seen in Parkinson's disease, including loss of facial expression, shakiness or tremor, drooling, slowness of movements and/or speech, difficulty getting movements started, stiffness in the arms and legs, poor balance (especially when turning), and a shuffling gait. *Akathisia* is an inner feeling of restlessness or unease. Patients with akathisia may pace, have difficulty sitting still, appear agitated, and feel sad or uncomfortable. *Dystonias* are involuntary, painful, tightening spasms of the muscles, particularly those in the face (eyes, tongue, and jaw) and neck. Although muscles in the face and neck are most commonly involved, dystonia can affect any muscle group including those in the trunk and extremities. Rarely, dystonia can affect the muscles used for swallowing and breathing. This constitutes a medical emergency and necessitates prompt medical attention.

Tardive dyskinesia (TD) is one of the most troublesome side effects associated with the use of antipsychotic medications. The disorder involves the development of abnormal movements of the mouth, tongue, face, neck, trunk, and limbs. Movements in TD are described as writhing or twisting. Movements may be subtle or very noticeable and are not purposely produced by the patient. Some examples include chewing movements of the mouth, protrusion of the tongue, puckering of the lips, and twisting movements of the fingers, toes, or trunk. These movements are more common in adults, particularly women; are associated with long-term use of these medications; rarely occur before 6 months after starting treatment; and may be irreversible. Your child should be examined by your doctor regularly for the appearance of TD.

The EPS side effects can be avoided or minimized by starting the medication at a very low dosage, increasing the medication slowly, and maintaining the medication at the lowest effective dosage. Once these symptoms appear, the dosage of medication should be lowered or the medication substituted with a different type of antipsychotic. In addition, medications such as diphenhydramine (Benadryl) and anticholinergic medications (i.e., benztropine [Cogentin], trihexyphenidyl [Artane], and procyclidine [Kemadrin]), may be added to counteract parkinsonism and dystonia. (Note: These medications, however, have their own side effects. Consult your child's doctor.) These medications are less effective in treating akathisia, which may respond better to medications such as propranolol, clonidine and benzodiazepines (i.e., lorazepam [Ativan] and clonazepam [Klonopin]). If your child experiences any of these side effects, contact your doctor.

- **Fever and stiffness.** One of the most serious side effects of these medications is the development of *neuroleptic malignant syndrome* (NMS). NMS is rare but can occur with any conventional antipsychotic medication and is characterized by fever associated with stiffness or rigidity and may be associated with confusion or a change in behavior and alertness. Make sure your child drinks plenty of liquids if he or she is active in sports and on hot days. This is a medical emergency and requires immediate medical intervention should symptoms appear.

> ### Counteracting EPS
> The medications used to counteract EPS have their own possible side effects, including problems with short-term memory, sedation, dry mouth, constipation, confusion, and increased heart rate.

- **Breast tenderness, nipple discharge, or missed periods.** These signs are indicative of high levels of prolactin in the blood. Contact your child's doctor.

First-Generation or Conventional Antipsychotic Medications: Laboratory Tests Needed Before and During Treatment

- Before starting your child on these medications, your doctor will measure your child's weight, blood pressure, and heart rate while your child is lying down and standing up. Your doctor will also obtain blood tests to determine the number of white blood cells, red blood cells, platelets, as well as liver and kidney function. An electrocardiogram (ECG) is indicated for the low-potency antipsychotics. Your doctor will also examine your child for any abnormal movements of the head, neck, tongue, trunk, hands, and feet.

- Throughout the course of treatment, an examination for abnormal movements will be repeated at least every 3 months. Other ongoing tests include periodic evaluation of weight, blood pressure, pulse, blood tests, and ECG if indicated.

Benzodiazepines

Benzodiazepines are a family of medications often used to treat symptoms of anxiety and seizures. These medications are not well studied in children, and the risk of developing dependence with long-term use makes them unpopular for use in youth. Therefore, benzodiazepines are usually used as a short-term treatment option only in children. In bipolar patients, benzodiazepines can be used to control agitation, insomnia, anxiety symptoms, and side effects associated with antipsychotic medications. Benzodiazepines are also used to ease the withdrawal side effects of discontinuing chronic alcohol use.

The benzodiazepines may reduce symptoms of anxiety quite quickly and are often prescribed temporarily at the beginning of treatment until the other medications begin to function.

Benzodiazepines: Presentation and Dosage

Many benzodiazepine medications are available. Benzodiazepines can be distinguished from one another by their potency (strength) and their duration of action (how long the medication stays and works in your body). The short-acting and long-acting benzodiazepines each have their own advantages and disadvantages that determine, in part, how they are used. The effects of the short-acting benzodiazepines (e.g., lorazepam, oxazepam, and temazepam) generally only last several hours. These medications leave the body quickly and, therefore, generally do not cause daytime drowsiness after a nighttime dosage. These medications are good for treating acute symptoms of anxiety or agitation.

The effects of the long-acting benzodiazepines (i.e., clonazepam and diazepam) may last 6 to 12 hours. These medications are therefore better for controlling symptoms that persist throughout the day. However, they are more likely to cause daytime drowsiness after a night dosage. Diazepam (Valium) is not recommended for children because its effects last too long and may produce significant cognitive side effects (slow thinking).

Your child may experience withdrawal symptoms (anxiety, nervousness, sweating, restlessness, difficulty sleeping) if a regular dosage of medication is missed. Withdrawal symptoms are more commonly seen with the short-acting benzodiazepines.

The most commonly used benzodiazepines in child psychiatry are alprazolam, lorazepam, and clonazepam (table 6.6).

TABLE 6.6.—ALPRAZOLAM, LORAZEPAM, AND CLONAZEPAM

Generic Name	Brand Name	Preparation	Dosage
Alprazolam	Xanax	Tablets: 0.25, 0.5, and 1.2 mg	0.25–4 mg 2–3 times a day
Alprazolam SR	Xanax SR	Tablets: 0.25, 1, 2, and 3 mg	0.25–4 mg once a day
Lorazepam	Ativan	Tablets: 0.5, 1.0, and 2.0 mg Liquid: 2 mg/ml Injection: 4 mg/ml	0.25–4 mg daily given 3 times a day or 0.25–2 mg at night for sleep
Clonazepam	Klonopin	Tablets: 0.5, 1.0, and 2.0 mg	0.25–4 mg daily given twice a day
	Klanopin (Orally disintegrating tablets)	Wafers: 0.125, 0.25, 0.5, 1, and 2 mg	0.125–4 mg daily given twice a day

Benzodiazepine: Precautions

- Benzodiazepines should be administered with caution to children with breathing problems, a history of substance abuse, and liver or kidney disease.

- Be cautious when giving your child other medications while he or she is taking benzodiazepines. Alcohol and prescription or over-the-counter medications that produce drowsiness (i.e., antipsychotic medications, cold and flu medications, and antihistamines such as Benadryl) may cause oversedation and decreased breathing rate. Taking benzodiazepines with food or antacids may reduce the effectiveness of these medications. Always ask your child's doctor or pharmacist for possible interactions between the benzodiazepine your child is being prescribed and other medications. Always inform your child's doctor and dentist of the medications being taken.

- Benzodiazepines should not be stopped abruptly unless otherwise indicated by your child's doctor because your child may experience a withdrawal syndrome, including anxiety, nervousness, irritability, sweating, restlessness, nausea, vomiting, and difficulty sleeping. If your child has been taking large dosages of these medications for several months or longer, sudden discontinuation may result in severe withdrawal symptoms, including seizures, out-of-control behavior, and hallucinations.

- *Unsupervised use of these medications may lead to abuse and dependence.* Do not change the dosage or schedule of medication without speaking to your child's doctor. Short- and long-term use of these medications are safe and do not lead to abuse or dependency if taken as prescribed. Always supervise your child's medications to ensure proper use.

    Do not give benzodiazepines to children and teens with suicidal behaviors. In addition to being dangerous in case of an overdose, benzodiazepines, like alcohol, may reduce the coping skills of your child and facilitate suicide.

Benzodiazepines: Common Side Effects

The most common side effect produced by the benzodiazepines is drowsiness. Drowsiness may occur during the day, especially in the morning, after taking a benzodiazepine the night before for sleep. This effect is more common with the long-acting medications. Drowsiness may also occur during the day after taking regularly scheduled daily dosages, which may interfere with your child's attention and concentration in the classroom and also slow your child's response time. Therefore, your child should avoid driving or operating any machinery if he or she experiences this side effect. Other side effects include unsteadiness, slowness in thinking, and dizziness.

Some children (especially children with ADHD) may become silly, giddy, excited, or agitated with these medications. If you notice a marked change in your child's behavior, notify your doctor.

For the management of these and other common drug side effects, including nausea, heartburn, vomiting, drowsiness, tiredness, cognitive problems, headaches, and allergic reactions, see the section on "Management of Common Side Effects."

Benzodiazepines: Laboratory Tests Needed Before and During Treatment

No laboratory tests or other investigations are necessary before using benzodiazepines.

OTHER BIOLOGICAL TREATMENTS

Of the many other types of treatment you may hear about, few have been studied for the treatment of mood disorders in children. In this section, we will discuss the few that have some scientific backing behind them: St John's wort, essential fatty acids, light therapy, electroconvulsive therapy, and transcranial magnetic stimulation. The use of these treatment modalities has not been evaluated in children and teens with mood disorder, so you should allow your child to use them only with caution and under careful medical supervision.

St. John's Wort

St. John's wort is reported to be useful for mild to moderate depressions. But recent studies in the United States with depressed adults have questioned the efficacy of St. John's wort for this purpose. Some reports in children found it useful for the treatment of major depression, but controlled studies are still necessary.

St. John's Wort: Presentation

The leaves, stem, and flowers of the St. John's wort herb contain the medicinal components (such as the chemicals hypericin and hyperforin) that are believed to be responsible for the antidepressant effects. The plant is native to Europe, the United States, and Canada and can be found growing wild in meadows and woods. It is available as the natural herb (which can be used to make tea), as a topical ointment, and as tablets. The tablets are the most common form of the herb used for the treatment of depression. The tablets are available over-the-counter in a variety of dosages.

St. John's Wort: Dosage

The dosage of St. John's wort used for adults with mild to moderate depression is most commonly 300 milligrams, taken three times per day.

St. John's Wort: Precautions

- St. John's wort should not be administered to children with schizophrenia as it may worsen psychotic symptoms.
- Effects in pregnancy are not known; therefore, the use of this herb during pregnancy is not recommended. If there is any possibility of your child becoming pregnant while receiving treatment, speak to your child's doctor regarding pregnancy prevention. If your child becomes pregnant during treatment, do

not administer the medication and inform your child's doctor immediately. In addition, St. John's wort is excreted in the breast milk of mothers who are taking this medication and could be harmful to the infant. Breast-feeding is not recommended for mothers who are taking St. John's wort.

- St. John's wort should be administered with caution to children with bipolar disorder due to the risk of inducing hypomania or mania.

- Be cautious when giving your child other medications while he or she is taking St. John's wort. Ask your child's doctor about possible interactions between St. John's wort and other medications. St. John's wort can reduce the effectiveness of many medications including heart medications (Lanoxin), the asthma medication Theophylline, birth control pills, and the blood-thinning medication Warfarin. If St. John's wort is used while taking the birth control pill, your daughter may experience abnormal menstrual bleeding (e.g., spotting between periods). In addition, the birth control pill may not be as effective while taking St. John's wort, and other methods of contraception should therefore be employed.

- If combined with other medications that increase serotonin levels, such as the SSRI antidepressants (i.e., Prozac, Paxil), monoamine oxidase inhibitor (MAOI) antidepressants (i.e., Parnate and Nardil), lithium, or tryptophan, there is an increased risk of developing serotonin syndrome (as explained further in the section on side effects).

- St. John's wort should be discontinued at least 2 weeks before having any kind of surgery as it may interact with the medication used for anesthesia.

- St. John's wort should not be stopped abruptly. Doing so may lead to withdrawal symptoms, which may include dizziness, weakness, nausea, headache, depressed mood, anxiety or nervousness, difficulty sleeping, poor concentration, and tingling sensations. These symptoms may be confused with worsening of the child's psychiatric disorder. If these symptoms occur, contact your doctor. Although these symptoms will resolve without treatment in several weeks, they may be extremely uncomfortable for patients and can be avoided by not missing dosages, taking it at the correct times, and gradual reduction in dosage if it is to be discontinued.

St. John's Wort: Management of Specific Side Effects

St. John's wort may be associated with nausea, vomiting, diarrhea or constipation, heartburn, headache, anxiety or nervousness, restlessness, difficulty with sleep, vivid dreams and nightmares, drowsiness, dizziness, and dry mouth. For treating common side effects, see the section on "Management of Common Side Effects" later in this chapter.

Other, less common side effects include the following:

- **Change in mood to markedly irritable or euphoric.** The development of manic symptoms is one of the main concerns when prescribing this medication to depressed children with bipolar disorder. Your child may experience a switch in mood from downcast and sad to silly, giddy, careless, or frustrated and irritable. His or her behavior may become bold or brazen and unusually animated. This switch in mood must be differentiated from onset of mania. If these symptoms arise, contact your doctor to determine whether these symptoms are indicative of mania.

- **Sun sensitivity.** St. John's wort can cause skin to become extrasensitive to the sun. Sun exposure can lead to skin rash and serious sunburn. Light- or fair-skinned individuals are the most susceptible.

- **Serotonin syndrome.** St. John's wort has rarely been associated with a syndrome characterized by extreme anxiety, confusion, high blood pressure and increased heart rate, called the *serotonin syndrome*. This syndrome may begin with diarrhea and restlessness, leading to extreme agitation, unstable heart rate and blood pressure, seizures, elevated temperature, stiffness, and confusion. Symptoms may progress further to coma and death if un-

treated. If you suspect that your child may be experiencing serotonin syndrome, stop the medication and seek medical attention
immediately.

The Essential Fatty Acids (EFAs)

The essential fatty acids (EFAs) are called "essential" because they cannot be made by our bodies and must be obtained through our diets. The
EFAs (e.g., linoleic acid) are found in cold-water fish (e.g., herring,
tuna), salmon, green leaves of plants, and some seeds (e.g., flax, canola,
perilla), walnuts, and legumes (e.g., soy). The EFAs are metabolized
(broken down) in the liver and converted into long-chain fatty acids:
the omega-3 fatty acids and the omega-6 fatty acids.

The EFAs are necessary for normal human fetal and newborn development, and for the functioning of many cells, including the nerve
cells (neurons). Lack of EFAs in the diet, problems with the metabolism
of these substances in the liver (e.g., viral infections, genetic illnesses),
or direct interference with the action of the omega-3 and omega-6 fatty
acids in the cells have all been associated with a variety of problems, including changes in immune, cardiac, and brain functioning.

Recent reports have suggested that lack of these substances in the
diet may be related to a propensity for depression and, possibly, bipolar
disorder. In a small preliminary study, the use of supplements of
omega-3 fatty acids together with other mood stabilizers was found
beneficial for adult patients with bipolar disorder who were not responding to usual treatment.

The National Center for Complementary and Alternative Medicine
and the National Institute of Mental Health recently funded two large
studies to evaluate the effects and safety of omega-3 fatty acids for the
treatment of depression and bipolar disorder in adults. These studies
will help clarify the benefits and safety of this substance for the treatment of mood disorder. At this time, together with traditional medications, EFAs seem to be useful as an adjunctive treatment for depression
and bipolar disorder, but further studies are necessary, especially in

children and adolescents. (No studies have yet been published on the use of the EFAs in children and teens.)

EFAs: Presentation and Dosage

EFAs are found in the following sources:

- **Food.** Walnuts, green leaves, soybeans, some fish (e.g., salmon, herring), and some oils (e.g., flaxseed, primrose, perilla oil). Flaxseed oil, for example, is a good source of omega-3 fatty acids. It can be taken as a supplement or used in salad dressings. Unlike fish oils, which contain a different combination of omega-3 fatty acids, flaxseed oil (and other oils) should not be cooked because heat can destroy the omega-3 fatty acids. Also, keeping fish oil refrigerated will reduce the risk of it becoming rancid.
- **Commercial products.** Many commercial products contain different proportions of omega-3 and omega-6 fatty acids alone or in combination with other vitamins and minerals. Check with your child's doctor as to which one he or she recommends.

The optimal dosage of EFAs for bipolar disorder is not known, but studies in adults with bipolar and major depression have used 2 to 9 grams per day, divided into three dosages per day. However, it is difficult and costly to take large amounts of these products. Ongoing studies will help clarify which are the optimal dosages for adults with bipolar disorder. We do not know the dosage of omega-3 or omega-6 fatty acids for children and teens with bipolar disorder. Until further studies, some investigators have recommended to administer up to 1 gram three times a day.

EFAs: Precautions

- Omega-3 fatty acids have not been evaluated in youth; therefore, the use of EFAs for children and teens needs to be done with caution and under the supervision of a physician.
- Until further studies, omega-3 fatty acids should be administered along with traditional treatments for bipolar disorder.

- Most supplements contain both omega-3 and omega-6 fatty acids. We do not know yet in what proportion these two fatty acids need to be taken.
- We do not know whether omega-3 or omega-6 fatty acids interfere with other medications.
- Check the product you are buying carefully because there are no regulations regarding the quality of these supplements. In addition, concerns have been raised regarding the levels of contamination (e.g., mercury and pesticides) in fish oil supplements.
- Heat may destroy or change some EFAs.
- Taking too much cod liver oil can be dangerous because it also contains vitamin A. Consult with your child's doctor.
- Although it has not been well studied, some authors have recommended taking antioxidant supplements, such as vitamins C and E, together with the EFAs to prevent the body from oxidizing the EFAs. Consult with your child's doctor before administering large quantities of vitamins to your child.

EFAs: Management of Specific Side Effects

Essential fatty acids supplements may cause nausea, abdominal discomfort, flatulence, and loose stools. These side effects depend on the dosage. For responding to common side effects, see the section on "Management of Common Side Effects" later in this chapter.

EFAs may also cause other side effects you should watch for:

- **Fishy odor/taste or burping.** Fish oil capsules can produce a "fishy" taste, odor, or burps. To reduce this effect, diminish the dosage, or change from fish oil capsules to other products, such as flaxseed oil. Some people have recommended trying clove of garlic or garlic tablets to counteract the fishiness. However, your child and you should decide which is worse, fish or garlic odor?
- **Weight gain.** EFAs may cause an increase in weight, particularly in children who are not active and eat too many carbohydrates. Talk with your child's pediatrician about nutritional and behavioral strategies to help manage your child's weight.

- **Possible increased risk for prostate cancer.** A few studies have suggested that flaxseed oil may promote the growth of prostate cancer in men, but further studies are necessary to validate these findings.

Light Therapy

Some people with bipolar disorder or unipolar depressions experience depressions mainly during the fall, winter, or beginning of spring. This type of depression is usually called *seasonal affective disorder* (SAD) and appears to be triggered by the short duration of daylight during these seasons. Although it is not known why this phenomenon occurs, it is believed that the lack of light changes the chemistry of the brain, producing the depressive symptoms. Studies in adults and a few studies in children and teens have suggested that bright light therapy is effective for treating SAD.

Light Therapy: Presentation and Dosage

Most commonly, a light box of 10,000 lux (the intensity of the light used for this treatment) is placed approximately 1 foot from the face of the person for 30 to 45 minutes per day. Treatment can be extended to 1 hour in cases where symptoms respond only partially. (Studies of light visors and other head-mounted light devices have yielded controversial results.)

The person undergoing treatment does not need to stare directly into the light and can engage in other activities while in front of the light box. Children may refuse to sit for too long in front of a light, but some parents have been successful by putting the light box next to the computer, the TV, or on the table while their children are reading or having breakfast.

It is unclear at which time of the day light exposure is more effective, but it appears that light therapy is better when done early in the morning before the sun rises. This is like tricking the brain into thinking that the amount of daylight is equivalent to a summer day. However, 30 minutes to 1 hour of light therapy in the morning may be difficult during the school year or for youth who refuse to wake up early. In this case, it is better to have the child use the light during the late afternoon near sunset.

The bright light therapy should be used for at least 2 weeks. If symptoms of depression have not responded, it is better to try different treatments, such as the SSRIs or venlafaxine.

Light Therapy: Management of Specific Side Effects

Bright light therapy has been associated with some side effects such as headaches and eye strain. But the most serious concern is the finding that in some individuals with bipolar disorder, treatment with light may induce episodes of hypomania or mania. Your child may experience a switch in mood from downcast and sad to silly, giddy, careless, or frustrated and irritable. His or her behavior may become bold or brazen and unusually animated. This switch in mood must be differentiated from the onset of mania. If these symptoms arise, contact your doctor to determine whether these symptoms indicate mania.

Electroconvulsive Therapy (ECT)

Electroconvulsive therapy (ECT) is used to treat severe depression and sometimes mania and schizophrenia. The treatment involves inducing a brief convulsion (seizure) through the short passage of small electrical pulses through the brain. The electrical pulses produce changes in the neurotransmitters in certain places of the brain, similar to the effects of antidepressant medications.

Many teens and their parents will rightfully get very uneasy and anxious even hearing the term *electroconvulsive therapy*. The media have devalued this type of treatment and presented a biased picture of it when, in fact, ECT can be life-saving for a person with severe depression, psychosis, agitation, and suicidal behaviors. In adults, ECT has been shown to be very effective and safe for the treatment of severe depressions, in particular those with psychotic symptoms.

This was the case for 17-year-old Helene. She had suffered from severe episodes of mania and depression since she was 12 years old. For the last 2 years, she had been having more frequent episodes of depression that did not respond well to treatment with medication and psychotherapy. During her last depressive episode, she heard voices that were telling her to commit suicide, and she became agitated and violent. She tried to hang herself but luckily was discovered tying the cord around her neck and was immediately admitted to the hospital. Because she did not respond to medications, treatment with ECT was offered.

Helene underwent eight treatments of unilateral ECT with excellent response. Her mood improved, the voices disappeared, and she was able to concentrate and relate to others. As expected, she does not have any memory of what happened during the ECT. Except for a mild temporary headache, she did not have any other side effects. In addition to the ECT, Helene began treatment with lithium and valproate. One year after her discharge from the hospital, Helene is still benefiting from her treatment with ECT and medications and is doing well.

ECT: Presentation

Before an ECT treatment, the person is mildly sedated and a brief course of general anesthesia administered to prevent the person from hurting him- or herself during the treatment. While the person is under anesthesia, special electrodes are placed on one side of the head (unilateral ECT) or both sides of the head (bilateral ECT). The electrodes pass a brief pulse of electricity through the brain, producing a convulsion (seizure). Because the person is under anesthesia, there are only very mild movements throughout the body, if any. The procedure is evaluated using an electroencephalogram (EEG).

ECT: Management of Specific Side Effects

A few reports have been published about the use and safety of ECT in teens, but no controlled studies have been done. ECT is used in teens only as the last resort for the treatment of severe depression, psychosis, agitated mania, and schizophrenia. The side effects are frequently mild and transient and include headaches, nausea, vomiting, and general muscle aches. The most significant side effect is gaps in memory for events that occurred during the treatment with ECT, but some people may have additional memory loss of earlier events. The memory losses are usually related to worldly events, rather than personal information, and tend to improve during the first months after ECT, but some events may remain forgotten. Headaches and memory loss are worse with bilateral ECT.

Parents and adolescents should weigh the consequences of the illness versus the side effects of ECT (including the anesthesia) and, in conjunction with their doctor, decide whether ECT is an appropriate option. ECT cannot be administered to people with brain tumors and needs to be administered carefully to people with heart conditions.

Also, the treatment team must consider the legal aspects of the treatment because some states do not permit the use of ECT in teens. *Before* administering ECT, it is recommended to get a second opinion from another child psychiatrist, and *after* ECT, the child must continue to take medications to prevent the development of further depressive or manic episodes.

ECT Education

Education is essential regarding ECT benefits, side effects, procedures, and outcome. Some videotapes of actual patients receiving ECT may be valuable in this regard: *Electroconvulsive Therapy: ECT: The Treatment, the Questions, the Answers* by Leon J. Grunhaus, Lisa Barroso-Wahl, and Kathy Krone (University of Michigan, Biomedical Communications Unit, Ann Arbor, 1988) and *Informed ECT for Patients and Families* by Max Fink, M.D. (Somatics Inc., Lake Bluff, IL, 1986).

Transcranial Magnetical Stimulation (TMS)

Transcranial magnetical stimulation (TMS) is a promising new treatment for depression and possibly other psychiatric disorders, such as schizophrenia and obsessive-compulsive disorder. In this treatment, a specific site of the brain is stimulated with a magnetic field produced by a special device placed over the head. Unlike ECT, TMS stimulates only a limited area of the brain, electrical current does not pass through the brain, the procedure does not require general anesthesia, and a seizure does not occur.

In adults, TMS appears to be effective for the treatment of depression, but further studies are necessary. So far, the main side effect is headaches. TMS has been safely used as a research tool to investigate the maturation of the nervous system in children ages 7 months to 18 years, but it has been used as treatment in only a small number of children with mood disorders. Thus, it is too early to know whether TMS will have a role in the treatment of youth with bipolar disorder.

MANAGEMENT OF COMMON SIDE EFFECTS

All medications have side effects. Whether or not your child will experience any negative effects depends on the medication being used, the dosage, the individual response to the medication, and how many medications your child is taking. For this reason, it is impossible to predict how your child will react to any prescribed medication. But you should know some basic facts about side effects if your child's treatment regime includes medications.

Facts About Side Effects

This list gives you some basic facts about side effects that will help you better understand when and how medications can act in undesirable ways:

- The timing of side effects is unpredictable. Common side effects often develop soon after the medication is started or after the dosage is increased, but they may also develop after several months or even more. Many of the side effects are short-lived and disappear once the body has adapted to the medication.

Most side effects disappear when the medication is discontinued or the dosage is lowered.

- Some side effects may require the temporary use of another medication to target and reduce specific side effects until your child adjusts to the medication.

- Several of the medications used to treat bipolar disorder (e.g., lithium, valproate) may produce slowness in thinking and mild difficulties with memory.

- Although many of the medications currently used to treat bipolar disorder in children and adolescents have been around for many years and have been well studied in adults, studies of the long-term use of these medications in youth are scarce or under way. Therefore, unless otherwise indicated, the side effects described are applicable to acute (short-term) rather than long-term treatment with these medications. You and your child's doctor must be alert to the possibility of unknown side effects with the use of these medications.

- Always ask your child's doctor or pharmacist about any possible interactions between the prescribed medication and other prescription or over-the-counter medications. Always inform your child's doctor and dentist of the medications being taken. *Interactions with other medications may be potentially harmful, result in increased side effects, and reduce the effectiveness of the medications.*

> **Caution**
> Ask your child's doctor whether the medication side effects can interfere with the child's functioning at school, sports, and driving. Keep all medicines out of the reach of children, especially if he or she has suicidal thoughts or has made prior suicidal attempts.

- Any medication can cause an allergic reaction. This reaction can be benign, with mild itching and skin rash, or more serious, with hives, swelling, and difficulty breathing. Most medication tablets and capsules contain fillers such as dyes and other substances in addition to the active medication. Sometimes the allergy can be attributed to one of these fillers and not to the medication itself. Therefore, a switch to another formulation of the medication may at times be a reasonable option. If your child experiences an allergic reaction while taking medication, stop the medication and inform your doctor. If your child develops hives, swelling, or has trouble breathing, take him or her to the emergency room.

Other Causes for Undesirable Symptoms

When determining whether a side effect is due to the medication(s) your child is taking, remember to consider other causes for the symptoms as well. Your child's undesirable side effects could be due to the following:

- Psychiatric symptoms that your child was already experiencing (e.g., tiredness or irritability due to depression, agitation due to mania or hypomania)
- New psychiatric problems
- Abuse of illegal drugs, alcohol, or nicotine
- Other medications, food, or the fillers and dyes in the medication pills
- The combination of various medications or only one of the medications that your child is taking
- Other medical or neurological illness
- Poor diet habits and/or lack of exercise
- Environmental factors. For example, your child may be tired and irritable because he or she is going to sleep late. Or, your child could be experiencing headaches and irritability related to conflicts with peers or family members. In both of these cases, the symptoms were due to environmental factors, not to the medication.

Management Options

The management of the most common medication side effects is described here, but you should always inform and consult with your child's doctor.

- **Allergic skin rash/itching.** If a rash or itching begins after administering the medication, do not give your child another dosage. Stop the medication and contact your child's doctor or nurse. If your child has any breathing difficulty or discomfort, take your child to the emergency room.

- **Cognitive (thinking) problems.** Some medications may produce slowed thinking or memory problems. Consider whether memory or thinking problems existed before the medications started or whether they are due to a specific medication or the combination of two or more medications. If these problems are due to the medication(s) and are interfering with your child's functioning, the dosage should be decreased, or the medication(s) should be discontinued. If the cognitive problems existed before the medications started, inform your child's psychiatrist or clinician.

- **Constipation.** Several medications may produce constipation, particularly in children who are prone to this problem. Make sure your child is drinking plenty of fluids. Try increasing bulk foods, such as bran and salads, in the diet. A bulk laxative, such as Metamucil, or a stool softener, such as Colace, may be helpful. If constipation persists, speak to your child's doctor or nurse.

- **Dizziness.** Some medications like the low-potency first-generation antipsychotics (such as Thorazine and Melleril) and the second-generation antipsychotics (such as Zyprexa and Risperdal) may lower the child's blood pressure and induce dizziness. Dizziness induced by low blood pressure is more pronounced when the person moves from a lying or seated position to a standing position quickly because of the fall in blood pressure. Let your child's doctor know that he or she is having these problems. To minimize dizziness, before your child stands, have him or her sit for several minutes and then stand up slowly. If the dizziness continues, have your child return to a seated or lying position and proceed more gradually. Caffeine and alcohol should be avoided. Have your child drink plenty of fluids, and add table salt to meals (do not overdo it—too much salt is not healthy). This side effect usually occurs when the medication is first started or when the dosage is increased and is usually temporary. If necessary, the dosage can be lowered or may be increased more gradually. If this side effect persists, the medication will need to be switched.

- **Drowsiness and tiredness.** With few exceptions, most medications produce drowsiness and tiredness. These side effects can be avoided by increasing the dosage of medications slowly, by initially administering the medication only at bedtime, and by using a larger dosage at night once an optimal total daily dosage is reached. Avoid using other medications that can also make your child drowsy, such as cold medications. Alcohol and drugs can also increase tiredness and drowsiness. If necessary, the medication dosage may be lowered or discontinued. Your child should avoid driving a car or operating machinery if the drowsiness persists. If appropriate, inform the school that your child is taking medication that may make him or her sleepy during class or not able to concentrate.

- **Dry mouth.** Medications such as lithium, antidepressants, antipsychotics, and others may produce dry mouth. In this case, your child may begin to drink high-calorie beverages or eat sweets, which may lead to increased weight and cause cavities. Instead try sugarless gum, drink water, and brush teeth regularly. In severe cases, consider switching medications. Since medications like lithium cause dry mouth because the child is urinating too much, he or she may need school permission to go to the bathroom frequently and to have a bottle of water in class.

- **Gastrointestinal problems: heartburn, nausea, vomiting, diarrhea.** These side effects often subside after several weeks of taking the medication and can be avoided or diminished by increasing the dosage of the medication slowly, lowering the dosage, dividing the dosage to three to four times a day, or administering the medication with food. If available, switching from an immediate-release to a slow-release preparation may be help-ful. If your child is experiencing severe nausea, vomiting, or diar-rhea, call your child's doctor or nurse.

- **Headaches.** Headaches can be managed with over-the-counter pain medication such as aspirin, ibuprofen (such as Motrin), or acetaminophen (such as Tylenol). One exception is that ibupro-fen or similar medications cannot be administered with lithium. A lower dosage of medication or increasing the dosage slowly may also help reduce your child's headaches. However, if the headaches persist and/or are severe, contact your child's doctor.

- **Mania—change in mood to markedly irritable or euphoric.** The development of manic symptoms is one of the main con-cerns when prescribing medications such as antidepressants and St. John's wort to depressed children with bipolar disorder. Your child may experience a switch in mood from downcast and sad to silly, giddy, careless, or frustrated and irritable. His or her behav-ior may become bold or brazen and unusually animated. If these symptoms arise, contact your doctor to determine whether these symptoms are indicative of mania. This switch in mood must be differentiated from the onset of mania.

- **Restlessness, excitability, irritability, nervousness, and/or anxiety.** Some patients experience these symptoms after starting treatment or after a dosage increase of some medications such as the SSRIs, venlafaxine, and bupropion. These symptoms may re-quire a reduction in the dosage of medication or a switch to an alternative medication. Your child's doctor will need to consider whether the medications are triggering a mixed episode or an episode of mania or hypomania.

- **Sleep problems.** Some children may experience difficulty sleep-ing for a few days after starting some medications, including ven-lafaxine, bupropion, or other SSRIs. Report the sleep difficulties to your child's doctor. This side effect can be addressed by low-ering the dosage or changing the dosing schedule of the medica-tion (taking the medication earlier in the day). Remember that your child needs to maintain a consistent sleep time. Establish regular bedtime routines, and avoid stimulating activities before bedtime. Avoid caffeinated beverages during the evening. If the medications have been effective in relieving bipolar symptoms and is otherwise well tolerated by your child, your child's doctor may consider adding a medication to improve sleep instead of switching to a different medication. If your child is not sleeping and appears more activated, restless, unusually talkative, irritable, or euphoric, speak to the doctor immediately. This behavior might indicate the beginning of a manic episode.

- **Sunburns or skin discoloration from sun exposure.** Some medications (such as St. John's wort and some antipsychotics) may increase your child's sensitivity to the sun. To avoid sunburns and the potential of skin discoloration, always have your child wear a sunscreen of SPF 15 or more as well as protective clothing and sunglasses when outdoors or in direct sunlight. Your child should also avoid exposure to artificial sunlight, such as tanning booths and sun lamps.

- **Sweating.** Medications like the SSRIs venlafaxine (Effexor) or bupropion (Wellbutrin), as well as St. John's wort, may increase sweating, particularly during the night. Deodorants and antiperspirants, talcum powder, wearing cotton undergarments, and frequent showering may be helpful. If your child develops skin irritation from the use of over-the-counter antiperspirants and other cosmetic products, he or she can try herbal, unscented, or crystal deodorants, which may be less irritating. If over-the-counter products are not strong enough, your doctor may suggest a prescription antiperspirant such as Drysol or Odaban. Always consult your child's doctor because some medical illnesses can also produce excessive sweating.

- **Weight gain.** Some medications, including lithium, valproate (Depakote), and most of the second-generation antipsychotics (such as Zyprexa and Risperdal), may induce weight gain. If you think that your child's increase in weight is due to the medications, consult with your child's doctor and a dietician to create a behavioral and nutritional plan to help your child manage his or her weight. Encourage your child to exercise, and offer your child plenty of healthy food options. Changes in diet and activity level may circumvent the weight gain associated with medications. If diet and exercise do not work, you should talk to your child's doctor about the possibility of changing medications.

- **Weight loss or loss of appetite.** Some medications, such as topiramate (Topamax), bupropion (Wellbutrin), and perhaps some SSRIs, may produce loss of appetite. Avoid forcing your child to eat meals. Instead, try administering these medications with or after meals, giving your child smaller meals more frequently, and using high-calorie supplements to help your child maintain his or her weight.

Other, less common side effects of medications used to treat bipolar disorder are listed in the chapter sections for each medication. If you notice any of those side effects, be sure to contact your child's doctor immediately.

SUMMARY

Several medications have been found to be helpful for the acute treatment and the prevention of episodes of mania and depression. The treatment of depression in bipolar patients has been challenging because antidepressant medications may trigger mania, rapid cycling, or mixed episodes. However, new treatments, such as lamotrigine and the second generation of antipsychotics, seem effective for the treatment of bipolar depression.

Most of the studies using mood stabilizers for bipolar disorder were carried out in adults, but it appears that these medications are also useful for the management of bipolar symptoms in youth. Ongoing investigations using mood stabilizers will give us further information about the use and side effects of these medications in children and teens (see Appendix II).

The next chapter will discuss the various psychosocial therapies that can be used, along with medications, to manage the acute symptoms of bipolar disorder and to prevent future episodes of mania, hypomania, and depression.

CHAPTER 7

Tools for Treating Bipolar Disorder: Psychological Therapies

ALTHOUGH THE FOUNDATION OF treatment for bipolar disorder is medications, this approach alone does not address the multiple problems of children and teens with bipolar disorder. Even with adequate medication, many children fail to show complete response to treatment, have recurrent episodes (in particular, depression), and have problems functioning at school, home, and with peers.

Therefore, researchers have established that psychosocial therapy in conjunction with pharmacological treatment is key in the management of bipolar disorder. While medications treat the biological roots of the disorder, psychosocial therapy helps the person with bipolar disorder understand the emotional and day-to-day issues that accompany a chronic mental health disorder, such as an acceptance of the illness, self-esteem issues, coping and problem-solving difficulties, adherence to treatment, family communication failures, and the risk of future episodes of mania and depression.

Several types of psychosocial therapies are possible. Some may be more helpful than others depending on your child's problems, family situation, attitudes and beliefs toward therapy, and cultural, ethnic, and religious background. Therefore, it is important for you to have information about the most common types of psychosocial therapies currently used to treat people with bipolar disorder and be able to judge, together with your child's clinician, whether the psychotherapy offered is the most appropriate for your child and your family.

This chapter will briefly describe the main principles for the following psychotherapies:

- Cognitive behavior therapy (CBT)
- Interpersonal psychotherapy (IPT)
- Interpersonal and social rhythm psychotherapy (IPSRT)
- Family focus therapy (FFT)
- Psychodynamic psychotherapy
- Supportive psychotherapy

Adults Versus Children and Teens

It is important to note that most psychosocial therapy studies for bipolar disorder have been carried out in adults with bipolar disorder. The results of these studies may not apply to children and teens.

COGNITIVE BEHAVIOR THERAPY

According to the principles of cognitive behavior therapy (CBT), people who tend to develop depression have a negative way of thinking or *negative cognitive style* about themselves, their world, and their future.[1–3] This style of thinking tends to focus more on negative thoughts, emotions, or life experiences instead of positive ones (seeing the "glass as half empty instead of half full"), and they feel hopeless and helpless about their future. They may be born with this tendency to be pessimistic, or they may learn it from the environment (home, peers, and daily situations). In either case, the goal of cognitive behavior therapy in the treatment of your child is to modify his or her negative or pessimistic way of thinking and in this way improve his or her mood.

Of course, everybody experiences sadness, but people with persistent negative cognitive style may develop severe depression, particularly when confronted with a stressful situation such as death of a loved one, separation from family or friends, poor grades, conflicts with peers, moving to another city, or a traumatic event (such as an accident). As shown in figure 7.1, when a negative situation occurs (1), a person who tends to think negatively (2) feels more hopelessness and helplessness (3). He or she feels pessimistic that "there is no light at the end of the tunnel" and gets depressed (4). The depression increases his or her negative way of thinking (2), exacerbating feelings of hopelessness and helplessness (3) and, ultimately, depression (4).

Figure 7.1—The Link Between Negative Thinking and Depression

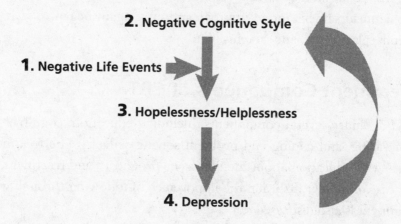

2. Negative Cognitive Style

1. Negative Life Events

3. Hopelessness/Helplessness

4. Depression

Using CBT to Deal with Self-Blame, Pessimism, and Generalizing

People with a tendency to become depressed often blame themselves excessively for past or present, real or imagined mistakes without considering that perhaps what has happened is not their fault or not related to them. They also tend to generalize their pessimistic thinking; they believe that if something bad happens in one situation, it will occur again. This type of negative thinking is common in children who are depressed or who have a tendency to develop anxiety or depression.[1,2]

Ten-year-old Mohammad, for example, is a pessimistic boy who got into a minor accident while riding his bike. He believed that the accident was his fault and that it would happen again. Despite the fact he loved to ride his bike, his fear prevented him from riding again. More-over, he generalized his fears to other sport activities and began to avoid them. He isolated himself from friends and became increasingly depressed. Mohammad's CBT therapist helped him consider that acci-dents can happen to anyone, that there is always the chance that an-other accident could happen, but with certain precautions, riding his bike and enjoying other activities will be safe. By modifying his nega-tive thoughts and behaviors, and with the support of his parents, Mohammad saw his mood improve and once again began to visit his friends, play sports, and ride his bike.

Treatment Components of CBT

CBT includes several components, including education, cognitive re-structuring, and coping and problem-solving skills.[1-3] The treatment starts with education about the illness, its prognosis, and treatment. In the case of bipolar disorder, the importance of following through with treatment is also discussed.

Cognitive restructuring focuses on mental exercises and daily moni-toring of mood. It addresses issues such as how many times a day the child has negative thoughts about him- or herself, what causes these thoughts, and what the child can do to modify them. This helps the child be more in control of the negative thoughts. It emphasizes the good events in the child's life, minimizes the real or imagined nega-tive ones, considers the child's strengths and weaknesses, and helps the child be less of a perfectionist. Cognitive restructuring provides the child with tools to regulate his or her emotions, and it also helps the child objectively evaluate daily life situations as well as his or her own fantasies.

CBT also fosters the development of new coping skills, giving the child alternative ways of responding to stressful events and problem-solving situations. The child learns to identify his or her problems and to create various strategies to solve them. Together with more posi-tive and realistic ways of thinking learned in therapy, the child practices in real life these coping and problem-solving skills and discovers whether they work, breaking the vicious circle described in figure 7.1.

This is a time-limited therapy, lasting approximately 12 to 16 weeks. During this time, the therapist will teach your child the skills necessary to become his or her own "therapist" and improve his or her mood to avoid future episodes of depression. You will also learn these skills and become the "therapist's assistant" by coaching your child at home.

INTERPERSONAL PSYCHOTHERAPY

Interpersonal psychotherapy (IPT) is a short-term psychotherapy developed for the treatment of depression.[5,6] It is based on the assumption that some people do not have the skills to find solutions to interpersonal problems or conflicts. When these people experience a stressful interpersonal event, depression is likely to occur.

IPT is a "here-and-now" treatment that focuses primarily on current symptoms, recent relationships, and recent life events or stressful situations. It includes a component of education about depression as a treatable medical illness. Because it is difficult for depressed people to resolve interpersonal conflicts or find solutions to interpersonal problems, IPT is useful therapy for people with depression in four problem areas: grief, interpersonal role disputes, role transitions, and/or interpersonal deficits.

- *Grief* or *sorrow* refers to symptoms that result from incomplete mourning or unresolved feelings about the death of an important person in someone's life. Grief can also be the result of lost hopes and ruined relationships. In addition, the loss of the healthy person the individual was before the illness started, or the person he

> ### CBT Study Results
>
> Several studies have found CBT helpful for the acute and preventative treatment of major depression, dysthymia (chronic depression), and anxiety in children and teens.[1,2] Recently, a study showed that CBT in conjunction with mood stabilizers reduced the number of manic and depressive episodes and the number of hospitalizations, and it promoted better social functioning in adults with bipolar disorder.[4]

or she could have become if not diagnosed with bipolar disorder, may produce grief and depression.

- *Interpersonal role disputes* refer to negative interactions with others. For example, teens can become depressed after several disagreements with parents about participating in certain activities, their personal relationships, or selecting a college.
- *Role transition* addresses significant life changes such as moving to a new city, being diagnosed with a psychiatric or medical illness, attending a new school or college, getting married or divorced, giving birth, and so forth.
- *Interpersonal deficits* refer to people with a long history of diminished or unsuccessful interpersonal relationships. These people usually have chronic depressions, and their depression is not necessarily due to stressful life events.

IPT was recently adapted for use with adolescents and has shown promise for the acute treatment of depression in depressed teens.[5] Some reports have also suggested that IPT is useful for treating bipolar depression.[6] It addresses common adolescent developmental issues such as separation from parents, exploration of authority in relationship to parents, development of interpersonal relationships, initial experience with the death of a relative or friend, peer pressure, and living in single-parent families.

INTERPERSONAL AND SOCIAL RHYTHM PSYCHOTHERAPY

Interpersonal and social rhythm psychotherapy (IPSRT) is based on the evidence that biological clocks that control the rhythms of the body (such as the sleep-wake cycles) are more sensitive to changes and disruptions in people with bipolar disorder.[7,8] Thus, positive life events (such as winning the lottery), negative life events (such as interpersonal conflicts, problems at school or work, separations from family or friends, or the death of a family member or a friend) or changes in the person's daily routine/schedule may disturb the biological clock and body rhythms, thus triggering an episode of mania or depression.

Together with medications, IPSRT will use the principles of education, interpersonal therapy, and behavioral techniques to help your child understand bipolar disorder, regulate daily routines, diminish interpersonal problems, cope with stressors, and follow through with medication treatment. Together these techniques are designed to control the biological, psychological, and social factors that may be disturbing your child's biological clock functioning.

> **IPSRT Study Results**
>
> Preliminary studies have shown that IPSRT improves depressive symptoms of adult with bipolar disorder, increases the person's adherence to medication treatment, and facilitates regulating the person's daily life routines (e.g., sleep schedule).[7,8]

FAMILY FOCUS THERAPY

There are many types of family therapy; however, only family focus therapy (FFT) has been tested for use in the treatment of bipolar disorder.[9,10] FFT is based on the fact that family education is a powerful addition to the successful treatment of people with bipolar disorder. Focusing treatment on the family makes sense for your child because he or she depends on the rest of the family for his or her well-being. Moreover, bipolar disorder runs in families, and medications can be difficult to dispense safely if your child is living in a chaotic family environment.

Family treatment is needed because negative family interactions often result in poor treatment response and worsening of the disorder. In fact, several studies have found that people with bipolar disorder who live with relatives (parents or spouses) and experience high levels of criticism, hostility, and/or emotional overinvolvement or who have relatives who are critical and/or hostile in face-to-face verbal interactions do worse than those who live with relatives who have less critical or negative interaction styles.[9,10]

The overall objectives of FFT are to help children and their relatives (1) come to a mutual understanding of the most recent mood disorder episode, (2) accept the child's propensity to develop more manic or depressive episodes, (3) understand the child's need for a lifelong treatment with mood-stabilizing medications, (4) distinguish the child's normal mood and behaviors from bipolar and other psychiatric disorders, (5) recognize and cope with stressors that trigger episodes, and (6) restore functional family relationships after the episode.

The treatment with FFT includes three components: education, communication, and problem solving. The educational component of this therapy is extensive. It includes information for families about the nature, symptoms, course, and treatment of bipolar disorder. It addresses detection of early symptoms, relapse prevention strategies, coping skills, and strategies for handling the social impact of the bipolar diagnostic label. The family also learns intervention techniques for times when the signs of the disorder appear. Parents and their children are educated about the rapid changes in normal emotional, cognitive, and social development and how to differentiate between what is bipolar disorder and what is normal childhood/teen behavior. Emphasis is placed on maintaining good sleep routines because sleep loss and irregular sleep-wake schedules may trigger mania in people with bipolar disorder. Discussion also focuses on preventing behaviors that can threaten the child's health and the health of others, including unsafe sex, substance and alcohol abuse, drunk driving, aggressiveness, and suicidal tendencies.

FFT also provides educational information about coexisting disorders and how they are different from bipolar disorder. It draws comparisons between managing bipolar disorder versus behavioral disorders. And it teaches anxiety management techniques, such as relaxation exercises. The educational component includes a strong focus on the safe and effective use of medication and the consequences of discontinuing treatment. When parents and siblings themselves have psychiatric disorders, they are encouraged to share with the child their past or present problems and how they learned to cope with these problems.

The second and third components, communication and problem-solving training, teach the child with bipolar disorder and family members coping strategies for dealing with illness-related conflicts. Families are taught how to communicate more positively and efficiently. Hostile communication patterns are changed through active, role-playing exercises that teach families to listen actively to each other, offer more positive feedback, make positive requests for changes in others' behaviors, and avoid negative feedback. These skills foster a feeling of collaboration among members of a family, encourage an open dialogue about difficult problem topics, and help develop skills for solving family problems. Solution-finding exercises are designed to promote healthy independence by giving the adolescent a greater role in his or her medication regime. Finally, help is always also offered to parents because whether or not they have a diagnosable psychiatric disorder, many parents have trouble raising a child with bipolar disorder due to their own emotional instabilities.

FFT Study Results

Researchers have found that FFT, when combined with mood stabilizer medications, is effective in delaying relapses of adult bipolar I disorder.[9,10] This approach can prevent hospitalizations, reduce levels of depression over 2-year follow-ups, enhance a person's adherence to treatment, and make family interactions more positive. An ongoing collaborative study between the University of Colorado and the University Pittsburgh will help determine whether FFT also helps teens with bipolar disorder.

PSYCHODYNAMIC PSYCHOTHERAPY

Although there is no empirical evidence to support the use of psychodynamic psychotherapy in treating bipolar disorders, as reviewed later, this type of therapy may be helpful for managing the child with bipolar disorder.

According to psychodynamic therapy, the goal of treatment is to treat the "whole person" rather than the symptoms, such as depressed mood.[11] To achieve this goal, psychodynamic therapy focuses on unconscious conflicts, interpersonal problems, and shortages at any of the psychological stages of development.

Several psychodynamic theories have proposed that we go through different psychosocial stages of development. At each stage we have to solve or master certain skills to be able to develop trust, autonomy, sense of self, independence, happiness, and so forth. Any person with problems at any of these stages may develop poor self-esteem, interpersonal problems, psychiatric disorder(s), and other challenges.

In general, psychodynamic psychotherapy proposes that our emotions, behaviors, and patterns and quality of our relationships with others are influenced by our early childhood relationships and experiences with significant others, particularly with our parents. During the first years of life, we develop internal models or mental representations of the person(s) to whom we are attached. When we encounter a new person and begin to develop a relationship with that person, we use the mental representations of early relationships as a guide. In a sense, we transfer or transmit our experiences with the original attachment figure to the new person. Thus, the way that we relate to our friends, spouse, and children is influenced by our original mental representations. We will repeat the same positive or negative pattern of interactions without being aware of this behavior. More recent theories proposed that we represent in our minds observations and habits not only from early childhood but from all our experiences, and each experience influences subsequent experiences.

The various types of psychodynamic psychotherapies differ according to the theoretical model they evolved from, such as the work of Sigmund Freud, Erik Erikson, Carl Jung, John Bowlby, and many others. But it is generally believed by psychodynamic psychotherapy practitioners that a symptom such as depression or mania indicates that the person is having unconscious unresolved problems. For example, a girl who is feeling anger against her parents can feel guilty. Instead of the child expressing her anger against her parents, she expresses anger against herself and feels depressed. Modern adaptations of this theory also take into account the existence of biological factors, temperament, and cognitive patterns, and they also address environmental factors that maintain problematic behaviors of the child in the family.

To achieve the goals of psychodynamic psychotherapy, most of these therapies rely on the ongoing patient–therapist relationships that can last many months or years, but short-term psychodynamic therapies have been created to focus on specific problems and issues. The treatment has traditionally been divided into a beginning phase, a middle phase, and a termination phase. During the first phase, the therapist establishes strong relationships with the child and his parents, indicates the nature of the work, and finds a comfortable mode of communication, whether verbally or in play. The middle phase involves interpretation of the child's problems using the relationship between the child and the therapist as a template of prior relationships (transference) and the repetitive themes that appears in the child's play, drawings, or speech. The termination phase is used to help the child separate from the therapist and reinforce the issues learned during therapy.

> ### Evaluating Unconscious Problems
>
> Often with psychodynamic psychotherapy, the therapist uses play, drawing, dreams, or talking to evaluate the child's unconscious problems and help him or her change. Because children cannot be counted on to maintain independent relationships with the therapist, throughout treatment the alliance with the child's parents must be maintained and fortified.

SUPPORTIVE PSYCHOTHERAPY

The main goal of supportive pyschotherapy is to develop a supportive and caring relationship among the child, parents, and the therapist. The therapist carefully listens, reviews, educates, and helps the child and his or her parents understand the problems that they may have experienced. They form a relationship based on trust, mutual respect, and genuine concern, in which they review problems and coping abilities. Together, they develop ways to deal with the child's problems and stressful circumstances. Time is devoted to allowing the child and parents to talk about their feelings and beliefs concerning bipolar disorder, as well as stressful experiences and other experiences important to the child and his or her parents. This therapy assumes that by developing a special relationship with the therapist and by allowing the child and his or her parents to determine what takes place during the session, they will be more optimistic about a specific problem and will show improvement in handling similar problems.

Supportive therapy should be included along with all modalities of your child's treatment (including pharmacotherapy), but it is usually not sufficient as a sole mode of therapy for bipolar disorder.

SUMMARY

Very few studies have been conducted on the use of psychosocial therapies for bipolar disorder, and even fewer studies have researched their use specifically with children and teens. But the studies that do exist have shown that psychosocial interventions such as CBT, IPT, FFT, and IPSRT help decrease the number of hospitalizations and the rates of bipolar recurrences, enhance medication adherence, and help with the overall improvement of the person with bipolar disorder, particularly the symptoms of depression. These interventions also help people with bipolar disorder better organize their daily routines (e.g., sleep patterns, meal times, and work schedule), improve communication among family members, and enhance the child's self-esteem. Although not specifically studied for the treatment of bipolar disorder, behavioral therapy is useful to modify the child's maladaptive behaviors or poor habits and comorbid conditions (e.g., ADHD, oppositional defiant disorder) that usually coexist with bipolar disorder.

Ideally, psychosocial therapy should help parents, children, and other relatives better understand the symptoms, course, complications, and treatment of bipolar disorder. It also should help families distinguish age-appropriate moodiness from bipolar disorder. In addition, psychosocial therapies educate parents and children about the warning signs of an upcoming episode of depression or mania and about how the family can help solve daily problems. (See chapter 8 for more information about the educational component of a treatment plan.) Other topics addressed during psychosocial therapy sessions include the role of stress in inducing symptoms, how to intervene should the symptoms appear, the importance of regular medication and blood monitoring, the social stigma attached to bipolar disorder, and the future of children with this disorder.

The following checklists will help you evaluate the use and expected outcomes of psychosocial therapy in the treatment of your child's bipolar disorder.

For children, psychosocial therapy should:

❑ Decrease the denial of the illness or discomfort with the bipolar disorder (and other disorders) diagnosis

❑ Improve the symptoms of the disorder

❑ Identify and manage the early warning signs of mania, hypomania, or depression and what to do

❑ Identify and manage suicidal ideation and suicidal behaviors and, if present, homicidal ideation

❑ Manage symptoms of coexisting psychiatric disorder(s)

❑ Improve self-esteem

❑ Help grieve for the healthy child your son or daughter was before the illness or could have become if he or she did not have bipolar disorder

❑ Improve coping and social skills including ways to make them feel better when they are upset

❑ Help cope with transitions and stressful events (such as moving to another city, transferring schools, going into junior high school, separation, or deaths)

❑ Improve social, academic, and occupational functioning

❑ Organize daily routines (such as sleep patterns, meal and activity times, and school homework) and help avoid overstimulation

❑ Teach about the dangers of discontinuing treatment and improving adherence to the pharmacological and psychosocial treatment

❑ Help children take a greater role in their treatment and, if appropriate, in the medication regime

❑ Prevent behaviors that can threaten the child's health and others' well-being, including unsafe sex, the use of caffeine and nicotine, substance and alcohol abuse, drunk driving, and aggressiveness or suicidal tendencies

❑ Reinforce the child's strengths (academic, artistic, athletic, social, etc.)

For the parents (and family), psychosocial therapy should:

❑ Help grieve for the healthy child they had before the illness or the child they could have had if the child did not have bipolar disorder

❑ Help parents to recognize the warning signs of an episode of mania or depression and teach them what to do

❑ Support parents' behavioral management efforts and reduce parents' enabling behaviors

❑ Decrease parental denial of the illness, and help them adapt to the idea that their child has a lifetime disorder and deal with the stigma of this illness

❑ Reduce the negative impact of the illness in the parents and family

❑ Develop strategies to cope with the child's and family's daily problems and crises at home and school

❑ Reduce family conflicts through open dialogue about difficult problems or topics and develop new coping and problem-solving skills

❏ Help parents solve their children's academic and other problems (such as retention, absenteeism, suspensions, and expulsions) at school

❏ Help parents to have continuing access to care and develop social networks for support

❏ Help parents recognize their own problems (and those of other family members) and, if necessary, seek treatment

Psychosocial therapies can change your child's life for the better—when used as one component of a carefully developed treatment program. The following chapter will help you become familiar with the way clinicians choose which treatment strategies to combine when managing acute symptoms and creating a maintenance program.

CHAPTER 8

Management of Bipolar Disorder: Using the Treatment Tools

To effectively manage your child's bipolar disorder, your child's doctor will evaluate all the biological and psychosocial treatments discussed in earlier chapters and create a treatment plan that is carefully tailored to your child's individual needs. Table 8.1 gives you important general facts about the treatment of bipolar disorder to keep in mind as your child begins the treatment plan. Then the chapter shows you how a treatment plan is divided into three stages: (1) *education* about the characteristics, long-term outcome, and consequences, causes, and treatment of bipolar disorder; (2) *acute treatment* to manage the symptoms that require immediate attention, such as agitation, psychosis, suicidal behaviors, and aggression; and (3) *maintenance treatment* to prevent further episodes of mania, hypomania, mixed symptoms, rapid cycling, psychosis, and aggressive or suicidal behaviors. This chapter also offers the information you'll need if your child shows no response to the prescribed treatment, and it will prepare you to recognize the signs of an upcoming episode so maintenance treatment can be adjusted.

Note: All medications mentioned in this chapter as part of treatment regimens are more fully explained in chapters 6 and 9.

TABLE 8.1—IMPORTANT FACTS ABOUT THE ACUTE AND MAINTENANCE TREATMENTS FOR BIPOLAR DISORDER

- The cornerstone treatment for bipolar disorder is medication to stabilize your child's mood.
- Psychosocial therapy, including education, increases the chance that your child will respond to treatment because it helps improve your child's coping and social skills, family relationships, and adherence to treatment, and it decreases the risk for recurrences, suicidal behaviors, and hospitalizations.
- The type of treatment and where the treatment will take place (e.g., hospital vs. clinic) will depend on the severity of the illness, the presence of aggressive or suicidal behaviors, and whether the child has mania, depression, mixed symptoms, rapid cycling, or psychosis.
- The major impediments for any effective acute and maintenance treatments are the child's (or parents') denial of his or her illness, poor adherence to treatment, and the clinician's lack of knowledge of how to treat bipolar disorder.
- The treatment needs to be optimized from the outset. The longer your child remains ill without treatment, the poorer the response to treatment.
- The efficacy and side effects of the medications need to be evaluated early in treatment as well as periodically throughout the treatment course.
- Medications need to be introduced one at a time. Otherwise, it will be difficult to determine which medication is helping or causing side effects.
- The medications used to treat bipolar disorder work slowly. You will not see changes immediately. Unless it is necessary (perhaps because of side effects), do not discontinue or keep changing medications frequently, as this will only delay your child's response to treatment.
- A series of medication trials may be needed before your child begins to respond to treatment. Frequently, your child's doctor will need to make educated guesses and several systematic trials until the best treatment for your child is found.
- The use of multiple medications is often necessary.
- Early discontinuation of medications may worsen the illness. Moreover, when the medications are restarted, the child may not respond as well as before.
- Rapid discontinuation of medication may cause early recurrences of depression or mania.

- The side effects of the medications need to be differentiated from the symptoms of the illness.
- Treatment of coexisting psychiatric (such as ADHD) and other environmental conditions (such as persistent conflicts at home or school) is also necessary. (See chapter 9 for the treatment of these conditions.)
- The possible presence of suicidal thoughts or plans to commit suicide must always be assessed (see chapter 10).
- The possible presence of thoughts to harm others must always be assessed. (The assessment and management of these thoughts are similar to the ones for suicidal behavior.)
- Family participation is crucial for treatment success.
- Parents and siblings may also require psychiatric evaluation and treatment.

A Word About Research Studies and Children

Most of the studies mentioned in this chapter have been performed with adults. However, physicians adapt the information to treat children and teens, and so the results are, in that way, of interest.

EDUCATION

The treatment of bipolar disorder cannot be carried out without educating the child, parents, siblings, other relatives, school counselors, and teachers about the nature and treatment of this disorder. Indeed, most of the psychosocial therapies reviewed in chapter 7 (e.g., cognitive behavior therapy, interpersonal psychotherapy, and family focus therapy) include an educational component at the initiation of the treatment.

Why Is Education Important?

Many of you have experienced the uncertainty of having a medical problem and finally being able to relax once your physician has explained the reasons for your illness and the most appropriate treatment. Similarly, for psychiatric disorders, learning about the causes of your child's mood and behavior problems may diminish your feelings of guilt, anxiety, and inadequacy, as well as thoughts that your child's illness is your fault or that your child is misbehaving on purpose.

For example, after a period of feeling extremely happy, energetic, and talkative, Rachel was brought to the clinic by her parents because of her irritability, sadness, temper outbursts, defiance at home and at school, verbal aggression toward family members, isolation from friends, and ensuing poor academic performance. Her parents were confused about their daughter's personality changes because she had always been a good student and never had any behavior problems. They began to think that Rachel was spoiled or lazy or that she might be using illicit drugs. They questioned their abilities as parents. Other relatives also blamed them for their daughter's problems. Rachel and her parents were having frequent arguments. These conflicts in turn were aggravating Rachel's symptoms to the point that her parents could not control her anymore and were contemplating admitting her into the hospital or sending her to a boarding school. Rachel was feeling depressed, angry, and hopeless about the situation. She could not understand why she was feeling so miserable and was considering suicide as a "solution" to her problems.

Rachel and her parents saw a child psychiatrist who diagnosed her with bipolar disorder and provided educational information about its symptoms, causes, consequences, and treatment. Rachel and her parents were reassured that Rachel's bipolar disorder is a disease that is not anyone's fault and that her poor grades were due to depression, not laziness. Upon hearing this, Rachel and her parents were greatly relieved and became very active in the treatment process. With Rachel's consent, her schoolteachers were informed about her problems and helped establish a plan to target her school issues. Rachel responded well to treatment and returned to her "normal self."

Similar examples can be given for episodes of mania in which children and adolescents may become hypersexual, very "wild," and sometimes "crazy," and nobody seems to understand what is happening to them. In this context, conflicts arise; others will misinterpret or misjudge the situation; members of the family will blame each other for the ensuing problems.

Several studies in populations of adults with depression and bipolar disorder have shown that educational programs that included the issues reviewed in this chapter improve patients' and families' understanding of the illness, enhance adherence to treatment, help avoid misunderstandings, diminish the family conflict, and encourage families to develop and improve coping, communication, and problem-solving strategies.[1–4]

Issues to Deal With in Treatment

In addition to understanding the acute or immediate symptoms, consequences, causes, and treatment of bipolar disorder, it is also very important to learn about the *psychological scars* that may remain after symptoms have improved, such as poor self-esteem, guilty feelings, and conflicts with family members, peers, and teachers. It is also crucial to discuss the effects of your child's bipolar disorder on you, siblings, and other relatives. In addition, you and your child may need to deal with the difficulties of accepting a lifelong diagnosis at an early age and of having to take medications to control the symptoms. You both may also need to learn how to cope with the stigma that your child is having a psychiatric illness.

The education program must also include information about a child's normal mood changes and age-appropriate behaviors in order to differentiate the expected normal behaviors and moods from the symptoms of bipolar disorder. For example, young children usually have low frustration tolerance, do not have a good concept of time, and cannot sit still for long periods of time. Teens, on the other hand, tend to want to spend more time away from home, may have a preoccupation with sex, challenge parental authority, and may have unpredictable sleep-wake patterns. (Chapter 2 discusses the differences between normal mood and behaviors and the symptoms of bipolar disorder in further detail.)

You and your family need to learn and practice coping and problem-solving skills to deal with daily stressful situations and to help avoid conflicts. You should all also be aware that many of the parents and siblings of youth with bipolar disorder may also have psychiatric disorders that need to be treated. Other important issues that should be included in a comprehensive education program are described in the summary section of chapter 7.

Moreover, the prevention of behaviors that can threaten the health and well-being of a child and others (including unsafe sex, substance and alcohol abuse, drunk driving, aggressiveness, and suicidal behaviors) should be discussed. You should also become familiar with the psychiatric disorders that often occur in conjunction with bipolar disorder and require separate treatments (chapter 9). Furthermore, it is important that you and your child understand the importance of following through with treatment and the practice of *mood hygiene* (keeping good sleep habits, for example) to prevent future bipolar episodes.

> **It Is Not Your Fault**
>
> You and your child need to know that it is no one's fault that your child has bipolar disorder. Although nothing can alter the fact that your child has bipolar disorder, if you, your child, and your family follow through with treatment, there is a good chance of preventing future episodes and limiting the damage caused by the bipolar disorder.

Types of Education Programs

Education can be done *individually* or in *groups*. A study of group education for parents of teens with depression showed improvement in the parents' understanding of their teen's problems, the symptoms of major depressive disorder, and the need for treatment.[3] Recently, Dr. Mary Fristad developed a 6-week multifamily psychoeducation group (MFPG) for families of children with bipolar disorder.[4] Preliminary results showed an increase in the parents' knowledge about the disorder, positive changes in the attitudes of family members toward bipolar disorder, and improvements in coping skills and support. Parents of our support/educational group in Pittsburgh have also reported that the group experience has helped them understand their children's problems and create an important support system.

I believe that group education is better than individual sessions because the group environment allows participants to share tips regarding the management of their children's daily behaviors and school and health insurance problems. Participants can discuss the benefits and side effects of medication, keep informed about new developments, support each other, and feel supported. A group forum also allows the clinician to hear from the participants about the most important issues regarding the diagnosis and treatment of their children and families.

The benefits of group sessions are better understood through the parents' responses to MFPG education:[4]

- I'm more aware and have more knowledge about bipolar disorder.
- My wife and I began to understand our child's mood and behavior problems.
- The program changed the way that we, and in particular my husband, interact with our child.
- We can make better decisions.
- Being in a group helped me realize that I am not the only one with these types of problems.
- It was helpful to listen to other people share the same problems.
- I got so much support, comfort, and relief.
- I do handle things differently now.
- Just being able to vent was wonderful.
- All these years I haven't had any support.
- It helped me believe that I can fight for the services my child needs.
- I don't feel like I have to hide—I can go out and ask for help.
- I feel that I am more in the driver's seat.

ACUTE TREATMENT

If your child has acute symptoms, he or she should be treated promptly to reduce the negative effects of the illness. The type of treatment depends on the severity of the illness and whether the child is in an episode of mania, hypomania, depression, mixed, rapid cycling, or psychosis.[5–12] The treatment of each one of these types of presentations of bipolar disorder is discussed in the following sections.

Treatment for Mania

The treatment of mania includes a mood stabilizer such as lithium or valproate (Depakote).[12] Because it takes about 2 to 4 weeks for these medications to work, an antipsychotic medication (usually a second-generation or novel antipsychotic) is added if your child is agitated, violent, or psychotic. These medications control agitation, violent behaviors, and mood faster than other mood stabilizers. A benzodiazepine (e.g., Klonopin or Ativan) can sometimes be added instead of an antipsychotic, but if your child is experiencing hallucinations or delusions, using an antipsychotic medication is preferred. Once the agitation or the psychosis has subsided, the antipsychotic or benzodiazepine may be very slowly tapered down and discontinued.

Recent reports[6–8,13] in adults with mania have shown that the second generation of antipsychotics such as olanzapine (Zyprexa), risperidone (Risperdal), quetiapine (Seroquel), and ziprasidone (Geodon) may be used *alone* for the treatment of acute manic symptoms, but this treatment has not been well studied in children.[12,14]

If your child is responding to treatment, you should see progressive improvement. For example, your child will be less agitated, impulsive, and talkative; he or she will have better judgment; and his or her sleep-wake habits will begin to normalize. But it is important to be patient because it takes time (2 to 4 weeks) for the mood stabilizers to take action. Moreover, some mood stabilizers need to be at a certain level in the blood to work effectively. These medications also need to be started

A Major Treatment Problem with Mania

One of the major problems encountered when treating a child during a manic phase is that he or she usually does not recognize the illness, refuses treatment, and becomes belligerent. For this reason, the child may need to be treated against his or her will.

at low dosages and slowly increased in order to avoid side effects, further adding to the lag in response time.

If your child has not shown improvement within 2 to 4 weeks, you must speak with your child's clinician since it is possible that the blood levels or dosages of the medication(s) are too low. If the dosage or blood level of the medications is appropriate, but your child is not responding to treatment, other medications may be added. For example, it is common to combine two mood stabilizers such as lithium and valproate. Psychosocial management strategies as well are always important for helping you and your child and family manage and cope with your child's manic symptoms.[1,3,4]

Hypomania

While hypomanic, your child may actually function better socially at home and at school. Therefore, if the symptoms are not severe, you may opt not to seek treatment for your child. (Moreover, your child may refuse treatment because he or she is feeling and performing well.) The problem with the decision not to treat, however, is that no one can predict whether the hypomania will escalate into a full-blown episode of mania or whether it will turn into an episode of depression. Therefore, it is best to seek treatment for a child who is hypomanic, especially if he or she has frequent episodes of hypomania that are followed by mania or depression or if the hypomanic episodes are affecting his or her functioning.

Mild, short-lived hypomanic periods may be treated with psychotherapy alone. If medication is needed, mood-stabilizing medications will treat the acute symptoms and may help prevent future bipolar episodes.

Depression

The treatment of bipolar depression is a challenge.[5–12] If a child has depression but not bipolar disorder, the current treatment of choice would be an antidepressant medication. But this strategy may not be appropriate for a child with bipolar disorder because antidepressants may trigger an episode of mania, mixed states, or rapid cycling. If antidepressants are used to treat bipolar depression, your child will need to be treated first with mood stabilizers. But even still, it is important to note that even if your child is taking the mood stabilizer, the antidepressant may still trigger a manic or a hypomanic episode.

Other ways your child's doctor may treat your child's bipolar depressive symptoms include the following:[5–12]

- The dosage of the mood stabilizers that your child currently takes may be increased.
- If your child is not taking lithium, this medication may be added to your child's current medications.
- Lamotrigine (Lamictal) may be added to your child's current medications. As stated in chapter 6, this medication may produce a severe rash, particularly in children; therefore, currently its use is restricted to youth older than 12 years old.
- A second-generation or novel antipsychotic alone or in combination with an SSRI may be used.
- A psychosocial therapy such as cognitive behavior therapy or interpersonal psychotherapy can be used in conjunction with the mood stabilizers.
- For children and teens with bipolar disorder whose depression occurs only during the fall, winter, or early spring, your child's doctor may consider using light therapy (as explained in chapter 6).
- Low thyroid hormone can produce symptoms of depression. If your child's thyroid gland is producing less thyroid hormone because of an illness or the effects of lithium, a thyroid hormone supplement may be added. If lithium is causing the low thyroid production, and lithium is not helping or is only partially help-

Do not be surprised if your child's doctor needs to make several trials until the best treatment for your child's depression is found.

ing, your child's doctor may consider discontinuing it.

- For teens who are severely depressed and are not responding to any treatment, the use of monoamine oxidase inhibitors (MAOIs) or electroconvulsive therapy (ECT) should be considered.

Do not be surprised if your child's doctor needs to make several trials until the best treatment for your child's depression is found. Sometimes parents and children may feel like "guinea pigs," but remember that your child's doctor is only trying to find the correct combination of medications for your child.

Importantly, bipolar disorder may initially present *only* with episodes of major depression. You might wonder how the clinician will know whether your child has bipolar disorder if she or he has never had a period of mania or hypomania. Currently, there are no tests to help determine whether the period of depression is part of bipolar disorder. However, as described in chapter 2, if your child has depression with psychosis, has a family history of bipolar depression, and/or experiences hypomania/mania induced by treatment with antidepressants, there is a good chance that he or she will develop mania in the future and fulfill the criteria for a diagnosis of bipolar disorder.[15,16]

Mixed Episodes

Mixed episodes include both symptoms of mania and depression. The child is usually confused and agitated and frequently has suicidal behaviors or psychotic symptoms. Mood stabilizers are the first choice when treating mixed episodes. Among the mood stabilizers, valproate (Depakote) is perhaps more helpful than lithium for the treatment of mixed episodes,[6–8,17] but this has not been evaluated in youth. Also, the second-generation antipsychotics seem to be useful; ongoing studies in children and teens will clarify their effectiveness for treating mixed symptoms in youth with bipolar disorder. *Antidepressants should be avoided for children with mixed episodes because these medications usually worsen the manic or hypomanic symptoms.*

Rapid Cycling

According to the American Psychiatric Association, a diagnosis of rapid cycling is made when a person has at least four cycles of mania/depression in a year.[6] In adults, the presence of rapid cycling has been associated with poor response to lithium,[6-9] but this is unverified in youth.[1-6] Also, children appear to have more rapid cycles than adults.[12,16] Thus, until further studied, it is recommended that a child with rapid cycling be treated first with valproate (Depakote) and then other mood stabilizers alone or in combination with valproate. The second-generation antipsychotics also seem to be useful for stopping the rapid cycling.[6-8,10,12,14]

Mania or Depression with Psychotic Features

Sometimes during an episode of mania, depression, or a mixed episode, your child may experience delusions (persistent false beliefs not shared by you or your community) or hallucinations (seeing or hearing things others do not). An antipsychotic medication, usually a second-generation or novel antipsychotic, is recommended in these cases. Sometimes, if the psychotic symptoms are mild, your child may respond to treatment with only lithium or Depakote.

MAINTENANCE TREATMENT

The main goal of the maintenance phase is to prevent further episodes of mania/hypomania, depression, mixed states, and rapid cycles.[6-12,16] This section will discuss who should have maintenance treatment and the type and duration of this treatment.

Who Should Receive Maintenance Treatment?

Most child psychiatrists believe that a child or a teen with two or more episodes of mania or bipolar depression should have maintenance treatment with medications and psychotherapy for long periods of time and perhaps a lifetime.

However, there is concern about keeping a child on medications for lengthy periods because no information is available on the long-term side effects of most of the medications used for the treatment of bipolar disorder, particularly when children begin taking these medications early in life.

> *Most child psychiatrists believe that a child or a teen with two or more episodes of mania or bipolar depression should have maintenance treatment with medications and psychotherapy for long periods of time and perhaps a lifetime.*

When faced with this dilemma, *you have to ask yourself what is worse—the side effects of medications or the side effects resulting from not treating the bipolar disorder (risk for suicide, poor academic, social and family functioning, etc.; see figure 8.1).* Moreover, some investigators have suggested that the more episodes of depression or mania that a person has, the poorer the treatment response.[6–8]

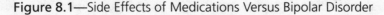

Figure 8.1—Side Effects of Medications Versus Bipolar Disorder

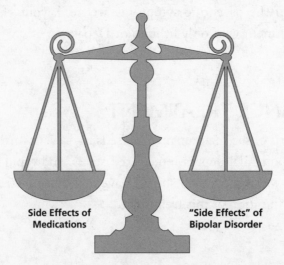

Side Effects of Medications   **"Side Effects" of Bipolar Disorder**

The question is *"What if my child has had only one episode?"* The jury is still out on this question. In general, if a child had a severe single episode (severe agitation, suicidal attempts, psychosis), particularly if there is family history of bipolar disorder, it is advisable to minimize the risk of a second episode as much as possible. On the other hand, children who have only had one (perhaps two) mild episodes of mania or a single episode of hypomania that did not considerably affect the child's functioning can be observed without maintenance medication treatment. If any symptoms worsen or reappear, the child should be treated immediately.

For example, 8-year-old Moses had a mild episode of mania. Moses's doctor advised the family to keep watch for symptoms of further episodes and only then to use medications. In his case, maintenance medication was not warranted, and Moses did not have any other episodes of mania or hypomania until he was 14 years old. In contrast, when Leroy was 15, he became talkative, energetic, inattentive, and impulsive; had poor judgment; and slept only a few hours a night. He was successfully treated with lithium, but 6 months later he and his parents decided to stop the lithium treatment. He did well for $1\frac{1}{2}$ years and then developed a severe episode of depression and tried to commit suicide. After his depression improved, Leroy agreed to take medications to prevent further episodes. Another child, Mary, was 12 years old when she had her first episode of depression. At age 14, she had her second episode, followed by symptoms of hypomania. She and her clinician decided to wait to see what would happen, but 6 months later Mary had a full-blown episode of mania. She may have avoided this episode with the use of maintenance medications. (Figures 3.1 and 3.2 in chapter 3 also show cases of children who had episodes of hypomania or depression and thereafter developed complete episodes of mania or mixed states.)

Which Maintenance Treatment?

Maintenance treatment programs are tailored to fit the specific type of bipolar disorder.

Mania, Mixed Episodes, and Rapid Cycling

The main treatments to prevent further episodes of mania/hypomania, mixed, and rapid cycling are lithium and the anticonvulsant medications, such as valproate (Depakote).[6–13,16,17] However, it appears that valproate may be better than lithium for the prevention of mixed episodes and rapid cycling.[17] Studies in adults with bipolar disorder have also shown that the second-generation antipsychotics alone or in combination with the anticonvulsants may be helpful in preventing mania and depressive episodes.[6–8,13] Also, recent studies in adult patients with bipolar disorder have shown that some psychosocial therapies, such as cognitive behavior therapy, may be useful for the prevention of manic episodes.[2]

Depression

Although medications such as lithium can be very effective in preventing further depressive episodes, *in general, the mood stabilizers are less effective in preventing episodes of depression than mania*.[6–10] One exception is lamotrigine (Lamictal). In adults with bipolar disorder, this medication appears to be more effective than other mood stabilizers for the prevention of depressive episodes.[18] Also, the combination of a second-generation or novel antipsychotic and an SSRI appears helpful.[6–12]

Other treatments described earlier for the acute treatment of depression, such as using light therapy and adding thyroid hormone, may also be helpful for the prevention of further episodes of bipolar depression.[6–10] Some children may respond to treatment with essential fatty acids, but the use of these substances for the prevention of bipolar episodes has not been well studied.[10]

The use of psychotherapy, particularly cognitive behavior therapy, interpersonal psychotherapy, interpersonal and social rhythm psychotherapy, and family focus therapy, has been shown to reduce the chance of further episodes of depression (see chapter 7 for a detailed description of each of these psychotherapies).[1] It is not clear whether these psychotherapies are useful because they directly treat the symptoms of depression or because they improve the person's adherence to treatment, reduce conflicts at home, and/or improve the person's support network. But by whatever means they work, they are important adjuncts to a maintenance program for depression.

Multiple Medications for Maintenance

The maintenance of bipolar disorder is complex. *To prevent mania/hypomania, depression, mixed episodes, and rapid cycling, your child may need multiple medications or combinations of medications and psychosocial therapies.*[6–12,16,19]

For example, 10-year-old Charles has rapid cycling and mixed episodes and ADHD. He responded only when he was treated with

---

Tips for Maintenance Treatment Programs

Remember the following important tips:
- Administer you child's medications consistently.
- Follow through with regularly checking your child's blood medication levels as ordered by his or her doctor. Some children may need lower blood levels of medications to prevent further episodes of bipolar disorder.
- Check for the presence of side effects. Some of these side effects can only be detected with a blood test or an electrocardiogram, so ask your child's physician about regular monitoring.
- Check for medication interactions.
- Manage family conflicts and other persistent stressors. This is important because ongoing stressors may prolong your child manic and depressive episodes or trigger further bipolar episodes (see chapters 3, 4, and 7).
- Seek treatment for your child's other psychiatric and learning problems.
- Seek treatment to teach your child to manage stress (chapter 7).
- Manage your child's behavior and academic problems (chapters 11 and 12).
- Manage your child's health insurance to ensure ongoing and optimal coverage (chapter 13).

lithium, valproate (Depakote), risperidol (Risperdal), and Concerta (a long-acting stimulant to treat ADHD, see chapter 9). In addition, he and his family received family therapy and in-home services (services available to your child are described later in this chapter).

Seventeen-year-old Stephanie, too, is on multiple medications to control depression, mania, and mixed episodes. Treatment with lithium or valproate (Depakote) alone was not successful. For the past 3 years, she has been doing well taking lithium, oxcarbazepine (Trileptal), olanzapine (Zyprexa), and a small dosage of an SSRI. She also participates in individual dialectical behavior therapy (described in chapter 10).

How Long Maintenance Treatment Should Be Continued

Similar to other chronic medical illness, the treatment of bipolar disorder is lifelong.[6–12,16] Of course, it may be difficult and painful to deal with this fact, and it's understandable that it may take several months or years before your child accepts that he or she has a chronic illness. However, it is crucial that your child continues to take the medications and participate in psychosocial therapy in order to manage and live with this illness.

WARNING SIGNS

The best treatment programs include plans for prevention. Even if your child carefully follows doctor's orders and gets his or her symptoms stabilized, over the course of a lifetime he or she may have repetitive episodes of bipolar disorder, particularly depression.[1–5,12] Therefore, note the importance of detecting early symptoms of bipolar disorder. Prior to a manic episode, for example, some children may experience persistent sleep problems, talkativeness, unusual energy or impulsiveness, or inappropriate sexual behavior. Prior to an episode of depression, they may have a lack of motivation, dif-

> *K*nowing the warning signs of an impending incidence of mania, hypomania, depression, mixed episode, or psychosis can help you prevent major problems.

ficulty falling asleep, increased irritability, or poor concentration. When you learn to recognize the telltale signs unique to your child, you can have the treatment intensified or revised before the illness becomes worse.

Here are some examples of children who have identified their warning signs:

- When Allen is going to have an episode of mania, he gets mildly "hyper" and talkative. He notices that he does not need to sleep as much and that he is more creative, productive with his school-work, gregarious, and silly.
- Before Rachel gets very depressed, she feels tired and mildly irritable, has a low frustration tolerance (minor issues bother her), and worries more.
- Leroy gets irritable and talkative before he gets manic.
- Mary begins to make sexual jokes in inappropriate places and flirts more. She sleeps only 6 hours (instead of her usual 9 hours) a night and cleans her house at 2 or 3 o'clock in the morning. Unless she is treated, she develops a full-blown episode of mania.
- Before Martha gets into one of her depressive episodes, she feels that her thoughts are in "slow motion"; it is difficult for her to concentrate, and even simple homework takes what seems like forever. Sometimes before she gets into a mixed episode, she laughs without any reason, "gets in peoples' faces," picks fights, and becomes more suspicious.

You and your child should look for patterns that accompany recurrent episodes of bipolar disorder. This is crucial to avoid or control the triggers. For example, you may notice that a bipolar episode is triggered by sleep deprivation, jet lag, use of drugs (caffeine, alcohol, illicit drugs, prescribed or over-the-counter medications), a medical illness, conflicts at home or with peers, before menstruation, or during the winter or summer.

When you see these symptoms, it's time to call your child's clinician immediately. Sometimes it is possible to stop or lessen the severity of the acute symptoms of bipolar disorders through psychotherapy or medications. For example, practicing progressive relaxation techniques, following a healthier sleep schedule, resolving conflicts, coping with stressful situations, increasing the dosage of lithium or other medications, temporarily using medications to help your child's sleep or reduce his or her anxiety or agitation, or using light therapy may help curtail an impending bipolar episode.

Without Warning

Although many people with bipolar disorder experience a notable pattern of behavior before a full-blown episode, sometimes mania or depression occurs without a warning or trigger. Your child may simply wake up on any given day and be very manic or depressed.

NO RESPONSE TO TREATMENT

When your child is not responding to treatment, many issues need to be systematically assessed and, together with your child's treatment team, solutions planned. Consider the following examples.

Mark was not responding to any treatment prescribed. He was feeling miserable, tired, and confused. After several appointments, he finally admitted that he was using alcohol and sometimes other drugs. When he stopped using drugs, his mood finally improved.

Kelly's depression was not responding to psychotherapy or antidepressants. One year later, she disclosed that she was constantly throwing up food, as well as her medications, and binging. Only with treatment of both her bulimia and her depression did her mood and physical well-being improve. In other cases, children simply refuse to take their medications.

Allen refused to take any SSRI antidepressants because of possible sexual side effects, but he was embarrassed to discuss this problem with his parents.

Another teen, Helen, did not want to continue psychotherapy because she was too depressed to do the "mental exercises" recommended in her cognitive psychotherapy sessions.

The solution for refusing to take medications or to participate in psychotherapy can be very easy, like altering the timing of the medications or changing the medication if your child experiences side effects. But a solution can't be found until you uncover the cause. The following list of possible causes for nonresponse to treatment should be carefully considered if you feel your child's treatment program is not effective:

- Is the diagnosis of bipolar disorder appropriate?
- Is the treatment appropriate (type, dosages, blood levels of the medications, type and intensity of the psychotherapy)?
- Is your child experiencing medication side effects?
- Are you, your child, and your family practicing what you have learned in psychotherapy?
- In addition to bipolar disorder, are there other psychiatric disorders (such as ADHD), use of illicit drugs or alcohol, or medical conditions (such as low thyroid functioning) that could be affecting the treatment outcome?
- Are you able to recognize the early warning signs that the illness may be recurring or coming back?
- Does your child have good mood hygiene (organized sleep schedule, moderate or no use of stimulants, such as caffeine)?
- Are environmental circumstances affecting your child's response to treatment (such as ongoing conflicts at home, abuse, problems with peers)?

A common and obvious reason for lack of response to treatment is the fact that the child is simply not taking the prescribed medications. If you know your child has a hit-or-miss approach to the treatment plan, you should take time to discover why. Consider these possible reasons:

- The child or family is in denial about the child's psychiatric disorder.
- The child and/or family lack the motivation necessary to work through treatment.
- The clinician is not motivating your child to follow the prescribed treatment.
- The dosage of the medications is inconvenient (such as too many pills or taking pills too frequently).
- The child is afraid to swallow pills.
- The child is experiencing unwanted side effects of the medication.
- The child is embarrassed that others will find out that he or she

is taking medications (especially if the medications need to be taken while at school).

- The child is suspicious that the medication will harm him or her.
- The child has oppositional behaviors.
- The child is living in a chaotic environment—the parents keep forgetting to administer the medications, or teens forget to take their medications (when it is appropriate for the teen to manage his or her own medications).

Keep digging until you uncover the most likely cause of your child's refusal to take medications properly. Then be sure to discuss the problem with your child's doctor. He or she needs to know what's going on in order to help your child. Sometimes, particularly when your child is too depressed, manic, or psychotic, you may have to force him or her to take the medications. In these cases, you will require help from your spouse, family, and the child's treatment team.

Financial Problems

Sometimes a child does not get the appropriate medications due to the family's financial situation. If the medications are expensive and the family does not have adequate health coverage, this situation can certainly interfere with proper treatment and response. If you find yourself cutting back on your child's prescribed medications for these reasons, be sure to talk to your child's physician so that he or she knows and understands the difficulty.

TREATMENT LOCATION

The main question regarding the place where your child should be treated is whether your child is safe to him- or herself and others. Depending on the answer to this question, children and teens with bipolar disorder can be treated in different settings, including outpatient clinics, partial or day hospitals, or residential facilities. Some clinics also offer in-home family services or crisis intervention teams that can come to your home as needed. These services are briefly described here. Ask your child's clinician if these services are available for your daughter or son and how you can obtain them.

Hospital Treatment

In general, if your child is agitated, aggressive, out of control, psychotic, suicidal, or homicidal, it is better to treat him or her in the hospital, but in some cases that child can be supervised and controlled just as well at home. For example, when Rachel was manic, one of her parents was able to stay at home with her and provide supervision so that she would not harm herself or others. Even though she was agitated and hearing voices, her parents managed to give her medications, and after 1 week of treatment her mood began to improve. In contrast, Allen became very disrespectful and aggressive, did not want to take any medications, wanted to run away from home, and needed to be admitted into the hospital against his will. At the beginning of the hospitalization, he was angry with his parents and clinician for sending him to the hospital. However, when he improved, he thanked them because he knew that, if they had not hospitalized him, he could have gotten into serious trouble.

Partial or Day Hospital

If your child does not have symptoms that are severe enough to require admission to the hospital, but he or she needs more intensive treatment than the one offered by a regular clinic, you and your child's treatment team may consider a partial or day hospital. Your child will go every day or several days during the week to the day hospital. He or she will get intensive therapy and usually attend school at the same place. Partial hospitalizations may last weeks to months depending on your child's response. The goal is to send your child back to the outpatient clinic and to his or her regular schools as soon as his or her symptoms are stable.

Intense Outpatient Treatment

Your child will be seen three to four times a week at the outpatient clinic until the current crisis is over or his or her symptoms stabilize. Your child will continue to go to his or her regular school as long as his or her symptoms permit. Similar to any medical illness (e.g., a cold or asthma), if your child's symptoms are too disturbing, it will be better for her or him to study at home until the manic or depressive symptoms improve.

Crisis Intervention Teams

Some clinics offer help as needed for emergencies, 7 days a week, 24 hours a day. The services can be very helpful to stop crises and avoid hospitalizations and further complications at home or school.

Home-Based Treatment

Some clinics send therapists to your home several times a week, depending on the severity of your child's problems. These therapists will offer individual and/or family psychotherapy and help you implement behavior modification plans. Some clinics also send their therapists to the child's school. Find out with your child's clinician if home treatment is offered.

Residential Placement

Children, and particularly teens, who continue to do poorly despite hospitalizations, day hospital treatment, and intensive treatment may need to be placed in a therapeutic residential facility. Your child will live, go to school, and get treatment at the residential facility until he or she is stable enough to come back home. As described in chapter 12, also available are private boarding schools that specialize in the management and education of children with mood and behavior problems.

THE NEED TO TREAT PARENTS AND OTHER MEMBERS OF THE FAMILY

The treatment of a child with bipolar disorder will be incomplete if his or her parent(s) and siblings are not screened for psychiatric disorders themselves and referred for a full psychiatric evaluation and treatment as needed. The psychiatric screen of family members is indicated for the following reasons:

- Conflicts at home with parents and/or siblings increase the chance that the child will have further episodes of depression[20] and mania (see chapter 4, "Causes of Bipolar Disorder").

- Parents and/or siblings of children with bipolar disorder frequently have psychiatric disorders (see chapter 4 for evidence that bipolar disorder runs in families).

Psychiatric disorders in a family member or continuous family stressors may interfere with treatment or aggravate your child's illness.[20,21] For example, Rachel's father also has periods of major depression. When he is depressed, he is very irritable and has low frustration tolerance, insomnia, and angry outbursts. These symptoms affect the whole family. Rachel's mood also goes down, and she has problems concentrating at school and socializing with friends. Another example is Ed, whose mother also has mood problems. Often, when Ed's mother has a period of depression or mania, he gets moody and anxious, has temper tantrums, and acts out at school. These symptoms get worse if his mother is admitted into the hospital.

One of the main problems regarding offering treatment to parents is that some parents are in denial of their own psychiatric problems or may refuse to seek treatment. For example, in one study of depressed teens, we found that 60 percent of the mothers were depressed.[21] We offered treatment to all of those, but only 30 percent accepted our recommendation for treatment. For persons in denial of their own illnesses, education about their own symptoms and the negative consequences of an untreated illness to themselves and their children, as well as establishing a trustful relationship with the clinician, may help promote treatment.

SUMMARY

The treatment of bipolar disorder must be individualized to your child's symptom characteristics (mania, depression, mixed or rapid episodes) and the severity of the episode. The type of intervention will also vary depending on whether the treatment is offered to treat an imminent crisis or to prevent a recurrence of the bipolar episodes.

Although your child's doctor will closely plan this treatment, it is very important that you take an active role in monitoring your child's health and become the dependable link between your child and proper health care. Be aware of symptoms, treatment response, problems, recurring episodes, and warning signs. And remember that as your child grows, his or her response to treatment, side effects, presence of coexisting psychiatric or medical disorders, and the surrounding environment will all routinely change. Be sure you are alert for these changes, and report them to your child's doctor so that your child continuously gets the best and most appropriate treatment.

To increase the likelihood that your child will improve, parents, siblings, other relatives, and teachers should be educated about the nature and treatment of bipolar disorder and the importance of following through with the treatment plan. Also, because bipolar disorder (and other psychiatric disorders) runs in families and affects the whole family, evaluation and, if appropriate, treatment should also be offered to family members living with the child with bipolar disorder.

The following chapter will add to your background of information on treatment plans so that you can better supervise not only your child's bipolar disorder but also any other coexisting psychiatric disorders.

CHAPTER 9

Treatment of Coexisting Psychiatric Disorders

ↀ

IN CHAPTER 2, we explored the fact that other psychiatric disorders often accompany bipolar disorder. The most common coexisting or comorbid disorders include: attention deficit hyperactivity disorder (ADHD), behavior disorders (oppositional defiant and conduct disorders), anxiety disorders (e.g., generalized anxiety, panic disorder, social anxiety), and substance abuse (alcohol and other illicit drugs).

If your child's psychiatrist feels your child has one or more of these disorders along with bipolar disorder, the treatment plan will be altered to include combined treatment of each disorder. This is a complex process that may require a period of trial-and-error to get the combinations of medications and therapies just right. Your input, feedback, and observations about your child's symptoms and reactions to medications will certainly help your child's health-care team determine the best form of treatment.

This chapter will give you an overview of the most commonly used treatments for coexisting conditions. You'll notice that in some cases, the medication and psychotherapy treatment for a coexisting condition is similar to the ones used for bipolar disorder. In those cases, you can refer back to the treatment information in chapters 6 and 7. The infor-

A Note About Medications
The general guidelines for administering medications and the management of common side effects described in chapter 6 also apply to the medications described in this chapter.

mation on safe and effective use of medications and the management of common side effects, also explained in chapter 6, again applies to the use of medications used to treat any coexisting condition. (Appendix II also includes some useful books to manage conflicts and behavior problems associated with your child's bipolar and other psychiatric conditions.)

GENERAL GUIDELINES

As your child begins the treatment regimen for bipolar disorder, be sure to ask his or her child psychiatrist whether, in addition to bipolar disorder, your child might have other psychiatric disorders or whether, perhaps, all symptoms can be accounted for by one other disorder. For example, 10-year-old Morris had severe temper tantrums, mood swings, hyperactivity, short attention span, and excessive worrying. He had problems with transitions from one activity to another, inflexibility with schedules, obsessions, and problems relating to other children. Initially, he was diagnosed with bipolar disorder, ADHD, and obsessive-compulsive disorder (OCD). After following him for 6 months, though, his clinician determined that most of his problems could be explained by a mild form of autism, called Asperger's disorder (see chapter 2).

Each psychiatric disorder should to be treated with the best available medication(s) for that disorder.[1-6] For example, as a general rule, physicians treat bipolar disorder with mood stabilizers, ADHD with stimulants, and OCD or anxiety disorders with selective serotonin reuptake inhibitors (SSRIs). *However, proper treatment can be difficult because some of the medications used to treat other disorders can worsen the symptoms of bipolar disorder.* For instance, treatment of anxiety with SSRIs may trigger an episode of mania or induce rapid cycling in a child with bipolar disorder, and stimulants may cause a youth with bipolar disorder to become more irritable. In these cases, the bipolar disorder must be treated before the other disorder(s) can be addressed.

You should also consider using psychosocial therapies to treat coexisting disorders. Cognitive behavior therapy has been found helpful for the treatment of depression, anxiety, and obsessive-compulsive disorders. In contrast to SSRIs, psychosocial therapies do not trigger mania or rapid cycling and can therefore be used without the risk of aggravating any bipolar symptoms.

> *In contrast to SSRIs, psychosocial therapies for mood and anxiety disorders do not trigger mania or rapid cycling and can therefore be used without the risk of aggravating any bipolar symptoms.*

Although it's understandable that you will want to get your child the treatment he or she needs as quickly as possible, it is very important to start the treatment of each disorder at separate times. If two (or more) medications are begun simultaneously, you and your child's doctor will not be able to differentiate between what is helping your child and what could be producing side effects. For example, after Moses, an 8-year-old boy with bipolar and ADHD, began treatment with valproate (Depakote) and a stimulant at the same time, he became tired and irritable. It was not clear which medication was producing these side effects.

After your child's initial evaluation has been completed, you still need to stay vigilant. All coexisting disorders need to be carefully monitored over time, and the benefits and side effects of each medication must be continuously assessed.

ATTENTION DEFICIT HYPERACTIVITY DISORDER (ADHD)

In general, it is better to treat bipolar symptoms first, and then, if the ADHD symptoms are still a problem, medications to treat ADHD may be added.

If your child needs additional treatment for ADHD, two types of treatments have been shown to be effective: (1) medications and (2) cognitive behavior therapies. For mild cases, cognitive behavior therapy and behavior therapy may be sufficient. However, for moderate or severe cases, a combination of psychotherapy and medications is the best approach.

Currently, the medications used to treat ADHD include stimulants, such as Adderall, Ritalin, and Concerta, as well as nonstimulants, such as tricyclic antidepressants (TCAs) (e.g., Imipramine and Nortriptyline), bupropion (Wellbutrin), atomoxetine (Strattera), and clonidine (Catapres) or guanfacine (Tenex).[1-6] These medications will be described in more detail below.

Stimulants for ADHD

Of all the recommended medications, stimulants have been studied most widely and have been found to be very effective and well tolerated by youth. In fact, up to 80 percent of the children with ADHD respond to stimulants.[1-6]

However, the use of stimulants, such as methylphemidate (Ritalin), in children with bipolar disorder is controversial. Some people think that stimulants should not be prescribed to youth with bipolar disorder because they may worsen the child's mood; others believe that it can be prescribed only with caution. However, without appropriate treatment for their ADHD symptoms, children with bipolar disorder and ADHD do not do well. While a few studies with small samples of children with bipolar disorder and ADHD have shown that the stimulants are effective and well tolerated, large well-controlled studies have yet to be conducted. Therefore, until results from such studies are available, it is recommended to use the stimulants carefully if clinically indicated.

Stimulants for ADHD: Presentations and Dosage

- Stimulant dosage and form depends on the child's clinical response to treatment and the presence of any side effects. Stimulants are available in short-acting (immediate-release), long-acting (slow-release), and mixed immediate-/slow-release forms (table 9.1). The effects of the short-acting stimulants usually lasts between 2 and 4 hours, depending on the preparation being used, and ADHD symptoms may reappear late in the morning or in the afternoon after a morning dose is given. Therefore, short-acting stimulants are usually given three times a day. The effects of the long-acting preparations can last up to 8 hours, depending on the preparation being used, and may therefore be given only once or twice a day (but these tablets cannot be chewed). The mixed stimulants may last up to 12 hours and are given once a day in the morning. Some children may require higher or lower dosages depending on their individual response to the medication prescribed. Also, some children may require a dose of a short-acting stimulant during the afternoon or evening after the effects of the long-acting or mixed stimulants have worn off.

TABLE 9.1—STIMULANTS

IMMEDIATE RELEASE STIMULANTS

Generic Name	Brand Name	Duration of Action (hours)	Preparations	Total Daily Dose
Methylphenidate	Methylphenidate	2–4	5, 10 and 20 mg tablets	5 mg–60 mg
Methylphenidate	Ritalin	2–4	5, 10 and 20 mg tablets	5 mg–60 mg
Methylphenidate	Methylin	2–4	5, 10 and 20 mg tablets	5 mg–60 mg
Dexmethyl-phenidate	Focalin	2–4	2.5, 5 and 10 mg tablets	2.5 mg–30 mg

IMMEDIATE RELEASE STIMULANTS (CONTINUED)

Generic Name	Brand Name	Duration of Action (hours)	Preparations	Total Daily Dose
Dextro-amphetamine	Dexedrine	4–6	5, 10, and 15 mg tablets	20 mg–40 mg
Dextro-amphetamine	Dextrostat	4–6	5 mg tablets	5 mg–50 mg
No generic name (this drug is a mixture of amphetamines)	Adderall	4–6	5, 7.5, 10, 12.5, 15, 20, and 30 mg tablets	5 mg–50 mg

LONG-ACTING (SLOW RELEASE STIMULANTS)

Generic Name	Brand Name	Duration of Action (hours)	Preparations	Total Daily Dose
Methylphenidate	Methylphenidate SR	4–8	20 mg tablets	20–60 mg
Methylphenidate	Ritalin SR	4–8	20 mg tablets	20–60 mg
Methylphenidate	Methylin ER	6–8	10 and 20 mg tablets	20–60 mg
Methylphenidate	Metadate ER	6–8	10 and 20 mg tablets	20–60 mg
Methylphenidate	Methy Patch	As long as patch is worn	Not available yet	N/A

Generic Name	Brand Name	Duration of Action (hours)	Preparations	Total Daily Dose
Dextro-amphetamine	Dexedrine Spansules (SP)	6–8	5, 10 and 15 mg capsules	5–50 mg
Pemoline	Cylert	8–12	18.75, 37.5, 75 mg tablets and 37.5 mg chewable tablets	37.5–112.5 mg

LONG-ACTING (MIXED IMMEDIATE-SLOW RELEASE STIMULANTS)

Generic Name	Brand Name	Duration of Action (hours)	Preparations	Total Daily Dose
Methylphenidate	Metadate CD	8–12	10, 20, and 30 mg capsules Can be opened and sprinkled	20–60 mg
Methylphenidate	Ritalin LA	8–12	20, 30, and 40 mg capsules	20–60 mg
Methylphenidate	Concerta	8–12	18, 27, 36, and 54 mg capsules	18–72 mg
No generic name (this drug is a mixture of amphetamines)	Adderall XR	8–12	5, 10, 15, 20, and 30 mg capsules Can be opened and sprinkled	5–50 mg

Stimulants for ADHD: Precautions

- Stimulants should be avoided during pregnancy, especially in the first 3 months, and in children with prior allergic reactions to these medications. Pemoline (Cylert) should not be used in patients with liver disease.

- Stimulants should be administered with caution to children with cardiac, thyroid, and seizure problems. Also, stimulants may worsen anxiety and bipolar disorders, psychosis, and tics. (It is important to note that studies have shown that stimulants can be safely administered to children with anxiety and tics.)

- Be cautious when giving your child other medications while he or she is on a stimulant. Always ask your child's doctor for possible interactions between the stimulant and any other medications. For example, consult your doctor when mixing stimulants with other prescription medications, such as anticonvulsants (i.e., carbamazepine and phenytoin), tricyclic antidepressants (e.g., imipramine), monoamine oxidase inhibitor antidepressants (e.g., Parnate and Nardil), and warfarin (Coumadin). Using over-the-counter cold medications (e.g., cough syrups) containing pseudoephedrine and allergy medications (antihistamines) while taking some of these stimulants may lead to increased irritability and behavior problems. Always inform your child's doctor and dentist of the medications your child is taking.

- Some medications require special diet considerations. For example, avoid taking Dexedrine with fruit juices as this combination may reduce the drug's effectiveness by lowering the amount of medication in the blood. Other medications must be taken on either a full or empty stomach. Again, ask your pharmacist or doctor to clarify directions for taking the medication.

- The long-acting and the mixed stimulants tablets cannot be chewed or cut.

- If your child has difficulty swallowing tablets, the Metadate CD and Adderall XR capsules can be opened and the beads inside mixed with a tablespoon of applesauce or ice cream. Ensure that the beads are not chewed; otherwise, they will lose their long-acting effect.

Stimulants for ADHD: Common Side Effects

Side effects of stimulants depend on the dosage, the dosing schedule, and the preparation used. Side effects also depend on how fast the stimulant dosage is increased. Many of the side effects are short-lived and disappear when the stimulant is discontinued or the dosage is adjusted. Report any side effects to your child's physician.

The most common side effects of stimulants are reduced appetite, weight loss, and difficulty falling asleep when the stimulant is given in the evening or close to bedtime. On the other hand, some children may be so hyperactive that they may require an evening dosage in order to settle down to fall asleep.

Depending on the dosage and how fast it is increased, stimulants may cause stomachaches, irritability or crankiness, skin picking and nail biting, sadness, excessive energy or excitability, headache, dry mouth, and a small increase in heart rate and blood pressure. Some children may be allergic to this medication, developing a skin rash and itching. Always discuss any side effects with your child's doctor.

For more about common medication side effects, such as nausea, loss of appetite, weight loss, excitability, irritability, headaches, and allergies, see the section "Management of Common Side Effects" in chapter 6.

Stimulants for ADHD: Management of Specific Side Effects and Laboratory Tests Needed Before and During Treatment

The management of some side effects specific for stimulants is described here. Do not alter your child's treatment without consulting with your doctor.

- **Difficulty sleeping.** If your child is having trouble falling asleep, consider administrating the medication earlier in the day. If a long-acting or mixed preparation is being used, consider switching to a shorter-acting preparation that will wear off in time for your child's bedtime. Alternatively, afternoon or evening dosages may be discontinued. Remember that your child should maintain a consistent sleep schedule. Establish regular bedtime routines, avoid stimulating activities before bedtime, and avoid caffeinated beverages in the evening. Consideration may be given to the addition of a medication to improve sleep.

- **Rebound or worsening of symptoms late in the day.** A worsening of symptoms, called *behavioral rebound*, may occur in the late afternoon or early evening when the effect of the medication begins to wear off. It is not clear whether these symptoms are really a rebound effect or whether, as expected, the child begins to show his or her regular ADHD symptoms as the effects of the stimulant diminish.

  Treatment of rebound symptoms may require an adjustment in dosage and/or scheduling of medication, switching to a long-acting preparation if short-acting stimulants are being used, using both short- and long-acting preparations, or switching to an alternative medication. The dosage or scheduling of medication should not be changed without speaking to your doctor.

- **Muscle twitching and tics.** Some children may experience muscle twitching or tics (e.g., frequent blinking, moving of the shoulder or nose). These side effects are rare in children who do not have a personal or family history of tics or Tourette's disorder (multiple body and vocal tics). Children with a history of tics or Tourette's disorder may experience a worsening of tics with these medications.

  If muscle twitching or tics occur with medications, treatment may require a decrease in the dosage of medication or switching to an alternative medication. If the stimulant is helping your child, your doctor may opt for combining the stimulant with a medication to treat the tics. The dosage of medication should not be changed without speaking to your doctor.

- **Growth.** Whether or not stimulants cause any significant slowing in your child's height is controversial. If any, it appears that the effect is minimal. In contrast, stimulants usually diminish your child's appetite and cause loss of weight, particularly during the first 6 to 9 months of treatment. Children who are not gaining weight will perhaps have a slowing in their height.

  If you are concerned that your child is not growing at a normal rate for his or her age, speak with your doctor. Ensure that your child is eating sufficiently and gaining weight normally. Lowering the dosage of medication or taking a break from the medication during the summer, holidays, and weekends may help. However, keep in mind that your child's potential height will likely reflect the average height of his or her parents and relatives. It is recommended to measure your child's weight monthly and height every 6 months.

- **Increased heart rate and blood pressure.** Stimulants may minimally increase your child's blood pressure and pulse, but these increases are usually not clinically important. However, if your child already has high blood pressure or cardiac problems, consult with your doctor.

- **Abuse.** Stimulants, particularly those with short-acting preparations, can produce a transient euphoric or "high" feeling in adolescents and adults and can be abused recreationally. It is therefore prudent to monitor medication use.

- **Liver problems.** Rarely, pemoline (Cylert) has been associated with liver failure and is now uncommonly used to treat ADHD in children. Signs of liver problems include unusual bruising or bleeding, nausea, vomiting, loss of appetite, weakness, fever, flulike symptoms, yellow tinge or discoloration of the skin or whites of the eyes, and dark-colored urine. These symptoms should be reported to your doctor immediately. Do not give your child another dosage, and take him or her to the emergency room for a liver function test.

Stimulants: Laboratory Tests and Other Evaluations

Your child's height, weight, heart rate, and blood pressure are all recorded before starting on a medication and are monitored throughout the course of treatment. If pemoline (Cylert) is prescribed, a blood test to check liver function will be done before starting the medication and periodically thereafter. An electrocardiogram (ECG) will be done if there is a history of heart problems.

Nonstimulants for ADHD

Several nonstimulant medications are used for the treatment of ADHD when the child does not respond or tolerate the stimulants.[1-6] Nonstimulants most commonly used to treat ADHD include tricyclic antidepressants (TCAs) (e.g., Imipramine and Nortriptyline), bupropion (Wellbutrin), atomoxetine (Strattera), and clonidine (Catapres) or guanfacine (Tenex). The use of each of these medications for the treatment of symptoms of ADHD in children with bipolar disorder will be described here, except bupropion, which was described in chapter 6.

Atomoxetine (Straterra)

Atomoxetine is a nonstimulant medication recently approved by the U.S. Food and Drug Administration (FDA) for the treatment of ADHD.

ATOMOXETINE (STRATERRA): PRESENTATION AND DOSAGE

Atomoxetine is available in capsules of 10, 18, 25, 40, and 60 milligrams. Atomoxetine lasts in blood up to 5 to 6 hours, but according to some studies, its effects can last up to 24 hours. Therefore, it can be administered once a day. A second dosage may be necessary depending on whether the child needs one to control symptoms of ADHD in the afternoon/evening.

The dosage of atomoxetine depends on the child's clinical response and presence of side effects. The dose in children up to 70 kilograms (154 pounds) should not exceed 1.2 milligrams/kilogram. For children who weigh more than 70 kilograms, the dosage also should not exceed 100 milligrams per day. Atomoxetine can be administered with food.

ATOMOXETINE (STRATERRA): PRECAUTIONS

- Atomoxetine *should not be taken* by a person with glaucoma (excessive pressure inside the eye). Atomoxetine cannot be administered with monoamine oxidase inhibitor antidepressants (e.g., Parnate and Nardil). Do not use atomoxetine if your child has experienced an allergic reaction in the past or develops an allergic reaction to this medication. Until further studies can be done, atomoxetine should be avoided during pregnancy, especially in the first 3 months. It is not known whether atomoxetine is excreted in human milk and should therefore not be prescribed to nursing mothers.

- Atomoxetine should be administered with caution to youth with bipolar disorder because it may trigger mania, mixed episodes, or rapid cycling (see chapter 1). Until further studies become available, if your child will be treated with atomoxetine, it is better to begin this medication after your child is well covered with one of the mood stabilizers (chapter 6).

- Atomoxetine should be administered with caution to children with high or low blood pressure or cardiac, thyroid, brain, and seizure problems. Also, although not well studied, atomoxetine may worsen anxiety disorders and tics and may trigger a manic or hypomanic episode in a child predisposed to bipolar disorder.

- Be cautious when giving your child other medications while he or she is on atomoxetine. Always ask your child's doctor or pharmacist for possible interactions between atomoxetine and other medications. Atomoxetine may have negative interactions when mixed with Prozac, Paxil, Luvox, and tricyclic antidepressants (e.g., imipramine). Make sure to monitor blood pressure when using atomoxetine in combination with other psychiatric medications that may alter blood pressure, such as clonidine (Catapres), guanfacine (Tenex), and the new antipsychotics (e.g., Risperdal and Zyprexa). As with stimulants, using over-the-counter cold medications containing pseudoephedrine while taking atomoxetine may produce more side effects. Inform your child's doctor and dentist of the medications your child is taking.

ATOMOXETINE (STRATERRA): COMMON SIDE EFFECTS

Side effects depend on the dosage, the dosing schedule, and how fast the dosage is increased. Many of the side effects are short-lived and disappear when atomoxetine is discontinued. The most common side effects include reduced appetite, weight loss, tiredness, nausea, vomiting, dizziness, mood swings, irritability, upset stomach, and difficulty falling asleep if a dosage is taken in the evening or close to bedtime.

For the management of these and other common side effects, see the section "Management of Common Side Effects" in chapter 6 and the management of side effects of the stimulants noted earlier.

ATOMOXETINE (STRATERRA): MANAGEMENT OF SPECIFIC SIDE EFFECTS AND LABORATORY TESTS NEEDED BEFORE AND DURING TREATMENT

Rare side effects that may be experienced include a small increase in heart rate, mild increase or decrease in blood pressure, and difficulty passing urine. It is also possible that this medication could trigger a manic or hypomanic state or cause muscle twitching or tics in children with a personal or familial history of this disorder. Notify your physician if your child experiences any of these side effects.

- **Increased heart rate and increased or decreased blood pressure.** Atomoxetine may minimally raise blood pressure and pulse, but these increases are usually not clinically important. Atomoxetine can also decrease blood pressure, particularly when a person has been sitting or lying down for a while and stands up quickly. If you suspect that your child has a problem with his or her blood pressure or if your child has a history of heart problems, consult with your doctor.
- **Change in mood to markedly irritable or euphoric.** Call your child's doctor immediately. This could indicate that atomoxetine

has triggered a manic or hypomanic state in your child and the treatment should be sought as soon as possible. See chapter 8 for the acute management of bipolar disorder.

- **Muscle twitching or tics.** Although not yet reported, it is expected that some children may experience muscle twitching or tics. These side effects are rare in children who do not have a history of tics or Tourette's disorder or a history of these problems in other family members. Children with a history of tics or Tourette's disorder may experience a worsening of tics with these medications.

ATOMOXETINE (STRATERRA): LABORATORY TESTS AND OTHER EVALUATIONS

A child's height, weight, heart rate, and blood pressure (sitting and standing) are recorded before starting the medication and are monitored throughout the course of treatment. Until further studies, it is recommended also to do an ECG before starting atomoxetine and repeating it when the maximum dosage is achieved.

Clonidine (Catapres) and Guanfacine (Tenex)

Clonidine and guanfacine were developed for the treatment of high blood pressure. These medications are also helpful in managing impulsivity, aggression, and agitation in children with ADHD or behavior disorders and tics, including Tourette's disorder.

CLONIDINE (CATAPRES) AND GUANFACINE (TENEX): PRESENTATIONS AND DOSAGE

Clonidine and guanfacine are similar medications, but guanfacine is longer acting than clonidine. Clonidine is available as tablets and as a transdermal (skin) patch. The transdermal patch is changed every 5 days in children. Guanfacine is available as tablets.

The dosage of clonidine or guanfacine used depends on the child's clinical response and the presence of side effects. Table 9.2 provides average daily doses, but the dosage used may vary from child to child.

TABLE 9.2.—CLONIDINE AND GUANFACINE

Generic Name	Brand Name	Preparations	Dosage
Clonidine	Catapres, Clonidine	Tablets: 0.1, 0.2, and 0.3 mg	0.05–1.2 mg daily given 2–3 times a day
Clonidine transdermal system	Catapres-TTS	Patches: 0.1, 0.2, and 0.3 mg per day	0.05–0.5 mg daily given every 5 days
Guanfacine	Tenex	Tablets: 1 and 2 mg	1–2 mg daily given 1–2 times daily

CLONIDINE (CATAPRES) AND GUANFACINE (TENEX): PRECAUTIONS

- Clonidine and guanfacine should not be administered to children with low blood pressure, a history of heart rhythm problems, or prior allergic reactions to these medications. Use of these medications should be avoided by pregnant women and nursing moms.
- Clonidine and guanfacine should be administered with caution in children with heart problems or circulation problems (i.e., Reynaud's syndrome). Clonidine and guanfacine are sometimes used along with stimulant medications (i.e., Ritalin and Dexedrine) in the treatment of ADHD.
- Several unconfirmed reports of fatality have been made about children taking clonidine and stimulants. However, it is not clear whether death was related to these medications.
- Be cautious when giving your child other medications while he or she is being treated with clonidine or guanfacine. Taking clonidine or guanfacine with other medications may cause drowsiness

or oversedation if alcohol is ingested. Always ask your child's doctor or pharmacist for possible interactions between clonidine or guanfacine and other medications, and always inform your doctor or dentist of the medications being taken.

- Clonidine or guanfacine should not be stopped abruptly unless otherwise indicated by your doctor. Suddenly stopping these medications or skipping a dosage may result in withdrawal side effects (anxiety, restlessness, sweating, nausea, vomiting, stomachache, headache, and a rise in blood pressure). These symptoms generally appear about 20 hours after missing a dosage.

CLONIDINE (CATAPRES) AND GUANFACINE (TENEX): COMMON SIDE EFFECTS

Clonidine and guanfacine may be associated with nausea or heartburn, constipation, dry mouth and eyes, fatigue, sedation, dizziness, headache, slow pulse, and low blood pressure. The transdermal patch may cause skin irritation and itchiness that can be minimized by changing the location of where the patch is placed when it is changed. These medications may be associated with a change in sexual interest or functioning.

For the management of common side effects including drowsiness, sedation, nausea, heartburn, headaches, dry mouth, allergies, and other common side effects, see chapter 6.

CLONIDINE (CATAPRES) AND GUANFACINE (TENEX): MANAGEMENT OF SPECIFIC SIDE EFFECTS AND LABORATORY TESTS NEEDED BEFORE AND DURING TREATMENT

Side effects more specific to clonidine and guanfacine include allergic reaction, a marked decrease in heart rate and/or blood pressure, as well as the following:

- **Dizziness/faintness.** Symptoms of very low heart rate and blood pressure include fatigue, dizziness, and fainting spells. If your child experiences these side effects, contact your doctor to have your child's blood pressure and heart rate checked. If your child's heart rate or blood pressure is too low, the medication may need to be gradually discontinued.

- **Allergic reactions.** Localized skin redness and irritation may occur on the area of skin where the clonidine transdermal patch is applied. To minimize this side effect, rotate where you apply the patch. If a generalized rash occurs with swelling around the face, stop the medication and contact your doctor as soon as possible. If your child experiences any discomfort or difficulty breathing, take your child to the emergency room immediately.

CLONIDINE (CATAPRES) AND GUANFACINE (TENEX): LABORATORY TESTS AND OTHER EVALUATIONS NEEDED BEFORE AND DURING TREATMENT

Your doctor should measure your child's blood pressure and pulse and obtain an electrocardiogram (ECG) before starting this medication and periodically thereafter. No other tests are necessary before using clonidine or guanfacine.

Tricyclic Antidepressants (TCAs)

Although the TCAs work for depression in adults, they are not effective for the treatment of youth with depression. However, in children and teens, TCAs are useful for the treatment of ADHD and enuresis (bed-wetting). They may also be used for pain and migraine headaches.

The use of TCAs is more complicated than with other medications used to treat ADHD. TCAs also have more side effects and can be very dangerous in case of an overdose. For these reasons, TCAs are currently utilized after treatments with other medications have failed.

TRICYCLIC ANTIDEPRESSANTS: PRESENTATION AND DOSAGE

There are many types of TCAs. The most common are imipramine (Tofranil), desipramine (Norpramine), nortryptiline (Pamelor, Aventyl), and amitriptyline (Elavil). The dosage of these medications depends on the child's response and side effects. Dosages for imipramine, desipramine, and amitriptyline range between 25 and 200 milligrams per day administered, once or twice a day, and for nortryptiline between 25 and 150 milligrams per day. The dosages of these medications when used to treat enuresis (bedwetting) are usually low and administered before bedtime.

TRICYCLIC ANTIDEPRESSANTS: PRECAUTIONS

- TCAs should not be administered to children with blood pressure problems or a history of heart rhythm problems. Use of TCAs should also be avoided by pregnant women and nursing moms.

- Special precautions are needed when giving TCAs to children with seizures, liver problems, and thyroid problems. Children with a history of suicidal behaviors must be closely monitored since an overdose of TCAs can be very dangerous. In these cases, an adult needs to be in charge of the administration of these medications and must keep them in a safe place.

- There have been several reports of deaths in children taking TCAs, particularly desipramine. However, it is not clear whether death was related to these medications.

- Be cautious when giving your child other medications while he or she is taking TCAs. TCAs may cause drowsiness, and taking them with other medications that may cause drowsiness or with alcohol may lead to oversedation. Also, TCAs cannot be administered with monoamine oxidase inhibitors (MAOIs). Always ask your child's doctor or pharmacist for possible interactions between the TCAs and other medications, and always inform your doctor or dentist of the medications being taken.

- TCAs should not be stopped abruptly unless otherwise indicated by your doctor. Suddenly stopping these medications or skipping a dosage may result in withdrawal side effects (anxiety, restlessness, sweating, nausea, vomiting, stomachache, headache, and a rise in blood pressure). These symptoms generally appear about 20 hours after missing a dosage.

TRICYCLIC ANTIDEPRESSANTS: COMMON SIDE EFFECTS

The side effects of TCAs as a group are similar, but some TCAs can produce more side effects than others. For example, amitriptyline and clomipramine (Anafranil) are more sedative and may produce more dry mouth, constipation, and urinary difficulties than do desipramine or nortryptiline.

For responding to common medication side effects, such as drowsiness, sedation, nausea, irritability, headaches, increased appetite, dry mouth, and allergies, see the section "Management of Common Side Effects" in chapter 6.

TRICYCLIC ANTIDEPRESSANTS: MANAGEMENT OF SPECIFIC SIDE EFFECTS AND LABORATORY TESTS NEEDED BEFORE AND DURING TREATMENT

The most common side effects of TCAs in particular include nausea or heartburn, rapid pulse, constipation, difficulties urinating, dry mouth, increased appetite, problems with near vision, fatigue, sedation, dizziness, headaches, confusion, and, rarely, seizures, as well as the following. Report any side effects to your doctor.

- **Changes in blood pressure.** TCAs may cause a decrease in blood pressure that may necessitate the gradual discontinuation of this medication. Symptoms of low blood pressure include fatigue, dizziness, and fainting spells.
- **Change in heart function.** TCAs may cause significant changes in the ECG. Therefore, it is important to have a baseline ECG and repeat this assessment during the treatment.

TRICYCLIC ANTIDEPRESSANTS: LABORATORY TESTS AND OTHER EVALUATIONS

Your doctor should measure your child's blood pressure and pulse, and obtain an ECG before starting this medication and periodically thereafter. No other tests are necessary before using TCAs.

BEHAVIOR DISORDERS: OPPOSITIONAL DEFIANT AND CONDUCT DISORDERS

If your child has bipolar disorder and a behavior disorder, he or she needs treatment for both disorders (see chapter 2). Psychosocial therapies, including cognitive behavior therapy and family therapies, are often helpful. Medications such as mood stabilizers (lithium and antipsychotics) and nonstimulants (clonidine and guanfacine) are also often used to manage behavior disorders.[1–6]

Mood Stabilizers for Behavior Disorders

A few studies have shown that medications such as lithium, valproate, and the new antipsychotics (e.g., quetiapine, risperidone) may help children and adolescents with irritability and aggressive behaviors. Luckily, the mood stabilizers also are beneficial for bipolar disorder. Among the mood stabilizers, lithium and the second-generation or novel antipsychotics seem to work the best. Importantly, antipsychotics are prescribed to children and adolescents with severe behavior problems to control aggression and moodiness, *not* because these children are psychotic, as the name may imply. The first-generation or conventional antipsychotics also seem to help, but because of their many side effects, this group of medications is usually avoided.

> *Antipsychotics are prescribed to children and adolescents with severe behavior problems to control aggression and moodiness, not because these children are psychotic, as the name may apply.*

Clonidine/Guanfacine for Behavior Disorders

Clonidine or guanfacine may be used to diminish aggressive behavior and anger, but more studies are still needed to confirm their effectiveness. Until such studies are completed, these medications may be utilized to reduce aggressive behaviors if others have not helped, but be sure that your child's doctor checks your child's blood pressure and pulse periodically. Also, be aware that these medications may produce drowsiness.

ANXIETY DISORDERS

Many types of anxiety disorders exist, including generalized anxiety disorder, panic disorder, separation anxiety disorder, social anxiety disorder, and obsessive-compulsive disorder (see chapter 2). It is common to see a child with both bipolar disorder and an anxiety disorder, and both problems need to be treated to improve the child's functioning.

In general, all anxiety disorders respond to similar psychosocial therapies and medications as those used to treat major depression[1-4] (as discussed in chapter 6). These include medications such as the SSRIs (e.g., Prozac, Luvox, Zoloft), venlafaxine (Effexor), benzodiazepines, and perhaps gabapentin (Neurontin) and buspirone (Buspar). Among the psychosocial therapies, the most extensively studied is *cognitive behavior therapy (CBT), which has been shown to benefit the acute symptoms and to prevent the anxiety symptoms from reappearing.*[7]

Selective Serotonin Reuptake Inhibitors (SSRIs) and Venlafaxine for Anxiety Disorders

The SSRIs (e.g., Prozac, Luvox, Zoloft) and venlafaxine (Effexor) have been shown to work for the acute treatment of anxiety in children and teens. *The main problem encountered when using SSRIs or venlafaxine to treat anxious children with bipolar disorder is that these medications may trigger mania, hypomania, rapid cycling, or mixed bipolar episodes.* Therefore, in most cases before attempting to use SSRIs or venlafaxine to alleviate the anxiety disorder, it is advisable to first control the bipolar disorder with mood stabilizers. (For further information regarding these medications, see chapter 6.)

If your child is going to take SSRIs or venlafaxine for his or her anxiety, he or she needs careful monitoring. If one of these medications helps ease anxiety symptoms, but your child gets manic or goes into a mixed episode, stop the medication, and consult with your child's doctor immediately. The dosage will need to be lowered, or the medication may need to be discontinued, in which case your child may be offered cognitive behavior therapy or a different medication.

Benzodiazepines for Anxiety Disorders

Benzodiazepines are used to treat anxiety disorders, agitation, and insomnia. Because benzodiazepines may cause addiction, they are usually avoided in youth. However, they can be used for the short-term treatment of agitation or anxiety problems until the other medication begins to work. If it is necessary to treat a child with benzodiazepines for a long time, the child should be carefully monitored by his or her doctor to prevent negative side effects. (For more information regarding the benzodiazepines, see chapter 6.)

Gabapentin (Neurontin) for Anxiety Disorders

Gabapentin (Neurontin) is a medication that is primarily used to treat seizures. It was thought that gabapentin might help treat bipolar disorder, but studies in adults have not shown a change in bipolar symptoms with administration of this medication. While more studies are necessary, gabapentin is also thought to help anxiety. If gabapentin is shown to be effective in treating anxiety, it would be a particularly good choice for the treatment of coexisting anxiety in youth with bipolar disorder because it does not worsen bipolar symptoms. It also does not generally interfere with other medications and produces very few side effects. Another medication similar to Neurontin, tiagabine (Gabitril), may also be useful to treat anxiety, but further studies in children are needed.

Buspirone (Buspar) for Anxiety Disorders

Buspirone (Buspar) has been found to be useful for the treatment of adults with general anxiety or worries. However, this medication has not been tested in children, and its effects on bipolar symptoms are unknown.

SUBSTANCE ABUSE

> *The optimal treatment of adolescents with substance abuse and bipolar disorder involves an integration of treatment types rather than merely consecutive treatments with a specific focus on either substance abuse or bipolar disorder.*

Teens with bipolar disorder are at high risk for abusing nicotine, alcohol, and other drugs, especially marijuana—and this is a bad combination. Youth with both disorders have poor response to treatment, get into trouble more often, do poorly at school, have more conflicts at home, and are at a higher risk of committing suicide. Therefore, it is important to treat both disorders at the same time.

The optimal treatment of adolescents with substance abuse and bipolar disorder involves an integration of treatment types rather than merely consecutive treatments with a specific focus on either substance abuse or bipolar disorder. But if your child is involved in substance abuse, it is difficult to be sure whether the bipolar diagnosis is accurate—his or her symptoms may be the result of drug or alcohol abuse. So unless your child's clinician is sure about the diagnosis of bipolar disorder, before you begin treatment for this disorder, your child must first stop using drugs or alcohol so that his or her true mood can be observed.

This observation period requires careful supervision through urine tests to ensure that the teen is not abusing alcohol or other drugs. But, unfortunately, urine tests are not always accurate and do not detect all types of drugs or alcohol. So, if you suspect that your teen is continuing to abuse drugs or alcohol, it will be necessary to admit him or her into a hospital, day hospital, or rehabilitation facility. In these facilities, the teen will hopefully not drink or use illicit drugs, allowing his or her true mood to be observed closely. If the teen has symptoms of bipolar disorder when not under the influence of drugs or alcohol, then treatment for bipolar disorder can begin immediately, and the problem of substance abuse can be addressed separately.

A Medical Controversy

Some clinicians believe that while teens are abusing drugs or alcohol, they cannot be medicated for bipolar disorder. This is not completely true. On the contrary, studies in adults and children have shown that treatment of mood disorders (depression and bipolar disorder) increases the chance of improving the substance abuse. Regardless, caution should be used when considering medications for bipolar teens with coexisting substance abuse.

If your teen is found to have both bipolar disorder and a problem with substance abuse, he or she is at increased risk for intentional or unintentional overdose with certain prescribed medications. Moreover, some commonly used medications, such as the stimulants and benzodiazepines, may have inherent abuse potential, especially in teens prone to substance abuse. For this reason, you should closely supervise the administration of your child's medication to alleviate concerns about potential abuse. You might also consider alternative agents with a lower potential for abuse, such as the newer long-acting stimulant preparations, bupropion or atomoxetine, due to their form of administration and the ability to monitor and supervise once-a-day dosing more easily.

Family interventions are also critical to the success of any treatment approach with teens involved with substance abuse. A number of family-related factors, such as parental alcoholism or other substance abuse, poor parent–child relationships, low parental support, inconsistent or ineffective discipline, and poor parent supervision and management of the teen's behavior have been identified as risk factors for the development of substance abuse among teens. *Family therapy is the most studied psychosocial therapy for the treatment of adolescents with substance abuse.* Based on the limited number of studies, several types of outpatient family therapy (e.g., functional family therapy, multisystemic therapy, and multidimensional family therapy) appear to be helpful.

SUMMARY

Many psychiatric and medical disorders may accompany bipolar disorder, such as ADHD, behavior disorders, anxiety disorders, and substance abuse. Each one of these coexisting conditions presents challenges for treatment. You should talk to your child's doctor about any plans for combining treatments for multiple symptoms and carefully supervise that treatment. This is especially true with the use of multiple medications because this combination increases the risk of side effects, medication interactions, and triggering mania, hypomania, mixed episodes, and rapid cycling.

Perhaps the most serious coexisting condition you may find in your child with bipolar disorder is suicidal tendencies. This circumstance requires special attention, as discussed in the next chapter.

CHAPTER 10

Recognizing and Responding to Suicidal Behaviors

$\mathcal{C}\!\mathcal{D}$

B Y THE END OF this chapter you will be familiar with the risk factors of suicide and what you should do if your child has suicidal thoughts or makes an attempt.

Chapter 3 presented the symptoms and factors that precipitate and protect children from having suicidal behaviors. This chapter provides an in-depth review of the suicidal behaviors in youth and their management.

SUICIDAL BEHAVIORS

Suicidal behaviors can be divided according to their severity into suicidal ideation or thoughts, suicidal attempts, and suicide or completed suicide.[1]

Suicidal Ideation

Suicidal ideation includes thoughts about wishing to kill oneself, making plans of when, where, and how to carry out the suicide, and thoughts about the impact of one's suicide on others.

*S*uicidal thoughts are common among high-schoolers, with approximately 1 in 4 females and 1 in 6 males having considered suicide in a twelve-month period.[1] Suicidal thoughts are more common in Hispanic students. The presence of suicidal thoughts does not indicate that the child has a psychiatric disorder; however, it needs to be taken seriously, particularly if it is persistent or if the child has prior suicidal attempts.

*I*n the United States it is estimated that approximately 700,000 teens receive medical attention for their suicidal attempts.[1]

Suicidal Attempts

Suicidal attempts involve any behavior that is intended to end the person's life. Suicide attempts are much less common than suicidal ideation.

The most common method used to attempt suicide in the United States is by overdosing with over-the-counter or prescribed medications. Other common methods include superficial cutting of the arms or neck, but the method used depends on the availability of the method, opportunity, and local customs. Suicide attempts are more common in girls than boys (approximately two girls for one boy) and in Caucasian populations but recently it has increased in African-American teens.

Suicidal attempts are more frequent in children and adolescents with psychiatric disorders, especially depression and bipolar disorder (see chapter 1), but it can occur in youth with other psychiatric disorders. Also, it can happen after a stressful situation even if the child does not have psychiatric problems.

Suicide or Completed Suicide

It is more common in Caucasian males but it has been steadily increasing in African-American males. Approximately 90 percent of teens who commit suicide have a psychiatric disorder, including bipolar disorder, major depression, conduct problems, and abuse of alcohol and illicit drugs.[1] Suicide is more common in those youth who have tried to attempt suicide, have a family history of mood disorders or suicide, and in those who have experienced stressful life situations such as physical and sexual abuse.

Even mild suicidal attempts may be indications that the child is at serious risk for committing suicide.

Suicide Behaviors in Bipolar Disordered Youth

It appears that suicidal attempts and completions are more frequent in bipolar disordered youth than in other psychiatric disorders. In a study of high school students,[2] 40 percent of bipolar teens had at least one suicide attempt in comparison with 20 percent in teens with unipolar depressions (see chapter 1 for definition of this disorder) and 1 percent in youth without any psychiatric disorders.

In adult bipolar patients, 25 percent to 50 percent will have at least one suicide attempt in their life and 10 percent to 15 percent will die from suicide.[3,4] Thus, it is important to take suicidal ideas and especially attempts in youth with bipolar disorder seriously.

Recognizing and Managing Suicide Behaviors

Since not all children and teens who have suicidal thoughts attempt suicide, and not all who attempt suicide end up committing suicide, you as a parent may wonder when you should consult a professional to evaluate whether your child is at risk for suicide or whether you should take your child's suicidal threats seriously. The following information will provide you with guidelines for recognizing suicide risk factors.

Steve Edwards and colleagues published a simple and straight-

A child who has had prior suicidal attempts is at high risk for eventually committing suicide, particularly if he or she has a mood disorder, substance abuse, or conduct problems and lives in a stressful and non-supportive environment.

Suicide occurs most commonly in older teens, but it can also occur in children as young as 6 years old. Approximately 2,000 U.S. teens commit suicide each year. In fact, suicide ranks as the third cause of death among 15-to-24-year-olds, just behind unintentional injuries (e.g., car accidents) and homicide.[1]

One important recommendation that will remain a theme throughout this chapter is to take all talk of suicide seriously, even when you doubt suicidal intent is present. It is much better to be cautious and "err on the side of safety."

forward guide for general medical practitioners to better recognize and respond to suicidal behavior in youth.[5] Their core concepts have been developed over many years of clinical practice with young people and have been utilized previously in a wide range of medical and allied health settings. I believe that their system can be helpful to parents, other relatives, and teachers with some modifications.

Steve Edwards and colleagues recommend the 4R's principles—a "ticket of entry" for parents and others wanting to help an emotionally distressed youth by recognizing and responding to suicidal behaviors.[6] The 4R's include:

1. Recognizing the signs
2. Raising the issue
3. Realizing the risks
4. Responding

1. Recognizing the Signs

The following signs or symptoms should alert parents (teachers and other relatives) that their children may be at risk to develop suicidal thoughts or attempts.

- Persistent symptoms of depression
- Bipolar disorder
- Conduct problems
- Anxiety disorders
- Abuse of illicit drugs or alcohol
- Psychosis (hallucinations or delusions)
- Borderline personality disorder
- Past or present attempts of suicide
- Recurrent suicidal ideation
- Male sex and older than 14 years old

Note: For the symptoms of the psychiatric disorders just mentioned, see chapters 1 and 2.

The risk of suicide further increases if in addition to one or more of the above noted signs your child has one or more of the following problems:

- Psychological, social or academic problems
  - Poor school performance
  - Employment problems
  - Few or no friends
  - Legal problems
  - Frequent conflict with others (friends, family, teachers)
  - Poor coping and problem-solving skills
- Family or environmental stressors
  - Physical or sexual abuse
  - Neglect
  - Interpersonal loss (girl- or boyfriend, death in the family, parental divorce)
  - Rejection by others
  - Family history of mood disorders or suicide
  - Exposure to stress and conflicts in his/her neighborhood/school
  - Exposure to media (e.g., television, radio, or newspapers) glorifying suicide
- Physical health
  - Poor physical health (chronic illnesses, AIDS, cancer)
  - Availability of method (e.g., guns at home, pills)

It does not necessarily mean that a child will commit suicide if she or he exhibits one or two of the above risk factors. However, the more signs a child has, the higher the risk for suicide.

2. Raising the Issue

If your child has several signs of the risk factors noted above, if your child has bipolar or depressive disorder, or if you have any suspicion that your child may be thinking about suicide, it is imperative to have him or her evaluated by a mental health professional. If you have a good relationship with your son or daughter, you can also ask the child whether he or she has any thoughts about hurting him or herself. However, remember that your child may deny having suicidal thoughts or having attempted suicide.

It is better to take your child for an evaluation by a professional than to wait until something bad happens.

There are some "myths" regarding suicide that you should know.

- **Talking about suicide will give the child ideas about suicide.** This is not true. The child may already be thinking about suicide and he or she may be relieved when an adult who cares acknowledges his or her suicidal ideation and shows them that they care.

- **Not talking about suicide or minimizing the talk about the ideas of suicide will distract the child and he or she will forget about it.** This is not correct. A person contemplating suicide thinks about it frequently and any stressor (e.g., separation from a girl- or boyfriend, poor grades, conflicts at home, and a friend who attempted suicide) can push him or her over the edge.

- **Children or adolescents who talk about suicide are manipulating or seeking attention.** Although this may be the case, you never know when the child is really considering committing suicide. Since many youth talk about suicide with their friends, relatives, and doctors before committing suicide, it is better to take their words seriously until a professional assesses your son's or daughter's risk for suicide. You should ask your child directly and clearly about suicide. For example, if your child is depressed or very distressed you can ask something like this, "When people are depressed (or very stressed) they may have ideas of hurting themselves. What about you?" "Have you been having any thoughts like that?" "If you were to have thoughts like that, could you tell me?" "Would you promise me to keep yourself safe?" (commonly referred to as a "no-suicide contract"; see below). The "no-suicide contract" is a promise/agreement that you ask your child to "promise" not to act on any suicidal thoughts or urges he or she may have. The child may deny suicidal thoughts but if you have any suspicion, take him or her for an evaluation with a professional. This is especially true if your child is engaging in suicidal behaviors such as taking pills, cutting him- or herself, or talking about

> *We usually tell children and adolescents that we keep confidentiality except regarding issues of safety to themselves or others.*

death. For example, if a child is repeating frequently "Life sucks, I wish I were dead" or "I hope tomorrow I won't wake up alive" or "I wish a car will hit and kill me" etc., never swear secrecy. Seek professional help immediately.

Acknowledge that it is difficult to talk about suicide and be patient and polite. Show your children that your main goal is to help and protect them.

3. Realizing the Risks

If your child has several of the signs described above, in particular depression or bipolar disorder, behavior problems, and use of illicit drugs, he or she may be at high risk for suicide. There is an even greater risk if your child is using alcohol or other drugs, is impulsive, has been abused, or shows

> *The combination of a mood problem, behavior problems, and use of alcohol highly increases the risk for suicide.*

strong feelings of hopelessness. While drinking alcohol or using drugs the person becomes more unpredictable and impulsive and can behave without thinking about the consequences.

The lack of hope or "no light at the end of the tunnel" indicates that the child is thinking that there is no way out of his troubles and he or she may be seriously considering committing suicide. Youth that cannot cope with stressful situations and cannot find solutions for their problems may become more hopeless when confronted with a stressful situation and try to commit suicide. In contrast, certain protective factors such as religious beliefs, caring about the effect of suicide on his/her parents, siblings and friends, and having a strong support sys-

Having an available method (e.g., a firearm) increases the chance to commit suicide. If a child is very hopeless and desperate and he or she knows there is a gun at home, they may use it without thinking twice. For that reason, we strongly recommend for families to remove all firearms from the home.

You have to remove all available methods, in particular guns (even if they are not loaded, teens can easily get the ammunition). If your child is taking medications, keep them in a safe place.

tem may delay or stop the suicidal behavior. Finally, having an available method (e.g., guns, pills) increases the risk that a person who is thinking about suicide will use the method.

For further information about the risk and protective factors, see chapter 3 and Figure 3.1.

Additionally, the suicide risk is greatest for bipolar patients:

- During a depressive or mixed episode
- While transitioning from the manic/hypomanic state to the depressive state
- Immediately following psychiatric hospitalization, particularly if the admission to the hospital was due to suicidal ideation or attempt

4. Responding

Your initial response should be to take the suicidal ideation or attempts seriously without panicking, becoming angry or judgmental with your child.

Explain to your child, in particular teenagers, that to avoid any accidents you are taking the pills from them until they feel better and the crisis is over. Let them know that even if they were adults, you would do the same to protect their life.

You will have to closely supervise your child and take him or her for an evaluation. In conjunction with your child's clinician develop a plan to help your child and decide:

- If it is not safe to keep your child at home until the crisis has passed, or if it is better to admit your child into the hospital. Cases in which it is better to admit a child into the hospital include a child that is psychotic or agitated and contemplating suicide; a child that cannot promise not to harm him- or herself; a child that seriously tried to commit suicide; or a child with a history of repetitive suicidal attempts.

in imminent danger and you can supervise him
ou may consider admitting him or her into a day
program.

tay at home, discuss the degree of supervision
ften your child needs to be taken to the clinic.
inician negotiates a "no-suicide contract." As
e contract is an agreement between the clini-
to do certain tasks instead of trying to com-
the next appointment. These tasks include
talking to parents, calling a special number
in Appendix II) if the suicidal thoughts are

uggest calling friends when they feel suici-
better than nothing, their friends may not
ion to a responsible adult. Moreover, if
ey will be very depressed, anxious, guilty,
suicide.

provided with "tools" to handle his or her
he current crisis (see chapter 7).

ortant to carefully
dal ideation can wax
our child feels frus-
alized due to suici-
discharge from the
prompt follow-ups
occur during the
the hospital.

> *Although "no-suicide contracts" are not "bullet proof" they can be helpful and parents should be involved in the process of negotiating these contracts. Agreeing to a "safety plan" is essential for the entire family.*

des psychosocial
ng on the under-
circumstances around the suicidal at-
and medications used for bipolar
6 and 7. Specific studies to help you

with suicidal behaviors have shown that cognitive behavior therapy (CBT), interpersonal psychotherapy (IPT), and psychodynamic psychotherapy are all options for the management of a suicidal youth but further studies are necessary.[1,7]

The only form of psychotherapy that has been well studied and found to reduce suicidal behaviors in adults with borderline personality disorder (for a description of this disorder see chapter 2) is Dialectical-Behavior Therapy (DBT).[8,9] In this type of therapy, suicidal behaviors are considered to be poor or maladaptive solutions to painful negative emotions. DBT also considers that suicidal behaviors may help regulate the person's mood and elicit help from others. The treatment involves strategies to increase the tolerance to stress, regulate emotions, solve interpersonal problems, improve skills to solve problems, and use both rational and emotional input to make balanced decisions. DBT also includes Zen meditation to help people become more aware of themselves and their surroundings. DBT has been adapted for adolescents, including strategies to improve the home environment and involving parents in the treatment.

> The medications used to manage suicide behaviors depend on the underlying psychiatric disorder.

For example, the selective serotonin reuptake inhibitors (SSRIs) and venlafaxine (Effexor) are used to treat depression, general anxiety, social anxiety, obsessive-compulsive, panic and post-traumatic stress disorders and the mood stabilizers more specifically for bipolar disorders (see chapters 6 and 7). In the past, some reports suggested that the SSRIs increased the risk for suicide. However, these reports were unfounded.[1] The main problem using the antidepressants listed above is the risk of inducing mania, mixed episodes or rapid cycling (chapter 1).

In bipolar adults, it appears that treatment with lithium greatly reduces the frequency of both suicide and suicide attempts. Moreover, discontinuing lithium treatment in bipolar patients is associated with an increase in suicide. The protective effects of lithium appear to be above and beyond its effects on the bipolar disorder.[1]

Studies on the efficacy of lithium for suicide in children and adolescents are needed. Importantly, lithium (and other medications) should not be self-administered by suicidal youth because it is very dangerous in case of an overdose (see chapter 6 for further information on lithium).

The use of medications that may increase disinhibition or impulsivity, such as the benzodiazepines (chapter 6), should be prescribed with caution because they may increase the risk for suicide and are dangerous in the case of an overdose.

It is important to mention that in cases where a child has committed suicide, his or her relatives, friends, and teachers may benefit from psychotherapy to facilitate grieving, reduce guilt and depression, and decrease the effects of guilt. Having the traumatic experience of a significant other committing suicide is often helped through psychotherapy. Moreover, the psychosocial interventions may minimize the risk of imitative or copycat suicides.[1]

> *The media should be alerted and educated on the dangers of excessive coverage and glorification of individual suicides. Studies have suggested that it can increase the risk that other children and adolescents (particularly if they were thinking about suicide) will commit suicide.*

SUMMARY

Suicidal ideation and attempts are common in youth with bipolar disorder. Recognizing the signs of mental illness and suicidal behavior and being able to raise the issue with a youth places parents, relatives and others in a better position to realize the risk and respond effectively. Suicide can be prevented by getting in early and recognizing the signs of a potential bipolar disorder, supported with prompt professional treatment.

CHAPTER 11

Managing Your Child's Behavior Problems

❧

I T IS SOMETIMES DIFFICULT to know which behavior problems are due to bipolar disorder and which ones are normal components of growing up. After all, as we discussed in chapter 2, not all misbehaviors are due to psychiatric disorders; children at any age may have "healthy" acting-out behaviors. For example, temper tantrums are not uncommon in children between the ages of 2 and 6, and a teenager may be normally "rebellious" and challenge the parents' or teachers' authority. *Only when these behaviors become too disruptive, affect your child's functioning, and are persistent or repetitive should you worry and consult a professional.*

Self-control can be learned through behavior modification therapy, which has been found to be effective in the management of behavior problems and other issues that frequently occur in children and adolescents with this disorder.[1-6] Although there are many ways to do behavior modification therapy, the overall goal of the plan is to reinforce the positive behaviors and diminish the negative ones.[1-6] (A *negative behavior* is a way of dealing with problems and conflicts that does not help the child but instead makes the situation worse, such as aggressive behaviors, recurrent and severe temper tantrums, and self-injurious behaviors. Phobias, excessive lying, stealing, inadequate homework habits, and

poor sleep habits are other examples of behaviors that can interfere with a child's normal functioning.)

This chapter will help you put together
and carry out a simple behavior modification
plan to help you manage your child's behavior problems. As you study this process, keep
in mind that behavior modification plans are
easier to carry out with young children. They
are less difficult to control while acting out or
having a temper outburst, and most of their

> ### Behavior Modification Therapy
> Although behavior modification therapy has not been specifically studied for use in children with bipolar disorder, it has been found to be effective in the management of behavior problems.

misbehaviors have not been in place for long periods of time, as in adolescents. Similar to any behavior that has been practiced repeatedly,
negative behaviors that have persisted longer are harder to change. For
this reason, the advice included in this chapter is more applicable to
children than to adolescents, but some of the tips relate to behavioral
therapy with all age groups. And remember, although it is necessary to
help your child control her or his disruptive behaviors, take into account that while your child is in an acute episode of bipolar disorder, it
may be very difficult to control him- or herself.

KEY GUIDELINES OF A SUCCESSFUL BEHAVIOR MODIFICATION PLAN

Before developing a behavior modification plan (a method used to reward positive behaviors and diminish negative ones) for your child, it is
important first to consider a few important guidelines that are vital to
designing a good program. Being familiar with these generalized considerations will improve your child's chances of success when you later
try to implement an individualized plan.

- **Rules must be simple and clear.** Tell your child what exactly
  you mean when you are trying to modify his or her behavior. For
  example, statements like "Behave well" or "Be good" are too

vague and can mean different things for you, your child, and the clinician.

- **Rules should not contradict each other.** Sometimes, obeying one rule means breaking another. This is the case when you say, "Don't rush while you brush your teeth; do a good job. Now hurry up, your school bus is coming in a few minutes." Be careful to set rules that do not contradict each other.

- **Give only one order or command at a time.** Do not give more than one command at a time. "Go clean your room, do your homework, and brush your teeth" is a complicated, long-term series of orders that your child is unlikely to carry out.

Never a Punishment

A behavior modification plan should never be used to punish a child. It is a method to teach correct behaviors by rewarding positive behaviors and diminishing negative ones.

- **Your child should enjoy and understand the rules of the behavior "game."** If your child sees the plan as a punishment, he or she is less likely to want to participate in the program at all. On the other hand, a plan designed to be fun and rewarding for the child will keep motivation high and improve chances of success.

- **The plan must be individualized.** No one plan fits all children. Your plan must take into consideration your child's age and intelligence. It must also consider the presence of any psychiatric disorder(s).

Note: *My experience indicates that children with significant psychiatric disorders usually cannot follow a behavior modification plan until the psychiatric disorder has been controlled.* For these cases, it will be impossible to plan a behavior treatment without treating the child's symptoms with medications or other types of treatment before implementing the behavior plan.

- **The plan should be easy at the beginning.** Your child may get discouraged and confused if the behavior modification plan is too demanding right from the start. Begin with an easy plan, and then, depending on your child's progress, steadily increase the demands being made on your child. This slow progression is the same that is used when a child first begins to play sports, an instrument, or a new board game. If the rules of the game are too difficult or too demanding to follow, the child is likely to refuse to participate.

- **You need to be patient.** Do not try to change more than one or sometimes two behaviors at one time; otherwise it can be too confusing for your child. Behaviors do not change overnight, particularly if the maladaptive behaviors have been occurring for a long time. Like excelling at a sport, playing an instrument, or learning a new subject, difficult times are to be expected at the beginning, and you'll need to keep your child feeling optimistic about the outcome of this "game." Always remember that small improvements slowly lead to large ones, and any improvements are a step in the right direction.

- **You must be consistent.** If you are consistent in the way you respond to your child, eventually he or she will learn that negative behaviors bring negative consequences and positive behaviors bring positive consequences. But lack of consistency will ruin the behavior plan and confuse your child. There's no way around it:

  In order for your child to learn to behave appropriately, those involved in the behavior program must always follow the rules of the plan—that includes you, your child's other parent, teachers, and clinicians. Just as it is unacceptable not to follow rules when playing a sport, it is also detrimental to the success of the behavior program.

- **Adults involved in the program need to be in agreement.** All those involved in the behavior plan must agree to the rules and the consequences outlined in the plan. A child who does not re-

> ### The Game Plan
> When creating a behavior modification plan under the supervision of your child's clinician, you might imagine the clinician as a "coach," yourself as the "coach's assistant," and your child as a "player" who must thoroughly understand the rules in order to play well and enjoy the game.

> *A lways remember that small improvements slowly lead to large ones, and any improvements are a step in the right direction.*

ceive the same reaction from all of the "coaches" will be confused about the plan and may take sides with one adult, creating conflict. While this is especially important for adults who live with the child, certain behaviors (such as not doing homework or talking back to teachers) require the participation of the child's teachers as well.

- **The plan must be flexible and revised periodically.** Behavior plans need constant monitoring and should be changed according to your child's response, environmental factors, and the development of new problems. But do not change the rules without discussing them with those involved *before* they are implemented. Your child must trust that the rules do not change spontaneously but that these rules will be discussed with him or her and changed as the "game" changes.

- **Adults involved in the child's life must change their own attitudes toward the child.** Once a behavior modification plan is developed, not only will your child need to change, but also parents, siblings, other relatives, and teachers must change their biases and attitudes toward the child. *Due to your child's past behaviors, many adults may always expect that the child is going to misbehave, or they may blame the child for whatever happens at home or school.* Under these circumstances, it will be very difficult for your child to change because those around him or her are expecting failure.

- **Set a good example.** You need to set an example for your child and avoid the behaviors you want your child to change, such as lying, swearing, or engaging in verbal or physical aggression. If you have trouble controlling these behaviors yourself or have any medical or psychiatric problems such as depression or bipolar disorder, you, too, should seek help. Not only does this show your child a constructive way of dealing with a problem, but it will also help you deal with important problems. Moreover, you should pay attention to the way you currently deal with your child's problems since we as parents may inadvertently reinforce our children's problems or be too negative with them.

- **You should consider any problems of your own that may unnecessarily lower your threshold or tolerance for your child's problems.** In addition to problems with your child, you may be dealing with issues such as mental illness, economic problems, substance abuse, lack of support networks, or other responsibilities (other children, work, etc.) that can affect your ability to focus on your child's behavior problems. If this is the case, you should consult with the child's clinician for help.

- **Take a break if you or your child is very upset.** When people are very upset, they can say or do things they do not mean. If you see that you or your child is getting out of control, it is better to get away from each other until you restore calm. Do not wait until the situation "explodes."[3] Like boxers, you have to go to neutral corners until you feel that you can talk without being too angry or argumentative.

- **Pick your "battles."** Sometimes it is not worthwhile to argue about minor things. Before making the formal behavior plan, you should choose the most important behaviors you wish your child to change and, if appropriate, ignore minor behavior problems (particularly if they are not frequent and not part of the behavior plan you are implementing). If you notice that you cannot ignore minor incidents, ask yourself whether your threshold to tolerate your child's normal acting out is too low. If you realize that your threshold is low, you may need to seek some professional help before you can help your child.

All adults involved with your child should be well informed about the nature of the child's problems and its management. Education is a key factor for the management of any psychiatric or medical disorder. When you understand the disorder, you will have greater insight into the child's behaviors and need for appropriate treatment plans.

The Root of the Problem

The behavior modification plan is a tool used to modify or manage your child's misbehaviors. But it cannot address problem behaviors that have serious physical or emotional roots. For example, your child may be acting out due to lack of attention, problems with peers, abuse, medical illness, poor vision or hearing, and the like. In these cases, the behavior plan alone is not sufficient to help your child—the underlying cause must also be considered. If the behavior modification plan does not initially work, consult with your child's clinician to help you decipher the cause of your child's problems.

IMPLEMENTING THE BEHAVIOR MODIFICATION PLAN

Now that you are familiar with the important concepts of a successful behavior modification plan, you are ready to begin creating one. Unless your child will not cooperate, it is good to develop this plan together with him or her, so that you and your child are in agreement.

When you and your child agree to all the terms of your plan, write down the terms. Both of you should sign it, and then keep one copy for yourself and give one to you child. This written record is particularly important when working with defiant and stubborn children because unless it is in writing, after the plan is established, they will try to renegotiate the deal.

There are many types of behavior plans, but in general a standard behavior modification plan includes the following components:

- A list of the behaviors that are interfering with your child's functioning at home, school, or other places
- A list of the positive reinforcements or consequences that will be used to reward your child

- A list of the negative consequences that will be used to control your child's misbehaviors
- A plan to help your child find more adaptive behaviors to avoid the negative consequences

Once you have established these issues, you and your child will be ready to start the behavior modification plan.

List the Behaviors That Are Interfering with Your Child's Functioning

As a first step, sit down and make a list of the behaviors that you feel are interfering with your child's functioning. Begin with the most severe problems first. Because it is impossible and very confusing to modify all these behaviors at the same time, choose only one behavior (or maybe two, if you must) on which to focus. If willing and able, your child may participate in this activity and help identify the problems. *Use simple language and be clear about which behavior(s) you expect the child to change.*

As stated earlier, vague or unclear rules about what you expect your child to do are bound to fail. Instead, define the specific behavior you would like your child to adhere to and state it clearly. Rather than make a very general rule such as "I want you to behave" or "Be good," define what you mean by "behave." You might say, "Do not hit your brother," "I do not want you to yell," or "You must finish your homework before you turn on the TV."

List the Rewards Your Child Can Earn

With your child, make a list of positive reinforcements (rewards) that are going to be used as a "prize" every time your child follows through with the behavior plan. *The reward must be well defined and agreed on in advance by those involved in the program.* The reward should be periodically changed so that it does not lose its effect if the child gets bored with it. Also, if you choose to use objects or promise to go to places, make sure you can afford them throughout the time the behavior modification plan is in place.

Types of Rewards

To make the program work, you must know what types of rewards your child will like—what will motivate him or her to obey the rules in order to get the prize. Young children often value stickers or small toys that can also be "earned" on a daily basis. These should not be expensive or difficult-to-obtain items. Hopefully, your child will earn a reward for good behavior every day, so make sure you can afford the prize and can offer it readily throughout the time the behavior plan is in place.

Older children may prefer money. If you decide to use money, it is a good idea to link the weekly allowance to the behavioral modification plan. For example, for each day that the stated goal is met, agree to give your child a certain amount of money, let's say 50 cents. In this way, depending on how many days in the week your child behaves, he or she can earn from $0 to $3.50 each week. This kind of reward helps your child feel in control of the plan and helps him or her understand that it is the child's responsibility, not yours, to gain as much money as he or she can. You can also add bonuses. For example, you might give an extra 50 cents for 3 days of successful behaviors (to make the behavior plan easy to follow at the beginning, make the 3 days nonsequential).

Some parents may be uncomfortable about using money to modify their children's behavior. If this is the case, you can use other objects or activities, but remember that in the adult world, people get paid for their work. In fact, one of our most potent rewards for improved performance at work is a cash bonus. Also, *remember that you are using the money (or any other reward) as a tool, and once the behavior is modified and your child is doing well, you will be able to give your child regular allowances and consequences for his or her behavior like any other child.*

A reward appropriate for children of all ages is the promise of a treasured activity, such as going to the movies, visiting the park, or playing a game. If the activity involves both of you, it has the added bonus of helping to improve your relationship with your child. Research has shown that the best way to increase ties between children and adults is through play. If you create a reward that allows you to spend time doing an enjoyable activity with your child, not only will you be rewarding your child for positive behavior, but you will also have a chance to focus positively on your child and on the things your child enjoys.

When to Give the Positive Rewards

A reward will work best when it is given close to the positive behavior. Consider the story of Ed: According to Ed's behavior modification plan, every 4 days he is to be rewarded for not having temper tantrums. He does well for 3 days, but on the fourth day Ed gets very upset and has a severe temper outburst. Should his mother give him a reward for the 3 good days? If she does, she may be reinforcing the temper outburst on the fourth. Opting not to give the prize is also unfair because the child tried his best for 3 days out of 4. Far better if Ed had been given a reward on day 1, another on days 2 and 3, and then none on day 4.

Figure 11.1—Example of a Time Schedule to
Track the Behavior Modification Plan

Monday	Tuesday	Wednesday	Thursday	Friday	Saturday	Sunday
☺	☺	☺	😢	☺	😢	☺

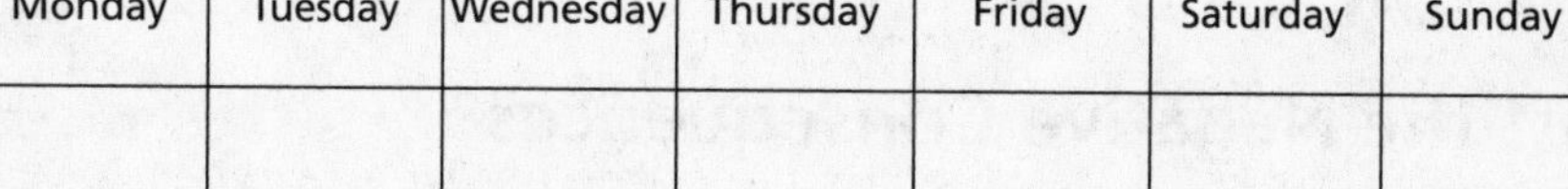

To keep track of your child's progress, you can make a calendar (like that in figure 11.1), and at the end of the day the child can draw a happy face or stick a star on the calendar if he or she has successfully accomplished the day's goal or a "sad" face if not. Immediately after placing a happy face or star on the calendar, you can then give your child the promised reward. In this way, your child can see how he or she is doing, and you can count the number of successful and nonsuccessful days to monitor the progress of the behavior plan. *The goal is to increase step-by-step the number of successful days.*

Treat Psychiatric Illnesses First

Children with significant psychiatric illnesses are unlikely to succeed in a behavior treatment plan. A child with significant impulsivity and hyperactivity will hardly earn any happy faces. A child that is easily distracted and forgetful will also lose the rewards often. This is especially bad for a child in a manic episode. In these cases, treatment of the child's symptoms with medications or other types of treatment is necessary before implementing the behavior plan.

List the Negative Consequences

Along with the positive rewards your child will receive for good behavior, make a list of the negative consequences that he or she will face if the behavior goal is not met. *The main goal of the negative consequences is not to punish the child but to discourage him or her from continuing the maladaptive pattern of behaviors.* If the behavior management goes well, the child will look forward to the positive rewards and avoid the negative consequences.

Avoid Physical Punishment

Although your child may *appear* to listen better if you use harsh methods, in the long run this approach will create more problems. The child may obey when physically punished, but he or she will become angry and sad and develop low self-esteem. Also, *the child will obey because he or she is afraid, not to because of a desire to change. And sadly, the child may learn to use physical punishment and do the same to his or her own children.* Their children will do the same, and the cycle of physical punishment will continue. Like a boomerang, harsh actions will "hit you back" because physical punishment and harsh or negative comments work against fostering the trusting, cooperative relationship between you and your child that is essential to overcoming maladaptive behaviors. In addition, always remember that in the United States and other countries, physical punishment is considered abuse, and parents may be penalized for their conduct, or sometimes the child may be taken away.

It's true that many parents punish their children physically because they do not know how else to do it. After all, nobody teaches parents how to raise their children. We usually raise our kids by trial and error or by using the techniques we saw our relatives use. It is amazing that we need to pass a test before we can drive a car, but we do not need to undergo such a process to have children.

Use Appropriate Negative Consequences

The first negative consequence will be losing the promised reward—for example, the 50 cents, small toy, trading card, or activity agreed on for good behavior. But it is necessary to have more than one negative consequence because a child who is not doing well may think, "I already lost my prize. I do not have anything left to lose, so I will continue to behave badly." The remainder of the negative consequences may involve time-outs and loss of some of the child's privileges. For example, an applicable consequence for a child who loves to play video games is not to be allowed to play video games for the rest of the day,

Be Consistent

Remember to be consistent with applying negative consequences. Even if your child says that he or she does not care and even if you feel "guilty," carry out the agreed-on consequence for poor behavior.

while for a teenager it may be more significant to take away the right to use the telephone or computer for the day. Whatever it is, the consequence should be meaningful for the child.

An example of consecutive negative consequences could be (1) losing a reward, (2) getting a time-out, (3) losing television viewing privileges, and (4) getting grounded for the day. But before applying the negative consequences, give your child a chance to change his or her behavior. For example, you can tell your child, "I am going to count up to 10, and at the end, if you do not stop doing _____, you will lose your reward. I am sure you can try. 1, 2, . . ."

Remember, do not change the negative consequences plan without the understanding and agreement of all the people involved. And do not enact a consequence on the child for more than 1 day unless the behavior was very severe (e.g., injury to others, vandalism). In these cases, consult with a professional.

Time-outs

Time-out is a consequence commonly used by families in response to poor behavior that is particularly useful with young children. Although it is difficult to make a teenager sit in a time-out chair, you can send your teen to his or her room until he or she has calmed down. (*Note*: While your child is alone in his or her room, monitor your child carefully if he or she has had suicidal thoughts.)

Time-outs do not necessarily need to take place in the child's room. Your child can go to a corner of the living room and sit in a chair designated "the thinking chair" or the "time-out chair." If you do send your child to his or her room for the time-out, make sure you can keep an eye on your child so you can be sure he or she is safe and, at the same time, cannot spend the time-out playing with toys.

For small children, a time-out should not be longer than 5 to 10 minutes. It's a good idea to place a large clock close to your child so you can show him or her what 5 to 10 minutes means in a concrete way. (Keep it at a safe distance in case your child has a temper tantrum and is tempted to throw it.) At the end of the 5 to 10 minutes, ask your child whether he or she is ready to leave the time-out area. If your child is ready, let him or her go, with a reminder that he or she will have to go back to the time-out area if behaving poorly again. If the child does repeat the misbehavior, he or she should go back to the time-out area as many times as is necessary. However, if the time-outs do not diminish your child's misbehaviors, or your child does not stay in the place designated for the time-out, you should consult with your child's clinician for further advice.

Find Behaviors That Will Help Your Child Avoid Getting in Trouble

The behavior modification plan needs to offer the child more appropriate ways to deal with his or her problems. Many times children act out because they do not know what else to do. Your child needs to learn how to control and cope with his or her behavior or emotions if you expect your child to change. With your help (under the supervision of your child's clinician if necessary), make sure your child learns more adaptive behaviors to calm him- or herself down when agitated or angry. Give your child alternatives to having a temper outburst or to screaming or swearing.

Help your child find what works for him or her. For some children, self-talking, listening to music, talking to friends, drawing, exercising, relaxing, punching a bag, dancing, or reading may help diffuse a temper outburst. For example, children can learn to talk themselves out of problems and to think about the consequences before they act. Young children may be read the book *The Little Engine That Could* and then taught to say, "I think I can control my temper." You have to help your child find what works for him or her to avoid trouble.

Children (many adults, too!) need to *"stop-think-act."* If your child can become accustomed to this, he or she can avoid trouble and earn rewards. Thus, you are rewarding your child for *avoiding* trouble and for fostering problem-solving skills. This is an important part of behavior modification that is often learned in complementary forms of therapy, such as cognitive behavior therapy or family therapy.

EVALUATING AND ENDING A BEHAVIOR MODIFICATION PLAN

For noncomplicated, mild to moderate behavior problems, a consistent and well-thought-out behavior modification plan should improve the child's misbehaviors in a few months. Once the identified behavior problem that was listed in the original contract has continuously improved, the behavior plan needs to be slowly tapered down. You should continue to monitor your child's behavior, but stretch out the reward periods to every few days and then eventually weekly. If the problem reappears, you should start the plan again. If the initial problem improves but your child has other behaviors that need to be modified, you can start a new plan following the same rules.

Do not overdo the behavior modification plan, and remember that the plan is not "written in stone" and requires a certain degree of flexibility. After all, nobody is perfect, and your child should be allowed to be a child. But if you see that the plan is not working at all, or if your child is not motivated, you need to keep revising the rewards and consequences until you hit on something that sparks an interest.

If the behavior management plan still does not work, you should consider the following causes:

- The behavior plan is not feasible or is not well done.
- You are not consistently carrying out the plan.
- Your child is not interested in or does not understand the plan.
- The behavior plan is well done, but it is inappropriate for your child's problems.

If the behavior modification plan is not working, your child's behaviors may be too complicated or severe, or if you suspect your child has a psychiatric or medical problem, consult a professional. He or she will assess the possible familial or environmental causes for your child's misbehaviors and, if appropriate, will help you to create and carefully monitor a new behavior modification plan.

SUMMARY

It is easy to talk about behavior modification plans, but they are time-consuming and sometimes difficult to carry out. This is especially true for children with psychiatric disorders such as bipolar disorder, major depression, or ADHD. In these cases, the behavior plan usually must be done in conjunction with medication treatment and other psychosocial therapies. Coexisting disorders such as ADHD sometimes also need to be addressed; otherwise the behavior plans will not work.

With patience, however, negative behaviors will change over time, and hopefully sooner or later you will not need to continue the behavior modification plan and be able to give your child regular prizes and negative consequences for his or her behavior like any other child. This is also true in situations where your child is having trouble at school. The next chapter will take a look at how to manage your child's academic problems.

CHAPTER 12

Solving Your Child's Academic Problems

Children with bipolar disorder often also have academic problems. Sometimes the difficulties are related to the symptoms of their illness; other times the difficulties are due to some other entirely separate cause. In either case, if your child is falling behind in school, he or she needs your help to find out why and to receive immediate support and academic help. Although it is beyond the scope of this chapter to cover all the possible educational plans for children with special needs, it will give you an overview of the possibilities you can explore as you strive to isolate the root of the problem and help your child achieve his or her potential.

REASONS FOR POOR ACADEMIC PERFORMANCE

As shown in table 12.1, a child may have trouble doing well in school for many reasons.[1] In a child with bipolar disorder, the symptoms of depression such as poor concentration, tiredness, lack of motivation, and slow thinking processes, and manic symptoms such as racing thoughts, hyperactivity, and lack of sleep can affect your child's ability to perform well academically.

270

If your child has any coexisting psychiatric disorders such as ADHD, anxiety disorder, or substance abuse, the reasons for academic difficulties naturally multiply. Your child may also have learning disabilities, cognitive problems, speech and language difficulties, conflicts at home or with peers, or medical problems (such as poor vision or hearing, thyroid problems, allergies, asthma, diabetes, anemia) that may interfere with his or her academic performance.

Moreover, the medications used to treat your child's bipolar disorder, other psychiatric disorders, or medical illnesses may also cause difficulties with your child's concentration and academic performance. For example, the mood stabilizers (e.g., lithium, alproate, topiramate) or the antipsychotics (risperidone, olanzapine, chlorpromazine) may directly affect your child's thinking processes or may produce sedation and tiredness that interfere with your child's ability to study. Corticosteroids (e.g., prednisone), anti-allergic, asthma, or antihypertensive (to lower blood pressure) medications also may cause tiredness or sedation.

> *The medications used to treat your child's bipolar disorder, other psychiatric disorders, or medical illnesses may also cause difficulties with your child's concentration and academic performance.*

Also, the use of illicit drugs or alcohol (not uncommon in teens with bipolar disorder) usually interferes with a child's ability to concentrate, think, and sit still. For example, teens using marijuana may become distracted, have memory problems, and lose their motivation to do many things, including academic work.

Children may also do poorly because they attend a school where they do not get enough reinforcement and stimulation to study. Or, they may be in the wrong environment (e.g., gangs) or have conflicts at home, with peers, or with teachers. Or, the academic problem may be rooted in something as simple as poor study habits; if your child comes home from school and watches TV until late in the night, without leaving time for homework, this alone could be the reason for his or her academic problems.

As table 12.1 indicates, the common causes of poor school performance are many and varied. The immediate challenge in solving the academic problems of a child with bipolar disorder is to find out if the academic difficulties are due to psychiatric problems or to one of the many other possible causes.

TABLE 12.1—MOST COMMON CAUSES OF POOR SCHOOL PERFORMANCE

- Child factors
  - Poor study habits and not doing homework
  - Disorganization
  - Poor motivation
  - Absenteeism or tardiness
  - Refusal to listen to the rules and instructions in class
  - Conflicts with peers or teachers
  - Psychiatric disorders (e.g., bipolar, attention deficit hyperactivity, anxiety, oppositional, conduct, pervasive developmental disorders)
  - Learning disabilities (reading, writing, math)
  - Low intelligence
  - Language disorders
  - Abuse of illicit drugs or alcohol
  - Side effects of medications
  - Medical and neurological problems (e.g., poor hearing or vision, allergies, seizures, diabetes, thyroid illness, anemia, poor nutrition)
- Home and other environmental factors
  - Lack of supervision at home
  - A chaotic home environment
  - Poor school instruction
  - Lack of positive reinforcement (home, school, and friends)
  - Stressors (e.g., abuse, conflicts)

As you consider all of these possible causes of school problems, make an effort to separate bipolar symptoms from other causes of academic problems. Consider these scenarios:

- Your child always did well at school until he or she developed bipolar disorder.
- Your child always did well, but now his or her academic performance fluctuates or changes among normal, excellent, and poor depending on his or her mood.
- One or both of the prior points apply, but in addition to bipolar disorder, your child is having other problems (e.g., substance abuse, poor study habits) (see table 12.1). In this case, perhaps the bipolar disorder is not the main cause of your child's academic difficulties.
- Your child had mild or severe academic problems (e.g., a learning disability), and the bipolar disorder is aggravating them. In these cases, it is necessary to evaluate and remediate all possible causes for the child's preexisting academic problems.
- Your child may have a mild learning disability. As long as she or he was in an "easy" class, he or she did well. Now, he or she may be in more difficult and demanding classes, and the learning disability becomes noticeable. The same may happen to a child that accepted his or her parent's mentorship and help. As soon as such children become teens, they do not want supervision with school work, and minor learning problems that may have existed before but that were not affecting their functioning are now evident.
- Check whether your child's poor academic performance is across all subjects or only in one class. If your child's learning problems are due to bipolar disorder, then most subjects should be affected. If only one subject is a problem, consider other causes, such as a specific learning problem with math or a challenge with a specific teacher.
- Successful treatment of your child's bipolar disorder was not accompanied by improvement in his or her academic performance. In this case:

- Consider that if your child has been depressed or manic for a while, he or she likely had difficulty studying and probably got behind in his or her schoolwork. Your child will need a period of rehabilitation similar to when an athlete injures a leg or an arm and needs time to recover his or her strength to be able to play again.
- Consider that something else is going on (see table 12.1) or that the medications used to treat your child are producing cognitive difficulties.

INITIAL ASSESSMENT

You, your child, your child's teachers, the school psychologist and social worker, the guidance counselor, and your child's clinician should all be involved in the prompt evaluation and implementation of an academic plan for your child.[1] Don't put this off or allow others to stall; the longer the problem continues, the more difficult it may be to solve.

If you or your child's teachers think he or she has a psychiatric problem(s), your child needs to be evaluated by a competent professional, as discussed in chapter 5. If necessary, psychological testing is recommended to evaluate your child for any cognitive problems, problems with attention span, and learning disabilities. Speech and language problems need to be evaluated using specific language tests. Your child may have problems expressing him- or herself or have difficulty understanding what others are saying despite normal hearing.

If your child was a good student or had a prior normal psychological test, retesting is indicated to assess whether the psychiatric or medical illness or the medications used to treat these disorders are affecting his or her cognitive processes. If a suspicion surfaces that the medications may be affecting your child's academic performance and it is possible to discontinue them, your child may need a psychological test with and without medications.

If your child is not seeing or hearing well or having any medical problem, he or she may require a medical evaluation and a vision and/or hearing test.

During and after this testing period, it is important that you and your child's clinician meet with the school's principal, teachers, guidance counselor or psychologist, and other appropriate people to inform them about your child's psychiatric problems and the academic and behavioral consequences of the disorder.

> **Look for Strengths**
>
> Remember that it is important not only to evaluate your child's problems but also to assess and reinforce your child's strengths.

Working with the School

Request a multidisciplinary evaluation and together with the school develop an *individualized education plan* (IEP) for your child.[1] Through the multidisciplinary evaluation process, your child may receive the psychological test at no cost. The problem obtaining a psychological test through the school system is that sometimes it can take too long to be performed. In this case, check whether the test is covered under your insurance company, and ask your child's clinician to order it. If you can afford to pay for the tests, you may get a private psychologist to do it.

In general, schools are interested in helping your child and making certain accommodations for your child to support optimum learning. Examples of some accommodations that may be made by the school include the following:

- Adjust the reading/math level.
- Provide extra tutoring.
- Allow the child to take classes with other students.
- Let the child use the computer to type homework.
- Allow a teacher's aid to provide one-on-one support to the child.
- Permit extra time to complete the work.
- Allow the use of dictionary or calculator during testing.
- Give extra time to complete work or test.

- Test the child in a less distractible environment.
- Modify his or her homework.
- Base grades according to the child's abilities.
- Allow extra-credit assignments.
- Seat the student near the teacher.
- Send daily/weekly reports to the parents.
- Supply your child with an organizer.
- Help your child to check and clean out his or her folders on a weekly (or more frequent) basis.
- Allow the child to go to the counselor or school nurse, if necessary.
- Allow the child flexibility in his or her schedule in order to accommodate the medication's side effects (e.g., goes more often to the bathroom or has a bottle of water if the child is taking lithium).
- Allow the child to catch up during summer school.
- Place the child in regular classes appropriate for his or her academic level (e.g., the child may be in ninth-grade English and eighth-grade math).
- Enroll the child in special classes such as one especially for children having trouble with math. (Always consider the psychological effects of having your child be taken out of his regular classes.)
- Try homebound instruction for your child until the crisis is over. (This approach can be helpful for children who do well at school except when they are acutely depressed or manic.)

Although your child's teachers and school administrators can make many changes to help your child, do not rely solely on their actions. Become an active partner yourself with your child and all the other people involved in your child's education. Also, consult with other parents and the special education department in your school. Contact advocacy groups and *be actively involved by taking the "driver's seat."* If you do not agree with the school and your child already has an IEP, request a review of that plan/program.

As a last resort, request a due process hearing, and, if necessary, seek judicial advice (as explained later in this chapter).

Special Schools

If the school has made the appropriate accommodations, you have exhausted all possibilities, and still your child is having academic difficulties, a special school should be considered. Usually the path and the funding to these special schools are through your child's public school, following a legally prescribed set of steps in making the placement decision. However, you may also consult with your child's clinician, visit several especial schools, check the Web (see Appendix II), and ask for advice from other parents who have sent their children to special schools.

Always involve your child in the decision and choice of special schools. Be aware that your child may feel like a failure. Changing schools, particularly to a school for children with emotional or learning problems, and losing his or her friends entail very significant stressors that may worsen your child's mood and behavior. Therefore, it is recommended that the process of accommodating and particularly placing your child in a special class or school will be done steadily and within the context of your child's psychotherapy.

Eventually, if appropriate, your child may return to regular school. In my experience, some children with severe mood problems have done well in special schools where the staff is prepared to manage psychological problems and the school is open to accommodating the child according to his or her needs.

Parents who can afford it may also consider sending the child to boarding schools. Again, the parents, the child, teachers, and the child's treatment team should meet and evaluate whether sending the child to these schools is appropriate for the case.

Several Web sites offer information about appropriate schools (see

Appendix II), but be careful because some of these sites may advertise unlicensed or poor-quality schools. Also, if you can afford their services, professionals who specialize in helping parents find appropriate schools for their children can be a valuable resource. For example, you can contact the Independent Educational Consultants Association for consultants in your area (www.iecaonline.com; telephone: [703] 591-4860), or explore the Children & Adolescent Bipolar Foundation Web site (www.bpkids.org).

Home Schooling

Some parents may consider home schooling. This issue, however, is controversial. Some parents and educators promote home schooling, while others disapprove. The parents, the child, teachers, and the child's treatment team need to evaluate the pros and cons of home schooling and consider whether this approach is in the best interest of the child's emotional, cognitive, and social development.

YOUR CHILD'S LEGAL RIGHTS

The United States and other countries have laws that guarantee public school compliance with requested special accommodations. Even nonreligious, private schools are required to provide some special accommodations for special needs children per the Americans with Disabilities Act (ADA), a 1990 civil law.

Two federal laws guarantee that children with special needs or disabilities receive appropriate education similar to children without problems: Section 504 of the Rehabilitation Act of 1979 and the Individuals with Disabilities Education Act (IDEA) of 1997.[2,3]

In general, Section 504 is for children with disabilities that are significantly impairing their functioning. The law guarantees special accommodations or services but does not necessarily indicate that the children need to be separated from the regular classroom. In general, children eligible under this law do not have severe disabilities.

In general, the second law, IDEA, is for children with more severe difficulties. To be eligible, the child's illness or problems need to be significantly affecting his or her functioning, be long-standing (chronic), or have a severe, immediate impact on the child's performance.

In contrast to Section 504, IDEA obligates the school district to have a multidisciplinary team evaluate the child. The evaluation needs to be comprehensive, and all the child's needs are to be identified and addressed. The plan needs to be written and periodically reevaluated. The plan can be carried out in regular classes, but if necessary, the child may be placed in special classes or a special school. Again, you should work with the multidisciplinary team, and if you do disagree with the placement, contest any school decision.

It is beyond the scope of this book to describe in detail each of these laws, but be sure to check your local libraries, schools, and government Web sites for further information (see Appendix II).

SUMMARY

If your child with bipolar disorder also has problems with schoolwork, a comprehensive evaluation and prompt remediation are absolutely necessary. The difficulties may be the result of bipolar symptoms, they may be caused by other coexisting psychiatric conditions, or they may be due to factors entirely separate from your child's mental health. In any case, school success is closely tied to issues of self-esteem and life accomplishments, so this matter cannot be ignored. Taking a proactive stand, you should use all resources available to you to make sure your child's academic needs are met. This chapter has given you an overview of how you can do this, but be sure to look over Appendix II for more sources of information.

CHAPTER 13

Handling Your Child's Health Insurance

As the parent of a child with bipolar disorder, you will quickly find out that your child may need expensive health services. Ongoing therapy, medications, treatment, and support services can financially ruin a family if you are required to pay for these services out of pocket. Because proper treatment is expensive, you should spend some time learning about and understanding the health insurance options that are available for your child. This can be a daunting task, but with patience and perseverance you will find the time to be well spent.

The specifics of your child's mental health insurance coverage will depend on your child's age, the state where you live, your child's diagnosis, and your child's specific health-care plan, but here is some general information that you need to know about health insurance as you begin your exploration.[1-5]

PRIVATE HEALTH INSURANCE

If your child's health-care coverage is provided by a private health insurance plan that you receive as a benefit through your employer, you should do the following things right away:

- Get a written description of the mental health coverage (also called *behavioral health coverage*) that your plan provides.
- Find out if the mental health coverage is different from the general medical coverage. In many cases, the coverage is very different.
- Find out which services are covered or not covered.
- Find out if your plan will cover the cost of medication.
- Find out whether your plan covers brand-name medications, generic medications, or both.
- Determine whether there is a financial limit on the mental health services that your child can use in a year or even during a lifetime.
- Understand the copays and deductibles that you are required to pay.

Generally, private insurance will cover all or part of the cost of hospitalization, emergency services, and outpatient services (including therapy and visits to a psychiatrist). A case manager may be assigned by the insurance plan to coordinate coverage of the services that have been recommended for your child. If a case manager is assigned to coordinate the services your child is eligible to receive, get to know this person. Ask questions and learn all that you can. Many families have received significant medical bills because they did not understand what is and what is not covered by their health insurance plan.

Most private health insurers also develop "networks" of doctors, therapists, and service providers from which you can select to treat your child. Usually these networks are fairly comprehensive, but you may find that the psychiatrist, therapist(s), or hospital that you want to use is not in your approved network. Of course, you may select any provider that you want to care for your child if you are prepared to pay for all or part of the services. However, if you want your health insurance plan to cover the cost, you should choose a participating health-care team.

PUBLIC HEALTH INSURANCE (MEDICAID)

If you have public health insurance, you probably have the major public program, Medicaid, that finances health and mental health care for eligible low-income people. Medicaid is run and financed jointly by the federal government and the states. Thirty-seven million people (and one-quarter of all children) are covered by Medicaid for their health care.

Children normally qualify for Medicaid because:

- they live in a low-income family;
- they have a disability severe enough to qualify them for federal disability benefits; or
- they live in a family that is financially eligible for Supplemental Security Income (SSI).

However, federal law permits (but does not require) states to expand Medicaid eligibility to certain other groups. Some states, such as Pennsylvania, allow children with certain mental health diagnoses (including bipolar disorder) to participate in the Medicaid program regardless of the family's income. Other states, such as Kansas, Vermont, and New York, have elected to provide Medicaid coverage to some children (including those with bipolar disorder) who would not otherwise be eligible. However, over half of the states do not allow participation in Medicaid unless the family is low-income.

Medicaid is supplemented by the State Child Health Insurance Program (S-CHIP), which covers children up to a slightly higher level of family income. States may provide S-CHIP children with either Medicaid coverage or coverage under a private health plan in the state.

Once approved to receive Medicaid, children are eligible to receive a significant range of mental health services. The services include inpatient hospital care, crisis services, outpatient clinical care (including therapy, medications, and visits to a physician), intensive in-home services, day treatment, substance abuse services, social and daily living

skills training, residential treatment center services, case management, and other intensive community-based care.

As you can see, Medicaid provides a broad array
of services that is much more comprehensive and
often more appropriate for a child with bipolar
disorder than the services offered by a typical
private health insurance plan. However, because
Medicaid is a program designed to cover low-
income individuals, its rules on financial eligibility
keep many families from qualifying.

> *Medicaid provides a broad array of services that is much more comprehensive and often more appropriate for a child with bipolar disorder than the services offered by a typical private health insurance plan.*

It is important that you take the time to investigate your state's
eligibility criteria to determine if you child is eligible for Medicaid or
S-CHIP. To do this, call your local Department of Public Welfare and
ask for a mental health advocate to help answer your questions.

MANAGED CARE INSURANCE

In recent years, states have been shifting their Medicaid programs to
managed care providers. In addition, many private health insurers offer
or require that mental health coverage be "managed." Managed care is
a way to control the cost of health-care services by providing the "right
care" at the "right time." Managed care companies keep costs down by
keeping track of the services a family uses and by covering only the services that the company considers to be "medically necessary."

If your child has health insurance that is provided by a managed care
company, it is important that you understand the mental health coverage for your child and the services that are considered medically necessary. You also need to clearly understand what your managed care plan
requires you to do before you make an appointment with a doctor or go
to an emergency room or hospital. Many managed care plans require
preplanning or preauthorization before using services. Like some pri-

vate health insurance plans, managed care plans almost always assign a case manager who will be responsible for coordinating services for your child. Get to know this person and work with him or her to learn how to make your family's managed care plan work for your child.

SUPPLEMENTAL SECURITY INCOME (SSI)

Depending on your family income, resources, and size, your child may be eligible for Supplemental Security Income (SSI). This is a federal income assistance program through the Social Security Administration for qualified individuals with a disability (including infants and children). Your child does not have to have a permanent disability to receive help. For more information, call the Social Security Administration office nearest you.

A Therapist's Help with Financial Planning

Parents should make financial plans (asset management, trusts designed to preserve the child's eligibility for benefits, government-funded services) for any child with disabilities. Because these issues are delicate and may trigger conflicts and guilty feelings, the planning may be done in the context of the psychosocial therapy and with the assistance of a lawyer with expertise in this field. Interested parents may read a booklet published by the Disability Law Project entitled *Estate Planning for Persons with Disabilities*. This booklet tells how to find appropriate help, discusses the pros and cons of common estate planning mechanisms, and defines terms you are likely to come across. This booklet is available at the office of Disabilities Law Project in your respective city.

CHALLENGES YOU MAY FACE

To initiate mental health services, to find the resources that your child needs, and to make sure that your child has adequate health-care coverage, you must be able to represent your child adequately. This requires that you act as an advocate for your child, making sure that your child's needs are met and that his or her rights are protected. To become an effective advocate, you can do the following:

- Identify the needs of your child, and note the areas in which he or she might need help.
- Gather information on available resources, such as books, Web sites, other parents, and local and national mental health organizations (see Appendix II).
- Start keeping your own records, including notes, on your observations.
- Prepare, in advance, for meetings or telephone calls. Know which questions you want to ask and which concerns you want to discuss.
- Follow up to make sure that things occur when promised.
- Complete all required paperwork in a timely fashion, and keep a copy for your records.
- Learn all that you can about your child's diagnosis and his or her rights.
- Monitor your child's progress, and express yourself if you have concerns.

You may need to stand up for your child in several vital situations:

When you face service restrictions. Depending on your child's health-care coverage, your child may or may not have access to the services he or she needs. Work with your child's health-care insurer or your state's Department of Public Welfare to get coverage for the services your child needs.

When you face pharmaceutical restrictions. Some health-care plans cover medications, and others don't. Some health-care plans cover generic medications only. Learn all that you can about your child's health-care coverage, and be prepared to advocate for your child's needs.

When you need to appeal. Every health plan has a formal appeal or grievance process. This process is different from filing or voicing a complaint. Many families find the appeal process to be intimidating and don't bother to take advantage of it. However, many health insurance companies respond favorably to a clear and concise appeal that is in the child's best interest.

Generally, you will be "appealing" to the health insurance company to cover the needed services. You will do this in writing. State your case clearly and explain why your child needs the services or medication that you are requesting. Ask your child's doctor to assist you in this process.

When your child turns 18 and is no longer a student. Most health insurance plans do not cover a child once he or she becomes 18 years of age and is no longer a student. But most plans will cover your child until he or she is 21 if he or she is still in high school, trade school, or college.

If your child's health-care coverage ends, you have several options:

- If your family is insured through an employer health plan, employers are required to allow you to pay for your child's continued coverage. This is expensive but less so than paying out of pocket for your child's health-care services.
- If this is not an option because your family does not receive health-care insurance through an employer, your child may be eligible for Medicaid coverage. Contact the Department of Public Welfare in your state to determine if Medicaid coverage is available to your child.

SUMMARY

As the parent of a child diagnosed with bipolar disorder, you have many challenges and issues with which to deal. In all instances, it is important to learn all that you can in order to advocate for your child's needs. In insurance matters, you need to stay especially vigilant. Fortunately, many useful organizations and resources can help you to learn more about all aspects of health insurance issues specific to your state. You might start by contacting organizations such as the National Alliance for the Mentally Ill (NAMI), the Federation of Families for Children's Mental Health, the Center for Mental Health Services (CMHS), and the Child & Adolescent Bipolar Foundation (CABF). For more information about their Web sites and telephone numbers, as well as information about other organizations, see Appendix II.

EPILOGUE

During the time I studied child psychiatry and until recently, bipolar disorder was rarely considered as a psychiatric diagnosis of children and adolescents. This was due in part to the difficulties encountered making this diagnosis in children, as described in detail in the first chapters of this book. Fortunately, because of the perseverance of some researchers, experienced clinicians, and parents, pediatric bipolar disorder is currently a diagnosis accepted and recognized by most clinicians.

The awareness of the presence of bipolar disorder in children and adolescents has already helped many children who were otherwise treated for other psychiatric conditions, and it has promoted the interest of researchers throughout the world. In fact, in the United States during the last few years the number of studies funded by the National Institute of Mental Health and other nongovernmental agencies have increased substantially. Currently several ongoing studies are evaluating the best way to diagnose children with bipolar disorder and how to recognize the early symptoms, the course and outcome, causes, and the most effective pharmacological and psychosocial treatments for youth with bipolar disorder.

The results of these studies, coupled with advances in the fields of neuroscience, genetics, neuroimaging (e.g., MRIs), pharmacology, and psychotherapy, among others, give us hope that in the near future your children will have the same chances to attain success and happiness as other children. Moreover, you will hopefully be able to enjoy your child without dedicating most of your time to "putting out fires" and worrying about the next recurrence of mania or depression. In the meantime, it is of utmost importance that your child is accurately diagnosed and managed with the current best-treatment practices as described in this book. However, remember, that it is important that you, your family, and child follow through with the clinician's recommendations.

With all my heart, I wish you and your child the best and hope this book will serve as a guide for your child's quick improvement.

APPENDIX I

Questionnaires

This appendix includes several questionnaires to be completed by children about themselves or parents about their children for the following psychiatric disorders:

- Bipolar disorder
- Depression
- Anxiety
- ADHD and behavior disorders
- General functioning

Also, included at the end of this appendix is an example of a mood diary to track the changes in your child's mood symptoms. ***Instructions on how to complete and interpret the mood diary are described in chapter 5.***

With the exception of the scale for bipolar disorder, instructions regarding scoring are included at the end of each questionnaire. Further information regarding the questionnaires is included in chapter 5 under the section about questionnaires. The bipolar disorder questionnaire is currently being studied, and information will be available soon.

Note: These questionnaires are helpful to make the diagnosis of mood, anxiety, or behavior disorders, but by themselves they do not make the diagnosis. A complete psychiatric assessment as described in chapter 5 is necessary.

CHILD MANIA RATING SCALE
Parent Version

INSTRUCTIONS: The following questions concern your child's mood and behavior. Please consider it a problem if it is causing trouble and is beyond what is normal for your child's age. For example, fill in the circle under "Never" if the behavior is not causing trouble.

DOES YOUR CHILD...	0 Never/ Not at all	1 Rarely/ Mild	2 Sometimes/ Moderate	3 Often/ Severe
1. Have periods of feeling super happy for hours or days at a time, extremely wound up and excited, such as feeling "on top of the world"?	O	O	O	O
2. Feel irritable, cranky, or mad for hours or days at a time?	O	O	O	O
3. Think that he or she can be anything or do anything (e.g., leader, best basketball player, rap singer, millionaire, princess) beyond what is usual for that age?	O	O	O	O
4. Believe that he or she has unrealistic abilities or powers that are unusual, and may try to act upon them, which causes trouble?	O	O	O	O
5. Need less sleep than usual; yet does not feel tired the next day?	O	O	O	O
6. Have periods of too much energy?	O	O	O	O
7. Have periods when he or she talks too much or too loud or talks a mile-a-minute?	O	O	O	O
8. Have periods of racing thoughts that his or her mind cannot slow down and it seems that your child's mouth cannot keep up with his or her mind?	O	O	O	O
9. Talk so fast that he or she jumps from topic to topic?	O	O	O	O
10. Rush around doing things nonstop?	O	O	O	O
11. Have trouble staying on track and is easily drawn to what is happening around him or her?	O	O	O	O
12. Do many more things than usual or is unusually productive or highly creative?	O	O	O	O
13. Behave in a sexually inappropriate way (e.g., talks dirty, exposing, playing with private parts, masturbating, making sex phone calls, humping on dogs, playing sex games, touching others sexually)?	O	O	O	O

DOES YOUR CHILD...	0 Never/ Not at all	1 Rarely/ Mild	2 Sometimes/ Moderate	3 Often/ Severe
14. Go and talk to strangers inappropriately or is more socially outgoing than usual?	O	O	O	O
15. Do things that are unusual for him or her that are foolish or risky (e.g., jumping off heights, ordering CDs with your credit card, giving things away)?	O	O	O	O
16. Have rage attacks, intense and prolonged temper tantrums?	O	O	O	O
17. Crack jokes or pun more than usual, laugh loud or act silly in a way that is out of the ordinary?	O	O	O	O
18. Experience rapid mood swings?	O	O	O	O
19. Have any suspicious or strange thoughts?	O	O	O	O
20. Hear voices that no one else can hear?	O	O	O	O
21. See things that no one else can see?	O	O	O	O

A total score of 35 or more suggests that your child *may* have bipolar disorder. Communicate this to your child's clinician.

MOOD AND FEELINGS QUESTIONNAIRE
Parent Version

INSTRUCTIONS: Please darken the circle next to the statement that best describes your child in the **past two weeks.**

	0 Not True	1 Sometimes True	2 True
1. S/he felt miserable or unhappy.	○	○	○
2. S/he didn't enjoy anything at all.	○	○	○
3. S/he was less hungry than usual.	○	○	○
4. S/he ate more than usual.	○	○	○
5. S/he felt so tired s/he just sat around and did nothing.	○	○	○
6. S/he was moving and walking more slowly than usual.	○	○	○
7. S/he was very restless.	○	○	○
8. S/he felt s/he was no good anymore.	○	○	○
9. S/he blamed her/himself for things that weren't his/her fault.	○	○	○
10. It was hard for her/him to make up her/his mind.	○	○	○
11. S/he felt grumpy and cross with you.	○	○	○
12. S/he felt like talking less than usual.	○	○	○
13. S/he was talking more slowly than usual.	○	○	○
14. S/he cried a lot.	○	○	○
15. S/he thought there was nothing good for her/him in the future.	○	○	○
16. S/he thought that life wasn't worth living.	○	○	○
17. S/he thought about death or dying.	○	○	○
18. S/he thought her/his family would be better off without her/him.	○	○	○
19. S/he thought about killing her/himself.	○	○	○
20. S/he didn't want to see her/his friends.	○	○	○
21. S/he found it hard to think properly or concentrate.	○	○	○
22. S/he thought bad things would happen to her/him.	○	○	○

	0 Not True	1 Sometimes True	2 True
23. S/he hated him/herself.	O	O	O
24. S/he felt s/he was a bad person.	O	O	O
25. S/he thought s/he looked ugly.	O	O	O
26. S/he worried about aches and pains.	O	O	O
27. S/he felt lonely.	O	O	O
28. S/he thought nobody really loved her/him.	O	O	O
29. S/he didn't have any fun at school.	O	O	O
30. S/he thought s/he could never be as good as other kids.	O	O	O
31. S/he felt s/he did everything wrong.	O	O	O
32. S/he didn't sleep as well as s/he usually sleeps.	O	O	O
33. S/he slept a lot more than usual.	O	O	O
34. S/he wasn't as happy as usual, even when you praised or rewarded her/him.	O	O	O

A score equal or above 40 is considered significant. If your child endorsed items 16, 17, 18, or 19 (particularly 18 and 19), immediately communicate this information to your child's clinician.

MOOD AND FEELINGS QUESTIONNAIRE
Child Version

INSTRUCTIONS: Please darken the circle next to the statement that best describes you in the **past two weeks.**

	0 Not True	1 Sometimes True	2 True
1. I felt awful or unhappy.	O	O	O
2. I didn't enjoy anything at all.	O	O	O
3. I was less hungry than usual.	O	O	O
4. I ate more than usual.	O	O	O
5. I felt too tired. I just sat around and did nothing.	O	O	O
6. I was moving and walking more slowly than usual.	O	O	O
7. I was very restless.	O	O	O
8. I felt I was no good anymore.	O	O	O
9. I blamed myself for things that weren't my fault.	O	O	O
10. It was hard for me to make up my mind.	O	O	O
11. I felt grumpy and upset with my parents.	O	O	O
12. I felt like talking less than usual.	O	O	O
13. I was talking more slowly than usual.	O	O	O
14. I cried a lot.	O	O	O
15. I thought there was nothing good for me in the future.	O	O	O
16. I thought that life wasn't worth living.	O	O	O
17. I thought about death or dying.	O	O	O
18. I thought my family would be better off without me.	O	O	O
19. I thought about killing myself.	O	O	O
20. I didn't want to see my friends.	O	O	O
21. I found it hard to pay attention or concentrate.	O	O	O
22. I thought bad things would happen to me.	O	O	O

	0 Not True	1 Sometimes True	2 True
23. I hated myself.	○	○	○
24. I felt I was a bad person.	○	○	○
25. I thought I looked ugly.	○	○	○
26. I worried about aches and pains.	○	○	○
27. I felt lonely.	○	○	○
28. I thought nobody really loved me.	○	○	○
29. I didn't have any fun at school.	○	○	○
30. I thought I could never be as good as other kids.	○	○	○
31. I felt I did everything wrong.	○	○	○
32. I didn't sleep as well as I usually sleep.	○	○	○
33. I slept a lot more than usual.	○	○	○

A score equal or above 40 is considered significant. If a child has endorsed items 16, 17, 18, or 19 (particularly 18 and 19), immediately communicate this to the child's clinician.

SCREEN FOR CHILD ANXIETY RELATED DISORDERS (SCARED)
Child Version

INSTRUCTIONS: Below is a list of sentences that describe how people feel. Read each phrase and decide if it is "Not True" or "Sometimes True" or "True" for you. Then for each sentence, fill in one circle that corresponds to the response that seems to describe you for **the last 3 months.**

	0 Not True	1 Sometimes True	2 True
1. When I feel frightened, it is hard to breathe.	O	O	O
2. I get headaches when I am at school.	O	O	O
3. I don't like to be with people I don't know well.	O	O	O
4. I get scared if I sleep away from home.	O	O	O
5. I worry about other people liking me.	O	O	O
6. When I get frightened, I feel like passing out.	O	O	O
7. I am nervous.	O	O	O
8. I follow my mother or father wherever they go.	O	O	O
9. People tell me that I look nervous.	O	O	O
10. I feel nervous with people I don't know well.	O	O	O
11. I get stomachaches at school.	O	O	O
12. When I get frightened, I feel like I am going crazy.	O	O	O
13. I worry about sleeping alone.	O	O	O
14. I worry about being as good as other kids.	O	O	O
15. When I get frightened, I feel like things are not real.	O	O	O
16. I have nightmares about something bad happening to my parents.	O	O	O
17. I worry about going to school.	O	O	O
18. When I get frightened, my heart beats fast.	O	O	O
19. I get shaky.	O	O	O
20. I have nightmares about something bad happening to me.	O	O	O
21. I worry about things working out for me.	O	O	O

	0 Not True	1 Sometimes True	2 True
22. When I get frightened, I sweat a lot.	○	○	○
23. I am a worrier.	○	○	○
24. I get really frightened for no reason at all.	○	○	○
25. I am afraid to be alone in the house.	○	○	○
26. It is hard for me to talk with people I don't know well.	○	○	○
27. When I get frightened, I feel like I am choking.	○	○	○
28. People tell me that I worry too much.	○	○	○
29. I don't like to be away from my family.	○	○	○
30. I am afraid of having anxiety (or panic) attacks.	○	○	○
31. I worry that something bad might happen to my parents.	○	○	○
32. I feel shy with people I don't know well.	○	○	○
33. I worry about what is going to happen in the future.	○	○	○
34. When I get frightened, I feel like throwing up.	○	○	○
35. I worry about how well I do things.	○	○	○
36. I am scared to go to school.	○	○	○
37. I worry about things that have already happened.	○	○	○
38. When I get frightened, I feel dizzy.	○	○	○
39. I feel nervous when I am with other children or adults and I have to do something while they watch me (for example: read aloud, speak, play a game, play a sport).	○	○	○
40. I feel nervous when I am going to parties, dances, or any place where there will be people that I don't know well.	○	○	○
41. I am shy.	○	○	○

SCORING:

A total score of ≥**25** may indicate the presence of an **Anxiety Disorder.** Scores higher than 30 are more specific.

A score of **7** for items 1, 6, 9, 12, 15, 18, 19, 22, 24, 27, 30, 34, 38 may indicate **Panic Disorder** or **Significant Somatic Symptoms.**

A score of **9** for items 5, 7, 14, 21, 23, 28, 33, 35, 37 may indicate **Generalized Anxiety Disorder.**

A score of **5** for items 4, 8, 13, 16, 20, 25, 29, 31 may indicate **Separation Anxiety Disorder.**

A score of **8** for items 3, 10, 26, 32, 39, 40, 41 may indicate **Social Anxiety Disorder.**

A score of **3** for items 2, 11, 17, 36 may indicate **Significant School Avoidance.**

SCREEN FOR CHILD ANXIETY RELATED DISORDERS (SCARED)
Parent Version

INSTRUCTIONS: Below is a list of statements that describe how people feel. Read each statement carefully and decide if it is "Not True" or "Sometimes True" or "True" for your child. Then for each statement, fill in one circle that corresponds to the response that seems to describe your child for **the last 3 months.** Please respond to all statements as well as you can, even if some do not seem to concern your child.

	0 Not True	1 Sometimes True	2 True
1. When my child feels frightened, it is hard for him/her to breathe.	○	○	○
2. My child gets headaches when he/she is at school.	○	○	○
3. My child doesn't like to be with people he/she doesn't know well.	○	○	○
4. My child gets scared if he/she sleeps away from home.	○	○	○
5. My child worries about other people liking him/her.	○	○	○
6. When my child gets frightened, he/she feels like passing out.	○	○	○
7. My child is nervous.	○	○	○
8. My child follows me wherever I go.	○	○	○
9. People tell me that my child looks nervous.	○	○	○
10. My child feels nervous with people he/she doesn't know well.	○	○	○
11. My child gets stomachaches at school.	○	○	○
12. When my child gets frightened, he/she feels like he/she is going crazy.	○	○	○
13. My child worries about sleeping alone.	○	○	○
14. My child worries about being as good as other kids.	○	○	○
15. When he/she gets frightened, he/she feels like things are not real.	○	○	○
16. My child has nightmares about something bad happening to his/her parents.	○	○	○
17. My child worries about going to school.	○	○	○

	0 Not True	1 Sometimes True	2 True
18. When my child gets frightened, his/her heart beats fast.	○	○	○
19. He/she gets shaky.	○	○	○
20. My child has nightmares about something bad happening to him/her.	○	○	○
21. My child worries about things working out for him/her.	○	○	○
22. When my child gets frightened, he/she sweats a lot.	○	○	○
23. My child is a worrier.	○	○	○
24. My child gets really frightened for no reason at all.	○	○	○
25. My child is afraid to be alone in the house.	○	○	○
26. It is hard for my child to talk with people he/she doesn't know well.	○	○	○
27. When my child gets frightened, he/she feels like he/she is choking.	○	○	○
28. People tell me that my child worries too much.	○	○	○
29. My child doesn't like to be away from his/her family.	○	○	○
30. My child is afraid of having anxiety (or panic) attacks.	○	○	○
31. My child worries that something bad might happen to his/her parents.	○	○	○
32. My child feels shy with people he/she doesn't know well.	○	○	○
33. My child worries about what is going to happen in the future.	○	○	○
34. When my child gets frightened, he/she feels like throwing up.	○	○	○
35. My child worries about how well he/she does things.	○	○	○
36. My child is scared to go to school.	○	○	○
37. My child worries about things that have already happened.	○	○	○
38. When my child gets frightened, he/she feels dizzy.	○	○	○
39. My child feels nervous when he/she is with other children or adults and he/she has to do something while they watch him/her (for example: read aloud, speak, play a game, play a sport).	○	○	○

	0 Not True	1 Sometimes True	2 True
40. My child feels nervous when he/she is going to parties, dances, or any place where there will be people that he/she doesn't know well.	○	○	○
41. My child is shy.	○	○	○

SCORING:

A total score of ≥25 may indicate the presence of an **Anxiety Disorder**. Scores higher than 30 are more specific.

A score of **7** for items 1, 6, 9, 12, 15, 18, 19, 22, 24, 27, 30, 34, 38 may indicate **Panic Disorder** or **Significant Somatic Symptoms.**

A score of **9** for items 5, 7, 14, 21, 23, 28, 33, 35, 37 may indicate **Generalized Anxiety Disorder.**

A score of **5** for items 4, 8, 13, 16, 20, 25, 29, 31 may indicate **Separation Anxiety Disorder.**

A score of **8** for items 3, 10, 26, 32, 39, 40, 41 may indicate **Social Anxiety Disorder.**

A score of **3** for items 2, 11, 17, 36 may indicate **Significant School Avoidance.**

DBD RATING SCALE

Parent Version

INSTRUCTIONS: Read each item below carefully and fill in the circle next to the number that represents your choice; do not mark between two choices. Please be sure to answer every item.

	0 Not at all	1 Just a little	2 Pretty much	3 Very much
1. Fails to give close attention to details or makes careless mistakes in schoolwork, work, or other activities	O	O	O	O
2. Has difficulty sustaining attention in tasks or play activities	O	O	O	O
3. Does not seem to listen to what is being said to him or her	O	O	O	O
4. Does not follow through on instructions and fails to finish schoolwork, chores, or duties in the workplace (not due to oppositional behavior or failure to understand instructions)	O	O	O	O
5. Has difficulty organizing tasks and activities	O	O	O	O
6. Avoids, expresses reluctance about, or has difficulties engaging in tasks that require sustained mental effort (such as schoolwork or homework)	O	O	O	O
7. Loses things necessary for tasks or activities (e.g., school assignments, pencils, books, tools, or toys)	O	O	O	O
8. Is easily distracted by extraneous stimuli	O	O	O	O
9. Is forgetful in daily activities	O	O	O	O
10. Fidgets with hands or feet or squirms in seat	O	O	O	O
11. Leaves seat in classroom or in other situations in which remaining seated is expected	O	O	O	O
12. Runs about or climbs excessively in situations where it is inappropriate	O	O	O	O
13. Has difficulty playing or engaging in leisure activities quietly	O	O	O	O
14. Is always "on the go" or acts as if "driven by a motor"	O	O	O	O
15. Talks excessively	O	O	O	O
16. Blurts out answers to questions before the questions have been completed	O	O	O	O

	0 Not at all	1 Just a little	2 Pretty much	3 Very much
17. Has difficulty waiting in lines or awaiting turn in games or group situations	O	O	O	O
18. Interrupts or intrudes on others (e.g., butts into others' conversations or games)	O	O	O	O
19. Loses temper	O	O	O	O
20. Argues with adults	O	O	O	O
21. Actively defies or refuses adult requests or rules	O	O	O	O
22. Does things that deliberately annoy people	O	O	O	O
23. Blames others for his or her mistakes or misbehavior	O	O	O	O
24. Is touchy or easily annoyed by others	O	O	O	O
25. Is angry and resentful	O	O	O	O
26. Is spiteful or vindictive	O	O	O	O
27. Often bullies or intimidates others	O	O	O	O
28. Often initiates physical fights	O	O	O	O
29. Used a weapon that can cause serious harm to others (e.g., a bat, brick, broken bottle, knife, gun)	O	O	O	O
30. Been physically cruel to people	O	O	O	O
31. Been physically cruel to animals	O	O	O	O
32. Stolen while confronting a victim (e.g., mugging, purse snatching, extortion, armed robbery)	O	O	O	O
33. Forced someone into sexual activity	O	O	O	O
34. Deliberately engaged in firesetting with intention of causing serious damage	O	O	O	O
35. Deliberately destroyed others' property (other than by firesetting)	O	O	O	O
36. Broken into someone else's house, building, or car	O	O	O	O
37. Lies to obtain goods or favors or to avoid obligations (i.e., "cons" others)	O	O	O	O
38. Stolen items of nontrivial value w/o confronting a victim (e.g., shoplifting, but without breaking and entering; forgery)	O	O	O	O

	0 Not at all	1 Just a little	2 Pretty much	3 Very much
39. Stays out at night despite parental prohibitions, beginning before age 13	◯	◯	◯	◯
40. Run away from home overnight at least twice while living in parental home or parental surrogate home (or once without returning for a lengthy period)	◯	◯	◯	◯
41. Often truant from school, beginning before age 13	◯	◯	◯	◯

HOW TO SCORE THE DBD

To determine if your child meets the symptom criteria for DSM-IV diagnoses of Attention-Deficit/Hyperactivity Disorder, Oppositional Defiant Disorder, or Conduct Disorder as measured by the DBD Parent / Teacher Rating Scale, count the number of symptoms that are endorsed "pretty much" or "very much" by either parent or teacher in each of the following categories: Note that impairment and other criteria (see chapter 2) must be evaluated in addition to symptom counts.

Attention-Deficit/Hyperactivity Disorder–Inattention Symptoms (items 9, 18, 23, 27, 29, 34, 37, 42, 44): 6 or more items must be endorsed as "pretty much" or "very much" to meet criteria for Attention-Deficit/Hyperactivity Disorder, Predominantly Inattentive Type. The six items may be endorsed on the teacher DBD, the parent DBD, or can be a combination of items from both rating scales (e.g., 4 symptoms endorsed on the teacher DBD and 2 separate symptoms endorsed on the parent DBD). The same symptom should not be counted twice if it appears on both versions (parent and teacher) of the rating scale.

Attention-Deficit/Hyperactivity Disorder–Hyperactivity/Impulsivity Symptoms (items 1, 7, 12, 19, 22, 25, 30, 33, 35): 6 or more items must be endorsed as "pretty much" or "very much" on the parent and/or the teacher DBD to meet criteria for Attention-Deficit/Hyperactivity Disorder, Predominantly Hyperactive-Impulsive Type.

If 6 or more items are endorsed for Attention-Deficit/Hyperactivity Disorder–Inattention and 6 or more items are endorsed for Attention-Deficit/Hyperactivity Disorder–Hyperactivity/Impulsivity, then criteria is met for **Attention-Deficit/Hyperactivity Disorder, Combined Type**. Some impairment from the symptoms must be present in two or more settings (e.g., school, home).

Oppositional Defiant Disorder (items 3, 13, 15, 17, 24, 26, 28, 39): A total of 4 or more items must be endorsed as "pretty much" or "very much" on either the parent or the teacher DBD to meet criteria for Oppositional Defiant Disorder.

Conduct Disorder: Aggression to people and animals (items 6, 20, 31, 32, 36, 40, 45); destruction of property (items 16, 41); deceitfulness or theft (items 4, 8, 43); and serious violation of rules (items 2, 11, 38). A total of 3 or more items in any category or any combination of categories must be endorsed as "pretty much" or "very much" on either the parent or the teacher DBD to meet criteria for Conduct Disorder.

MOOD DIARY

Name: _____

Instructions: On the 0–10 scale, please mark the number that best describes your mood for the day.
0 = very sad, 5 = feeling okay, 10 = super-happy

Monday/Date: _____
☹ 0   1   2   3   4   5   6   7   8   9   10   ☺

Comments: _____
_____
_____

Tuesday/Date: _____
☹ 0   1   2   3   4   5   6   7   8   9   10   ☺

Comments: _____
_____
_____

Wednesday/Date: _____
☹ 0   1   2   3   4   5   6   7   8   9   10   ☺

Comments: _____
_____
_____

Thursday/Date: _____
☹ 0   1   2   3   4   5   6   7   8   9   10   ☺

Comments: _____
_____
_____

Friday/Date: _____
☹ 0   1   2   3   4   5   6   7   8   9   10   ☺

Comments: _____
_____
_____

Saturday/Date: _____

☹   0   1   2   3   4   5   6   7   8   9   10   ☺

Comments: _____

_____

_____

Sunday/Date: _____

☹   0   1   2   3   4   5   6   7   8   9   10   ☺

Comments: _____

_____

_____

Instructions on how to complete the mood diary are described in chapter 5.

APPENDIX II

Resources for Parents of Children with Bipolar Disorder

This appendix includes the following information regarding adult and child bipolar disorder and other relevant topics:

- National Bipolar and other Mental Health Organizations
- Internet/Web Sites
- Education Resources
- Research Clinics in North America studying bipolar disorder in youth
- Books for parents, children, and clinicians about bipolar disorders and other related issues

Unless indicated, I am not endorsing any particular resource. However, I think that it is important to compare different sources of information.

NATIONAL BIPOLAR AND OTHER MENTAL HEALTH ORGANIZATIONS

American Psychiatric Association (APA), 1000 Wilson Boulevard, Suite 1825, Arlington, VA 22209-3901; phone: (888) 35-PSYCH (77924) or (703) 907-7300; www.apa.com. A scientific and professional organization that represents psychiatrists in the United States. The Web site contains information about books, conferences, tips on choosing a psychiatrist, research news, and other resources.

American Psychological Association (APA), 750 First Street, NE, Washington, D.C. 20002-4242; phone: (800) 374-2721 or (202) 336-5500; www.apa.org. The APA is a scientific and professional organization that represents psychology in the United States. On this site, you can find about conferences, books for parents and children, psychologists in your area, testing research, and other information that might be helpful for the management of your child.

Child & Adolescent Bipolar Foundation (CABF), 1187 Wilmette Ave., #PMB 331, Wilmette, IL 60091; phone: (847) 256-8525; www.bpkids.org. CABF is a unique parent-led organization whose goal is to provide information and support to family members, health-care professionals, and the public concerning bipolar disorder in the young. CABF advocates for health services and research on the nature, causes, and treatment of early-onset bipolar disorder. On its Web site, you will find many resources and education for parents of children with bipolar disorder. In addition, you will find information regarding child psychiatrists interested in the treatment of bipolar disorder or discover news about new studies and information regarding other reliable Web sites.

National Alliance for Research on Schizophrenia and Depression, 60 Cutter Mill Road, Suite 404, Great Neck, NY 11021; phone: (800) 829-8289; www.narsad.org. This is the largest donor-supported, nongovernmental organization dedicated to raising and distributing funds for research into the nature, causes, treatments, and prevention of severe mental illnesses, including bipolar disorder, schizophrenia, depression, and severe anxiety disorders. The Web site includes up-to-date information about the diagnosis and treatment of severe psychiatric disorders.

National Alliance for the Mentally Ill (NAMI), 200 N. Glebe Road, Suite 1015, Arlington, VA 22203-3754; phone: (800) 950-NAMI (6264); www.nami.org. NAMI is a self-help, support, and advocacy organization for people with severe mental illnesses, their family members, and friends. On its Web site, you will find reliable information about diagnoses, treatment, sources of support, books, and many other relevant issues for people with psychiatric disorders. In some states NAMI offers a program for families called Hand-by-Hand.

American Academy of Child and Adolescent Psychiatry (AACAP), 3615 Wisconsin Ave., N.W., Washington, D.C. 20016-3007; phone: (202) 966-7300; fax: (202) 966-2891; www.aacap.org. The AACAP is a scientific and professional organization that represents child psychiatrists in the United States. Its Web site is designed to serve members, parents, and families. You will find information about child and adolescent psychiatry, current research, conferences, information for parents, and other resources. It has information for parents in English and Spanish.

Depressed and Bipolar Support Alliance (DBSA) (previously known as the **National Depressive and Manic-Depressive Association**), 730 N. Franklin St., Suite 501, Chicago, IL 60610-7204; phone: (800) 826-3632 or (312) 642-0039; fax: (312) 642-7243; www.dbsalliance.org. The DBSA is devoted to educating consumers and their family members about mood disorders, decreasing the public stigma of these illnesses, fostering self-help, advocating for research funding, improving access to care, and it also has a link to find mental health and professionals in your area and other resources.

National Mental Health Association, 2001 N. Beauregard St., Alexandria, VA 22311; phone: (800) 969-NMHA (6642); www.nmha.org. The National Mental Health Association is the country's oldest and largest nonprofit organization addressing all aspects of mental health and mental illness. NMHA works to improve the mental health of people with mental disorders, through advocacy, education, research, and service.

INTERNET RESOURCES/WEB SITES

Internet Resources Specific to Children with Bipolar Disorder

The Bipolar Child (www.bipolarchild.com)
This Web site provides general information about bipolar disorder in youth, news about new research, an e-mail newsletter, and other resources.

Bipolar Significant Others (BPSO) (www.BPSO.org)
This is an Internet support group for people in relationships with someone who has a bipolar disorder (children, parents, siblings, spouses, etc.).

Bipolar World Web Site (www.bipolarworld.net)
This site provides general information on bipolar diagnosis, treatments, and suicide; an "ask the doctor" link; personal stories; information on disabilities and stigma; community and family support; relevant books; a bipolar message board; and chat rooms.

Child & Adolescent Bipolar Foundation (CABF) (www.bpkids.org)
This is the best and most reliable Web site for parents of children with bipolar disorder. It offers online support groups, chat rooms, message boards, a learning center, a database of professional members and local support groups, a resource page with information on Social Security, educational laws, a drug database, information about studies and publications, books, and international resources. It also provides a list of psychiatrists interested in treating bipolar children across the world.

Juvenile Bipolar Research Foundation (JBRF) (www.bpchildresearch.org)
This site provides general information about bipolar disorder in youth, news about new research, screening questionnaires, professional listservs for physicians and thera-

pists treating children, Grand Rounds Program (bimonthly online clinical case conferences with parental questions addressed by international experts), and discussion forums for parents and educators.

Lithium Information Center c/o Madison Institute of Medicine (www.wpic.pitt.edu/STANLEY/images/othrnws/lithinfo.htm)

This center compiles all information available regarding lithium.

National Institute of Mental Health Publications (www.nimh.nih.gov/publicat/bipolar.cfm)

This site provides excellent up-to-date information on the symptoms, course, causes, and treatment of bipolar disorder in children and adults. Separate sections are devoted to child and adolescent bipolar illness, suicide, medical treatments and their side effects, co-occurring illnesses, psychosocial treatments, sources of help for individuals and families, and clinical research studies.

Suicide Hotline (www.suicidehotlines.com)

This Web site includes toll-free phone numbers for all states in the United States for teens and parents of teens who are in crisis and have suicidal thoughts.

Note: For more information regarding help during a crisis, you can check the front of your phone book for suicide prevention, hotlines: crisis or suicide, crisis intervention, or mental health centers or emergency rooms.

Other important Web sites are described under "National Bipolar and Other Mental Health Organizations" earlier.

Other Relevant Internet Resources

Anxiety Disorders Association of America (www.adaa.org)

This Web site may be useful because many children and teens with bipolar disorder also have anxiety disorders.

Bridge to Understanding (www.bridgetounderstanding.com)

This Web site will inform about special schools for children and teens with mood and behavior problems.

Children and Adults with Attention-Deficit/Hyperactivity Disorder (CHADD) (www.chadd.org)

This Web site gives reliable information regarding education, support, and research for youth and adults with ADHD. Since children with bipolar disorder usually have ADHD, this site is a very important source of information for parents and clinicians.

Federation of Families for Children's Mental Health (www.ffcmh.org)

A national parent-run advocacy and support organization for children and youth with emotional, behavioral, or mental disorders and their families.

National Attention Deficit Disorder Association (www.add.org)

This Web site offers support and information for parents of children with ADHD and adults with this disorder.

National Library of Medicine (www.nlm.nih.gov/medlineplus)

Free access to Medline, where over 4,000 biomedical journals are archived. Click on "Other Resources" and then on "MEDLINE" to conduct a search of articles dating back to the 1960s. Some full-text articles are available; others are abstracts.

National Association of School Psychologists (www.nasponline.org)

This Web site includes numerous tips for parents and teachers on helping children with school related issues like how to manage off-task behaviors, impulsivity, violent behaviors, and learning disabilities and how to advocate for your child. It includes several links to other important Web sites.

Pendulum Resources (www.pendulum.org)

Offers information about the *DSM-IV* diagnostic criteria, current medical treatments, books favored by mental health consumers and family members, articles on how to cope with depression on bipolar disorder in yourself or a loved one, writings and poetry by people with bipolar disorder, links to other relevant sites, and updates on research studies.

Struggling Teens (www.strugglingteens.com)

This is an Internet resource for parents who are struggling with their children. You'll find a wide variety of resources for your child such as special camps (e.g., for ADHD, boot, and wilderness camps), keep up-to-date on current news, and ideas from and about schools and programs (e.g., residential), educational consultants, chat rooms, and news.

Teaching LD.Org (www.teachingLD.org)

The Web site for the Division of Learning Disabilities for the Council of Teaching Exceptional Children is a good resource for parents and teachers who have or are working with children with psychiatric disorders.

Center for Mental Health Services (CMHS) (www.mentalwealth.org)

The Child, Adolescent and Family Branch of the federal Center for Mental Health Services promotes and ensures that the mental health needs of children and their families are met within the context of community-based systems of care.

Education Resources

ADA, IDEA, and Section 504. ERIC Digest E537. Educational Resources Informational Center (ERIC) Web site. Available at www.ed.gov/databases/ERIC_Digests/ed389142.html.

ADA, IDEA, and Section 504. Update 2001. ERIC EC Digest #E606. Educational Resources Informational Center (ERIC) Web site. Available at www.ldonline.org/ld_indepth/legal/legislative/update_504_2001.html.

Child & Adolescent Bipolar Foundation (CABFS). The CABFS's Web site, www.bpkids.org, also is a very helpful resource for information regarding accommodations of school to fit the needs of children with bipolar disorder.

National Association of School Psychologists (www.nasponline.org). This Web site also includes numerous tips for parents and teachers on helping children with school-related issues such as how to manage off-task behaviors, impulsivity, violent behaviors, and learning disabilities and how to advocate for your child. It includes several links to other important Web sites.

The National Information Center for Children and Youth with Disabilities (NICHCY) (www.nichcy.org)

NICHCY is a national information center that provides information on disabilities and disability-related issues. For example, this Web site has information about special education and related services, individualized education programs, parents' materials, disability and professional associations, laws, and education rights. It also connects you with resources in your state.

The National Association of State Directors of Special Education (NASDSE) (www.nasdse.org)

This Web site contains useful information regarding education for children with and without disabilities.

Negotiating the Special Education Maze (www.ldonline.org/ld_indepth/parenting/maze.html)

Learning disabilities OnLine: LD. This Web site provides guides and information regarding resources for special education.

Office for Dispute Resolution ([800] 222-3353). This group provides service coordination on mediation and due process hearings for school districts and mutually agreed-on written agreements (MAWAs) in technical assistance and scheduling.

Parent Education Network, Consultation, and Office of Dispute Resolution.
There is one for each state. For example, Pennsylvania has the following: Parent Education Network, (800) 522-5827, is a statewide federally funded project through the Office of Special Education Programs (OSEP) to provide information and support to parents of children with disabilities throughout Pennsylvania.

Special Education Regulations (www.ed.gov). Visit the U.S. Department of Education, in particular the policy section and parents' guides.

Special Education Consultline ([800] 879-2301) is a program of the Department of Education, Bureau of Special Education, for use by parents or parent support organizations to answer questions about school-related concerns, special education, and the compliant system. It is designed to be a one-stop service on special education services and programs for parents.

Teaching LD.Org (www.teachingLD.org). The Web site for the Division of Learning disabilities for the Council of Teaching Exceptional Children is a good resource for parents and teachers who have or are working with children with psychiatric disorders.

Research Clinics in North America Studying Bipolar Disorder in Youth

Some of the following clinics are conducting numerous studies about the symptoms, course and outcome, biology, and treatment of bipolar disorder in children and teens. However, by the time this book is published, the studies may be completed, and new investigations across North America and other countries might have been initiated. Even if your city or state is not mentioned in this list, it is recommended that you call the investigators and ask whether they are aware of any other ongoing bipolar research studies in your area.

Baltimore, Maryland: Johns Hopkins Hospital, Johns Hopkins Children's Center, Division of Child & Adolescent Psychiatry, 600 North Wolfe Street, Baltimore, MD 21287; phone: (410) 955-5823; John Walkup, M.D. Dr. Walkup and colleagues are evaluating the effects of medications for the treatment of youth with bipolar disorder.

Baltimore, Maryland: The George Washington University, 2121 Eye St., Washington, D.C. 20052; phone: (202) 994-4949; Joshi Paramjit, M.D. Dr. Paramjit and colleagues are evaluating the effect of medications for the treatment of bipolar youth.

Bethesda, Maryland (National Institute of Mental Health): NIMH Public Inquiries, 6001 Executive Blvd., Room 8184, MSC 9663, Bethesda, MD 20892-9663, phone: (301) 443-4513; fax: (301) 443-4279; TTY: (301) 443-8431; Ellen Leibenluft, M.D. Dr. Leibenluft and colleagues are carrying out medication studies for children with bipolar disorder who have not responded well to prior medications and medications for children and teens with irritability, trouble handling frustration (severe temper tantrums and rages), and "hyper" behavior (distractible, hyperactivity, trouble sleeping).

Boston, Massachusetts: Massachusetts General Hospital, Pediatric Psychopharmacology Unit, Wang Building, Room 725, 15 Parkman St., Boston, MA 02114; phone: (617) 724-4644 or (617) 724-9734; Joseph Biederman, M.D., Janet Wozniak, M.D., Tim Willens, M.D., Tom Spencer, M.D. The Massachusetts General Hospital group is currently involved in medication studies for depression in children with and without bipolar disorders, youth with bipolar disorder who also have ADHD, and teens with substance abuse (use of illicit drugs or alcohol) and bipolar disorders.

Belmont, Massachusetts: The McLean Hospital Child Outpatient Clinic in Belmont, MA, 02478; phone: (617) 855-2880; Jean A. Frazier, M.D. Dr. Frazier is evaluating the brain of children with bipolar disorder or ADHD using magnetic resonance imaging (MRI).

Boulder, Colorado: University of Colorado at Boulder, Department of Psychology, Boulder, CO 80309-0345; phone: (303) 492-1411; David Miklowitz, Ph.D. Dr. Miklowitz and colleagues are studying the usefulness of family therapy for the treatment of teens with bipolar disorder.

Chapel Hill, North Carolina: University of North Carolina, Department of Psychology, Campus Box 3270, Davie Hall, Chapel Hill, NC 27599-3270; phone: (919) 962-1000; David Miklowitz, Ph.D. Dr. Miklowitz and colleagues are studying the usefulness of family therapy as adjunctive treatment for teens with bipolar disorder.

Chicago, Illinois: University of Illinois at Chicago, Institute for Juvenile Research (MC747), Section of Child Psychiatry, 840 South Wood St., Chicago, IL 60612; phone: (312) 996-2200 or (312) 413-1722; Mani Pavuluri, M.D. Dr. Pavuluri and colleagues are studying the use of a parent rating scale to screen for bipolar disorder in children and teens. In addition, they are evaluating the biological causes of bipolar disorder using functional magnetic resonance imaging (fMRI) of the brain and neuropsychological testing.

Cincinnati, Ohio: Pediatric Bipolar Program at Children's Hospital Medical Center of Cincinnati, 3333 Barnet Ave., Cincinnati, OH 45229; phone: (513) 636-4124; Robert A. Kowatch, M.D., and Melissa DelBello, M.D. Drs. Kowatch and DelBello are carrying out medication studies for children and teens with bipolar disorder.

Cleveland, Ohio: The Stanley Research Center, Case Western Reserve University; University Hospitals of Cleveland, Department of Psychiatry, 11100 Euclid Ave., Cleveland, OH 44106; phone: (216) 844-3881; Robert L. Findling, M.D. Dr. Findling is carrying out medication studies for children and teens with bipolar disorder.

Columbus, Ohio: Division of Child and Adolescent Psychiatry, The Ohio State University, 1670 Upham Dr., Columbus, OH 43210-1250; phone: (614) 292-6446; Mary Fristad, Ph.D. Dr. Fristad is studying the usefulness of group education as an adjunctive intervention to existing treatment for families of children who have mood disorders.

Dallas, Texas: Pediatric Bipolar Disorders Program, Southwestern Medical Center at Dallas and Children's Medical Center of Dallas Children's Medical Center of Dallas, 6363 Forest Park, UT, 5323 Harry Hines Blvd., Dallas, TX 75390-8589; phone: (214) 648-5322 or (214) 456-2416; fax: (214) 456-5941; Russell Scheffer, M.D., and Graham Emslie, M.D. Drs. Scheffer and Emslie are evaluating the effects of medications for treating youth with bipolar disorder.

Galveston, Texas: University of Texas, Galveston, TX 77555-0425; phone: (409) 772-2885; Karen Wagner, M.D. Dr. Wagner and colleagues are evaluating the effect of medications for the treatment of youth with bipolar disorder.

Glen Oaks, New York: Long Island Jewish Medical Center, Adolescent Mood Disorder Program, Hillside Hospital, 75-59 263d St., Glen Oaks, NY 11004; phone: (718) 470-8556; Vivian Kafantaris, M.D. Dr. Kafantaris is studying the effects of medications for children and teens with bipolar disorder with and without psychosis.

Halifax, Nova Scotia, Canada: Dalhousie University Medical School, Department of Psychiatry, The IWK-Grace Health Sciences Center, 5850 University Ave., P.O. Box 3070, Halifax NS B3J 3G9 Canada; phone: (902) 428-8375; Stan Kutcher, M.D. Dr. Kutcher and colleagues are investigating the effects of medications for youth with bipolar disorder.

Hamilton, Canada: Chedoke Child and Family Center—Mood Disorders Team, Hamilton Health Sciences, POB 2000, 1200 Main St. West, Hamilton, Ontario L8N 3Z5, Canada; phone: (905) 521-2100, ext. 77350; Mood Disorders Program, St. Joseph's Healthcare Hamilton, Center for Mountain Heath Services, 100 West 5th St., Hamilton, Ontario L8N 3K7, Canada; phone: (905) 522-1155, ext. 5419; Kathy MacDonald, M.D.; and Khrista Boylan, M.D.

Los Angeles, California: Adolescent Mood Disorders Program, University of California Los Angeles (UCLA), Neuropsychiatric Institute, 760 Westwood Plaza, Los

Angeles, CA 90024; Pablo Davanzo, M.D. (phone: [310] 825-0469) and Michael Strober, Ph.D. (phone: [310] 825-5730). Dr. Davanzo is investigating the biological causes of bipolar disorder in children and adolescents, and Dr. Strober is studying the course and outcome of bipolar disorder in youth.

Milwaukee, Wisconsin: Children's Hospital of Wisconsin, 9000 W. Wisconsin Avenue, MS #750; phone: (414) 266-2932. Russell E. Scheffer, M.D. Dr. Scheffer is pursuing treatment studies for children with bipolar disorders and comorbid ADHD.

Montreal, Canada: Bipolar Disorder Clinic, Department of Psychiatry, Montreal Children's Hospital, 4018 Ste-Catherine West Montreal, QC H3Z 1P2, Canada; phone: (514) 412-4449; fax: (514) 412 43 37; Fiona Key, M.D., and Eric Fombonne, M.D.

Philadelphia, Pennsylvania: Children's Hospital of Philadelphia, Department of Child and Adolescent Psychiatry, 34th Street and Civic Center Blvd., Philadelphia, PA 19104-4399; phone: (215) 590-7573; Elizabeth Weller, M.D.

Philadelphia, Pennsylvania: Thomas Jefferson University, 833 Chestnut Street, Suite 210-D, Philadelphia, PA 19107; phone: (215) 955-8180; Gail Edelsohn, M.D. and Harris Ravinovich, M.D.; Drs. Edelsohn and Ravinovich are currently performing a treatment study for teens with bipolar disorder.

Pittsburgh, Pennsylvania: Child and Adolescent Bipolar Services (CABS), 100 North Bellefield Ave., Bellefield Towers, #612, Pittsburgh, PA 15213; phone: (412) 624-CABS (2227) or (877) 851-CABS; David Axelson, M.D., and Boris Birmaher, M.D. Drs. Axelson and Birmaher are studying the biological causes, course and outcome, and medication and family therapy treatment of bipolar disorder in youth. In addition, they are evaluating the first manifestations of bipolar disorder in children whose parents have bipolar disorder.

Providence, Rhode Island: COBY Study, 345 Blackstone Blvd.; Providence, RI; phone: (866) 279-KIDS (5437); Martin Keller, M.D., and Henrietta Leonard, M.D. Dr. Keller and colleagues are investigating the course and outcome of bipolar disorder in youth.

Richmond, Virginia: Virginia Commonwealth University, MCV Campus, 515 North 10th Street, P.O. Box 980489, Richmond, Virginia 23298; phone: (804) 628-0088; Directors Julie Linker, Ph.D., and Bela Sood, M.D. Drs. Linker and Sood are studying the symptoms and treatment of bipolar children.

San Antonio, Texas: University of Texas Health Science Center at San Antonio, 7703 Floyd Curl Drive, San Antonio, TX 78229; phone: (210) 567-5492; Jair Soares, M.D.

Dr. Soares and colleagues are studying the biological causes of bipolar disorders in children and teens using MRI.

Stanford, California: Stanford Pediatric Mood Disorders Clinic, Stanford University School of Medicine, 401 Quarry Road, Stanford, CA 94305; phone: (650) 723-5511; Kiki Chang, M.D. Dr. Chang and colleagues are evaluating the use of medications, genetics, early manifestations. and biological causes of bipolar disorder in children and teens.

St. Louis, Missouri: Washington University Child Psychiatry Clinic at Children's Hospital, Montclair Building, 24 South Kingsway, St. Louis, MO 63108; phone: (314) 286-1740; Barbara Geller, M.D., and Joan Luby, M.D. Drs. Geller and Luby are studying the manifestations, course and outcome, and medication treatment of children and teens with bipolar disorder.

Stony Brook, New York: Division of Child and Adolescent Psychiatry, State University of New York at Stony Brook, Putnam Hall—South Campus, Stony Brook, NY 11974; phone: (631) 632-8850; Gabrielle Carlson, M.D. Dr. Carlson and colleagues are studying the manifestations and response to medications for children and teens with bipolar disorder.

There are other particular child psychiatrists and psychologists treating children and teens with bipolar disorder. A list of these doctors across the world can be found on the Web site of the Child & Adolescent Bipolar Foundation (CABF), described above.

BOOKS AND ADDITIONAL RESOURCES ABOUT BIPOLAR DISORDERS AND OTHER RELEVANT ISSUES

Note: The Child & Adolescent Bipolar Foundation (CABF) maintains an updated list of books relevant for bipolar disorder in their Web site bpkids.org.

Books and Videos Written for Parents About Children with Bipolar Disorder

Clinicians, teachers, and counselors can also benefit from reading these books.

Carlson, T. *The life of a bipolar child: What every parent and professional needs to know* (originally published as *The Suicide of My Son*). Duluth, MN: Benline, 2000. The year-by-year description of a boy's life with emerging bipolar disorder and the effects of his illness on functioning through each year of school until his death at age 14.

Fristad, M., and J. Goldberg Arnold. *Raising a moody child: How to cope with depression and bipolar disorder*. New York: The Guilford Press, 2004. Two esteemed child therapy experts explain the numerous medical and therapeutic options in lay language for parents seeking help for their child with depression or bipolar disorder.

Isaac, G. *Bipolar, not ADHD: Unrecognized epidemic of manic depressive illness in children*. Writers Club, 2001. Carlsbad, CA: This book discusses how to differentiate bipolar disorder from ADHD, conduct disorder, and other related behavioral disorders. Also, it includes a brief discussion of the etiology and treatment available for this illness and the social ramifications of this illness and its misdiagnosis in children.

Koplewicz, H. S. *More than moody*. New York: Putnam's, 2002. This is an informative book for parents whose teens have depression. It includes symptoms, course and outcome, treatment, and useful tips for the management of this disorder.

Lederman, J., and C. Fink. *The ups and downs of raising a bipolar child*. New York: Simon and Schuster, 2003. Provides a firsthand account of parenting a child with bipolar disorder and tips for juggling family and work life while finding (and recognizing) good medical care for your child.

Lynn, G. T. *Survival strategies for parenting children with bipolar disorder: Innovative parenting and counseling techniques for helping children with bipolar disorder and the conditions that may occur with it*. London, UK: Jessica Kingsley, 2000. This book offers practical advice on recognizing the symptoms, understanding medication, and accessing the necessary support at school, as well as managing the day-to-day challenges of parenting a child with bipolar disorder.

Mondimore, F. M. *Bipolar disorder: A guide for patients and families*. Baltimore: Johns Hopkins University Press, 1999. A practical introduction to bipolar disorder, treatment, and self-care for affected individuals and advice for families.

Papolos, D. F., and Papolos, J. *The bipolar child*. New York: Broadway Books, 1999. This book reviews the literature of bipolar disorder in children and new developments in the field. It has helpful chapters on neuropsychological testing and how to do an individualized education plan (IEP) at school.

Steel, D. *His bright light: The story of Nick Traina*. New York: Delacorte, 1998. This book portrays the personal story of the childhood and adolescence of a gifted and talented boy with early-onset bipolar disorder.

The Josselyn Center. *In our own words: Teens with bipolar disorder: Facts about bipolar disorder* (2001). A video in which a group of teens and young adults share their individual stories about living with bipolar disorder. Josselyn Center, 405 Central Avenue, Northfield, IL 60093, phone: (847) 441-5600, www.josselyn.org.

Torrey, E. F., and Knable, M. B. *Surviving manic depression: A manual on bipolar disorder for patients, families, and providers.* New York: Basic Books, 2002. This book provides an overview of diagnostic and treatment of bipolar disorders and important family issues associated with this disorder.

Waltz, M. *Bipolar disorders: A guide to helping children and adolescents.* Sebastopol, CA: O'Reilly, 2002. A very good book about the diagnosis, treatment, and management of school, insurance, transition to adulthood, and other issues in children with bipolar disorder.

Books Written for Parents About Psychiatric Disorders or Behaviors

These are additional resources that are relevant for the management of your child's bipolar disorder.

Barkley, R. A. *Your defiant child;* and Barkley, R. A. Edwards, Gwenyth H., and Robin, Arthur L. *Defiant teens.* New York: Guilford, 1997 and 1998, respectively. These books present practical advice on how to manage children and teens with oppositional or defiant behaviors.

Barkley, R. A. *Taking charge of ADHD*, rev. ed. New York: Guilford Press, 2000. A step-by-step plan for behavior management for children with ADHD. Diagnosis, treatment, and neurological research of what causes ADHD. Practical advice for parents on managing stress and keeping peace in the family. This book includes descriptions of books, organizations, and Internet resources that families can trust.

Green, R. W. *The explosive child: A new approach for understanding and parenting easily frustrated, chronically inflexible children.* New York: HarperCollins, 1998. This book teaches parenting techniques for children with severe behavior problems, mood swings, and temper outbursts.

Patterson, G. R. *Families: Applications of social learning to family life.* Champaign, IL: Research Press, 1975. This book informs parents on how to manage their children's behavior problems.

Patterson, G. R. *Living with children: New methods for parents and teachers.* Champaign, IL: Research Press, 1976. This book teaches parents and teachers how to manage children with behavior problems.

Patterson, G. R., and Forgatch, M. S. *Parents and adolescents living together. Part 1: The basics and parents and adolescents living together; part 2: Family problem solving.* Castalia, 1989. In volume 1, authors provide practical, useful and effective suggestions on how to improve your parenting skills and thereby improve the behavior of your children. It suggests methods to replace negative, coercive parent–child interactions with more positive, reciprocal interactions. Volume 2 covers communication skills, problem solving, sex, drugs, and alcohol, school problems and more.

Wilens, T. E. *Straight talk about psychiatric medications for kids.* New York: Guilford, 1999. An overview of common childhood psychiatric disorders (including bipolar disorder) and medications used to treat them.

Woolis, R., and Hatfield, A. *When someone you love has mental illness: A handbook for family, friends, and caregivers.* Los Angeles: Tarcher, 1992. An essential resource for quick reference guides for parents, siblings, and friends of people with mental illness, as well as professionals in the field.

Books for Children with Bipolar Disorder

Angiade, Tracie. *Brabdon and the Bipolar Bear.* A fictional history about a young boy with bipolar disorder. Suitable for children ages 4 to 10 years old. This book can be purchased by direct order from www.bipolarchildren_bigstep.com.

Anglada, T. *Turbo Max: A story for siblings of bipolar children.* Self-published, 2002. For siblings (ages 8 to 12) of children with bipolar disorder. A boy's summer diary describes his understanding and feelings regarding his sister's illness.

Children & Adolescent Bipolar Foundation (CABF). *The storm in my brain: Kids and mood disorders* (Bipolar Disorder and Depression). For kids 6–12 (teens and adults too), filled with artwork by kids living with mood disorders, describes in child-friendly language what depression and mania feel like and how to cope. Contains tips for parents and tips for teachers. Published by Child & Adolescent Bipolar Foundation and Depression and Bipolar Support Alliance. Free to download at www.bpkids.org or www.dbsalliance.org or order printed copies from 1-800-826-3632.

Cobain, B. *When nothing matters anymore: A survival guide for depressed teens.* Minneapolis: Free Spirit, 1998. This book was written by Kurt Cobain's sister. It is geared toward teens with depression and suicidal behaviors.

Dubuque, N., and Dubuque, S. E. *Kid power tactics for dealing with depression;* and Dubuque, S. E. *A parent's survival guide for childhood depression.* Chicago, IL: Center for Applied Psychology, 1996. Written by an 11-year-old and his mother for children dealing with depression and parents for dealing with depressed kids.

McGee, C. C. *Matt the moody hermit crab*. Nashville, TN: McGee & Woods, 2002. A story for children (ages 8 to 12) with bipolar disorder. Over the course of one school year, Matt undergoes the onset, diagnosis, and treatment of this mental illness.

Sommers, M. A. *Everything you need to know about bipolar disorder and manic depressive illness*. New York: Rosen, 2000. A book with nice illustrations intended for adolescents upon first diagnosis of bipolar disorder. Very straightforward, with examples, and a glossary of terms at the back.

Books Written for Clinicians About Bipolar Disorder in Children
These titles can also be helpful for parents.

Barkley, R. A., Edwards, G. H., and Robin, A. L. *Defiant teens: A clinician's manual for assessment and family intervention*. New York: Guilford, 1999. An 18-step program designed to teach clinicians and parents the skills they need to manage difficult adolescent behavior and to improve family relationships.

Conners, C. K., and Jett, J. L. *Attention deficit hyperactivity disorder (in adults and children)*. Kansas City, MO: Compact Clinicians, 1999. Authors describe the diagnosis, course and outcome, causes, and treatment of ADHD.

Dudley, C. D. *Treating depressed children: A therapeutic manual of cognitive behavioral interventions*. Oakland, CA: New Harbinger, 1999. This book shows through cartoons the principles of cognitive behavior therapy for depressed youth.

Edwards, S. J., and Pfaff, J. J. *The 4R's. Managing youth suicidal behavior*. Ramsay Health Care, 1996. Subiaco, Australia. This book gives excellent guides for the assessment and management of suicidal behaviors.

Findling, R. L., Kowatch, R. A., and Post, R. M. *Pediatric bipolar disorder: A handbook for clinicians*. London: Martin Dunitz, 2003. This book reviews the most current literature about the causes, manifestations, and treatment of pediatric bipolar disorder.

Geller, B., Delbello, M. P., and Frome, M. P. (eds.). *Bipolar disorder in childhood and early adolescence*. New York: Guilford, 2003. Review of current knowledge on bipolar disorder in children, including prevalence, diagnosis and assessment, comorbid conditions, treatment, and outcomes.

Goodwin, F. K., and Jamison, K. R. *Manic-depressive illness*. New York: Oxford University Press, 1990. This is the "bipolar bible." It is written for professionals but it may be informative for parents. A new edition will be published soon.

Kendal, P. C., and Braswell, L. *Cognitive-behavioral therapy for impulsive children*. New York: Guilford, 1985. This book explains the techniques and theory of cognitive behavior therapy for children that have problems controlling their impulses (like bipolar children).

Kutcher, S. *Child and adolescent psychopharmacology*. Philadelphia: Saunders, 1997. A good book on medications used to treat pediatric psychiatric disorders, medications side effects, and rating scales to assess symptoms. Many real cases are included.

Martin, A., Scahill, L., Charney, D. S., and Leckman, J. F. *Pediatric psychopharmacology: Principles and practice*. New York: Oxford University Press, 2003. The latest and more comprehensive book published about the use of medications in children and teens.

Robin, A. L., and Foster, S. L. *Negotiating parent-adolescent conflict*. New York: Guilford, 2002. This is an excellent book on the management and treatment of parent–adolescent conflict.

Books for Adults with Bipolar Disorder and Their Families

Fawcett, J., Golden, B., and Rosenfeld, N. *New hope for people with bipolar disorder*. Roseville, CA: Prima Health, 2000. This book is a good source of information for adults with bipolar disorders.

Duke, P., and Hochman, G. *A brilliant madness: Living with manic-depressive illness*. New York: Bantam, 1993. The author gives a self-report of her bipolar disorder and successful treatment, and she explains facts of the disease and methods of treatment available.

Hinshaw, Steve. *The years of silence are past: My father's life with bipolar disorder*. Cambridge, U.K.: Cambridge University Press, 2002. Dr. Hinshaw writes about growing up with a father with bipolar disorder. It describes the effects that this illness can have on a family and the fact that, despite all the problems, a child and his/her relationships with his/her parents may survive.

Jamison, K. R. *Touched with fire: Manic-depressive illness and the artistic temperament*. New York: Maxwell Macmillan International, 1993. This book reviews the lives of famous people who have mood problems and quite probable bipolar disorder.

Jamison, K. R. *An unquiet mind*. New York: Knopf, 1995. Dr. Jamison, a known researcher in the area of bipolar disorder, recounts her personal experiences living with this disorder.

Garnet, R., and Ferber, E. *Why am I up, why am I down?* New York: Dell, 1999. This book discusses the symptoms of both manic and depressive episodes and their common triggers, what causes bipolar disorder and who is at risk, how to get the very specific kind of help you need, and current treatments.

Miklowitz, D. J. *The bipolar disorder survival guide: What you and your family need to know.* New York: Guilford, 2002. This is an excellent book for people with bipolar disorder. This book can also be read by parents of children with bipolar disorders. It gives excellent tips on how to manage the symptoms of bipolar disorder.

NOTES

Chapter 1

1. Lewinsohn PM, Klein DN, Seeley JR (1995), Bipolar disorders in a community sample of older adolescents: prevalence, phenomenology, comorbidity, and course. *J Am Acad Child Adolesc Psychiatry* 34(4):454–63.

2. American Psychiatric Association (APA) (1994), *Diagnostic and statistical manual of mental disorders*, 4th ed. *(DSM-IV)*. Washington, D.C.: American Psychiatric Association.

3. Biederman J (2003), Pediatric bipolar disorder coming of age. *Biological Psychiatry* 53:931–934.

4. American Psychiatric Association (APA) (1994), Practice guideline for the treatment of patients with bipolar disorder. *Am J Psychiatry* 151(Dec. supplement).

5. Goodwin FK, Jamison KR (1990), *Manic-depressive illness.* New York: Oxford University Press.

6. Geller B, Zimerman B, Williams M, Bolhofner K, Craney J, DelBello MP, Soutullo C (2000), Diagnostic characteristics of 93 cases of a prepubertal and early adolescent bipolar disorder phenotype by gender, puberty, and comorbid attention deficit hyperactivity disorder. *J Child Adoles Psychopharmacol* 10:157–64.

7. Nottelmann E (2001), National Institute of Mental Health research roundtable on prepubertal bipolar disorder. Consensus Development Conference. *J Am Acad Child Adolesc Psychiatry* 40:871–8.

Chapter 2

1. Egeland J, Hostetter A, Pauls D, Sussex J (2000), Prodromal symptoms before onset of manic-depressive disorder suggested by first hospital admission histories. *J Am Acad Child Adolesc Psychiatry* 39:1245–52.

2. Biederman J, Faraone S, Mick E, Wozniak J, Chen L, Ouellette C, Marrs A, Moore P, Garcia J, Mennin D, Lelon E (1996), Attention-deficit hyperactivity disorder and juvenile mania: an overlooked comorbidity? *J Am Acad Child Adolesc Psychiatry* 35(8):997–1008.

3. Carlson GA (1995), Identifying prepubertal mania. *J Am Acad Child Adolesc Psychiatry* 34(6):724–26.

4. Carlson GA (1998), Mania and ADHD: comorbidity or confusion. *J Affec Disord* 51:177–87.

5. Geller B, Luby J (1997), Child and adolescent bipolar disorder: review of the past 10 years. *J Am Acad Child Adolesc Psychiatry* 36:1168–76.

6. Kovacs M, Pollock M (1995), Bipolar disorder and comorbid conduct disorder in childhood and adolescence. *J Am Acad Child Adolesc Psychiatry* 34:715–23.

7. Weller E, Weller RA, Fristad M (1995), Bipolar disorder in children: misdiagnosis, underdiagnosis, and future directions. *J Am Acad Child Adolesc Psychiatry* 34:709–14.

8. Carlson GA, Fennig S, Bromet EJ (1994), The confusion between bipolar disorder and schizophrenia in youth: where does it stand in the 1990s? *J Am Acad Child Adolesc Psychiatry* 33(4):453–60.

9. Wozniak J, Biederman J, Kiely K, Ablon S, Faraone S, Mundy E, Mennin D (1995), Mania-like symptoms suggestive of childhood onset bipolar disorder in clinically referred children. *J Am Acad Child Adolesc Psychiatry* 34:867–76.

10. American Psychiatric Association (APA) (1994), *Diagnostic and statistical manual of mental disorders*, 4th ed. *(DSM-IV)* Washington, D.C.: American Psychiatric Association.

11. Strober M, Carlson G (1982), Bipolar illness in adolescents with major depression: clinical, genetic, and psychopharmacologic predictors in a three- to four-year prospective follow-up investigation. *Arch Gen Psychiatry* 39:549–55.

12. Geller B, Fox LW, Clark KA (1994), Rate and predictors of prepubertal bipolarity during follow-up of 6- to 12-year old depressed children. *J Am Acad Child Adolesc Psychiatry*, 33(4):461–68.

13. Fristad MA, Weller EB, Weller RA (1992), The Mania Rating Scale: can it be used in children? A preliminary report. *J Am Acad Child Adolesc Psychiatry* 31:252–7.

14. Biederman J, Wozniak J, Kiely K, Abbon S, Faraone S, Mick E, Mundy E, Kraus I (1995), CBCL clinical scales discriminate prepubertal children with structured interview-derived diagnosis of mania from those with ADHD. *J Am Acad Child Adolesc Psychiatry* 34(4):464–71.

15. Geller B, Warner K, Williams M, Zimerman B (1998), Prepubertal and young adolescent bipolarity versus ADHD: assessment and validity using the WASH-U-KSADS, CBCL, and TRF. *J Affect Disord* 51:93–100.

16. Axelson D, Birmaher B, Ulloa RE, Williamson D, Brent D, Ryan N (1998), Bipolar children and adolescents from a mood disorder clinic. Presented at the 45th Annual Meeting of the American Academy of Child and Adolescent Psychiatry, Anaheim, CA.

Chapter 3

1. Strober M, Schmidt-Lackner S, Freeman R, Bower S, Lampert C, DeAntonio M (1995), Recovery and relapse in adolescents with bipolar affective illness: a five-year naturalistic, prospective follow-up. *J Am Acad Child Adolesc Psychiatry* 34(6):724–3.

2. Lewinsohn PM, Klein DN, Seeley JR (1995), Bipolar disorders in a community sample of older adolescents: prevalence, phenomenology, comorbidity, and course. *J Am Acad Child Adolesc Psychiatry* 34(4):454–63.

3. Geller B, Craney JL, Bolhofner K, Nickelsburg MJ, Williams M, Zimerman B (2002), Two-year prospective follow-up of children with a prepubertal and early adolescent bipolar disorder phenotype. *Am J Psychiatry* 159(6):927–33.

4. Birmaher B (2001), Follow-up of adolescents with bipolar disorder. Presented at the 4th International Conference on Bipolar Disorders, Pittsburgh, PA, June.

5. Judd LL, Akiskal HS, Schettler PJ, Endicott J, Maser J, Solomon DA, Leon AC, Rice JA, Keller MB (2002), The long-term natural history of the weekly symptomatic status of bipolar I disorder. *Arch Gen Psychiatry* 59:530–7.

6. Strober M, Morrell W, Lampert C, Burroughs J (1990), Relapse following discontinuation of lithium maintenance therapy in adolescents with bipolar I illness: a naturalistic study. *Am J Psychiatry* 147(4):457–61.

7. Jamison KR (1993), *Touched with fire: Manic-depressive illness and the artistic temperament.* New York: Maxwell Macmillan International.

8. Cobain B (1998), *When nothing matters anymore: a survival guide for depressed teens.* Minneapolis, MN: Free Spirit.

Chapter 4

1. Findling RL, Kowatch RA, Post RM (2003), *Pediatric bipolar disorder: a handbook for clinicians.* London: Martin Dunitz.

2. *Breaking ground, breaking through: the strategic plan for mood disorders research of the National Institute of Mental Health.* August 2002.

3. Goodwin FK, Jamison KR (1990), *Manic-depressive illness.* New York: Oxford University Press.

4. Faraone S, Tsuang MT, Tsuang DW (1999), *Genetics of mental disorders.* New York: Guilford.

5. Malkoff-Schawartz S, Frank E, Anderson B, Sherrill JT, Siegel L, Patterson D, Kupfer DJ (1998), Stressful life events and social rhythm disruption in the onset of manic and depressive bipolar episodes. *Arch Gen Psychiatry* 55:702–7.

Chapter 5

1. American Psychiatric Association (APA)(1994), *Diagnostic and statistical manual of mental disorders,* 4th ed. *(DSM-IV).* Washington, D.C.: American Psychiatric Association.

2. World Health Organization (2000), *International statistical classification of diseases and related health problems*, 10th rev. (ICD-10).

3. Kaufman J, Birmaher B, Brent D, Rao U, Ryan ND (1995), Schedule for Affective Disorders and Schizophrenia in School-Aged Children—Present and Lifetime Version (K-SADS-PL). Western Psychiatric Institute and Clinic, Pittsburgh, PA.

4. Shaffer D, Fisher P, Lucas CP, Dulcan MK, Schwab-Stone ME (2000), NIMH Diagnostic Interview Schedule for Children Version IV (NIMH DISC-IV): description, differences from previous versions, and reliability of some common diagnoses. *J Am Acad Child Adolesc Psychiatry* 39:28–38.

5. Costello AJ, Benjamin R, Angold A, Silver D (1991), Mood variability in adolescents: a study of depressed, nondepressed and comorbid patients. *J Affect Disord* 23:199–212.

6. Birmaher B, Brent DA, Chiappetta L, Bridge J, Monga S, Baugher M (1999), Psychometric Properties of the Screen for Child Anxiety Related Emotional Disorders (SCARED): a replication study. *J Am Acad Child Adolesc Psychiatry* 38(10):1230–36.

7. Pelham WE, Gnagy EM, Greenslade KE, Milich R (1992), Teacher ratings of DSM-III-R symptoms for the disruptive behavior disorders. *J Am Acad Child Adolesc Psychiatry* 31:210–18.

8. Shaffer D, Gould MS, Brasic J, Ambrosini P, Fisher P, Bird H, Aluwahlia S (1983), A Children's Global Assessment Scale (CGAS). *Arch Gen Psychiatry* 40:1228–31.

9. Axelson D, Birmaher B, Brent D, Williamson D, Ryan N, The K-SADS Mania Rating Scale for Pediatric Bipolar Disorder. *J Child Adolescent Psychopharmacol* (submitted for publication).

10. Poznanski EO, Freeman LN, Mokron HB (1984), Children's depression rating scale-revised. *Psychopharmacol Bull* 21:979–89.

Chapter 6

1. Martin A, Scahill L, Charney D, Lekman JF (eds.) (2003), *Pediatric psychopharmacology: principles and practice*. New York: Oxford University Press.

2. Wilens, TE (2002), *Straight talk about psychiatric medications for kids*. New York: Guilford.

3. Kutcher S (1997), *Child and adolescent psychopharmacology*, Philadelphia: Saunders.

4. Werry JS, Aman MG (1999), *Practitioner's guide to psychoactive drugs for children and adolescents*. New York: Plenum Medical.

Chapter 7

1. Brent DA, Gaynor S, Weersing VR (2002), Cognitive behavioral approaches to the treatment of depression and anxiety. In *Child and adolescent psychiatry: modern approaches*, Rutter M, Taylor E, eds. (4th ed.). London: Blackwell Scientific, pp. 921–37.

2. Kendall PC (ed.) (2002), *Child and adolescent therapy: cognitive behavioral procedures*. New York: Guilford.

3. Dudley C (1997), *Treating depressed children: a therapeutic manual of cognitive behavioral interventions*. Oakland, CA: New Harbinger.

4. Lam DH, Watkins ER, Hayward P, Bright J, Wright K, Kerr N, Parr-Davis G, Sham P (2003), A randomized controlled study of cognitive therapy for relapse prevention for bipolar affective disorder: outcome of the first year. *Arch Gen Psychiatry* 60:145–52.

5. Mufson L, Dorta KP (2000), Interpersonal psychotherapy for depressed adolescents: Theory, practice, and research. In *Adolescent psychiatry: developmental and clinical studies*, Esman, AH, Flaherty LT, eds. Vol. 25. Annals of the American Society for Adolescent Psychiatry, pp. 139–67.

6. Swartz HA, Markowitz JC, Frank E (2002), Interpersonal psychotherapy for unipolar and bipolar disorders. In *Treating chronic and severe mental disorders: a handbook of empirically supported interventions*, Hofmann SG, Tompson MC, eds. New York: Guilford.

7. Frank E, Swartz HA, Kupfer DJ (2000), Interpersonal and social rhythm therapy: managing the chaos of bipolar disorder. *Biol Psychiatry* 6:593–604.

8. Frank E, Hlastala S, Ritenour A, Houck P, Tu XM, Monk TM, Mallinger AG, Kupfer DJ (2000), Inducing lifestyle regularity in recovering bipolar disorder patients: results from the maintenance therapies in bipolar disorder protocol. *Biol Psychiatry* 41:1165–73.

9. Miklowitz DJ, Frank E (1999), New psychotherapies for bipolar disorder. In *Bipolar disorder: clinical course and outcome*. Goldberg JF, Harrow M, eds. Washington, D.C.: American Psychiatric Press.

10. Miklowitz DJ (2002), Family-focused treatment for bipolar disorder. In *Treating chronic and severe mental disorders: A handbook of empirically supported interventions*, Hofmann SG, Tompson MC, eds. New York: Guilford.

11. Gabbard GO (2002), Mood disorders: psychodynamic aspects. In *Comprehensive textbook of child psychiatry*, Benjamin J. Sadock and Virginia A. Sadock, eds. Baltimore: Lippincott Williams & Wilkins.

Chapter 8

1. Miklowitz DJ, Frank E (1999), New psychotherapies for bipolar disorder. In *Bipolar disorder: clinical course and outcome*, Goldberg JF, Harrow M, eds. Washington, D.C.: American Psychiatric Press.

2. Lam DH, Watkins ER, Hayward P, Bright J, Wright K, Kerr N, Parr-Davis G, Sham P (2003), A randomized controlled study of cognitive therapy for relapse prevention for bipolar affective disorder: outcome of the first year. *Arch Gen Psychiatry* 60:145–52.

3. Brent D, Poling K, McKain B, Baugher M (1993), A psychoeducational program for families of affectively ill children and adolescents. *J Am Acad Child Adolesc Psychiatry* 32:770–4.

4. Fristad MA, Goldbert-Arnold JS, Gavazzi SM (2002), Multifamily psychoeducation groups (MFPG) for families of children with bipolar disorder. *Bipolar Disorders* 4:254–62.

5. American Academy of Child and Adolescent Psychiatry (AACAP) (1998), Practice parameters for the assessment and treatment of children and adolescents with depressive disorders. *J Am Acad Child Adolesc Psychiatry* 37(10 Suppl):63S–83S.

6. American Psychiatric Association Practice Guidelines (2002), Practice guideline for the treatment of patients with bipolar disorder (revision). *Am J Psychiatry* (Suppl), 159.

7. Grunze H, Kasper S, Goodwin G, Bowden C, Baldwin D, Licht R, Vieta E, Moller HJ (2002), World Federation of Societies of Biological Psychiatry Task Force on Treatment Guidelines for Bipolar Disorders. World Federation of Societies of Biological Psychiatry (WFSBP) guidelines for biological treatment of bipolar disorders. Part I: Treatment of bipolar depression. *World J Biol Psychiatry* 3(3):115–24.

8. Suppes T, Bennehy EB, Swann AC, Bowden CL, Calabrese JR, Hirschfeld RMA, Keck PE Jr., Sachs GS, Crismon ML, Toprac MG, Shon SP (2002), Report of the Texas Consensus Conference Panel on Medication Treatment of Bipolar Disorder 2000. *J Clin Psychiatry* 63 (4):288–98.

9. Goodwin FK, Jamison KR (1990), *Manic-depressive illness.* New York: Oxford University Press.

10. Martin A, Scahill L, Charney D, Lekman JF, eds. (2003), *Pediatric psychopharmacology: principles and practice.* New York: Oxford University Press.

11. Weller EB, Danielyan AK, Weller RA (2001), Somatic treatment of bipolar disorder in children and adolescents. *Child Adolesc Psychiatry Clin N Am* 11(3):595–617.

12. Findling RL, Kowatch RA, Post RM, (2003), *Pediatric bipolar disorder: A handbook for clinicians.* London: Martin Dunitz.

13. Gonzalez-Pinto A, Tohen M, Lalaguna B, Perez-Heredia JL, Fernandez-Corres B, Gutierrez M, Mico JA (2002), Treatment of bipolar I rapid cycling patients during dysphoric mania with olanzapine. *J Clin Psychopharmacol* 22(5):450–4.

14. Delbello MP, Schwiers ML, Rosenberg HL, Strakowski SM (2002), A double-blind, randomized, placebo-controlled study of quetiapine as adjunctive treatment for adolescent mania. *J Am Acad Child Adolesc Psychiatry* 41(10):1216–23.

15. Strober M, Carlson G (1982), Bipolar illness in adolescents with major depression: clinical, genetic, and psychopharmacologic predictors in a three- to four-year prospective follow-up investigation. *Arch Gen Psychiatry* 39:549–55.

16. Geller, B., Delbello, M.P. & Frome, M.P. (eds.) (2003). Bipolar disorder in childhood and early adolescence. New York: Guilford.

17. Bowden CL, Calabrese JR, McElroy SL, et al. (2000), A randomized, placebo-

controlled 12-month trial of divalproex and lithium in treatment of outpatients with bipolar I disorder. Divalproex Maintenance Study Group. *Arch Gen Psychiatry* 57:481–9.

18. Calabrese JR, Shelton MD, Rapport DJ, Kimmel SE, Elhaj O (2002), Long-term treatment of bipolar disorder with lamotrigine. *J Clin Psychiatry* 63 Suppl 10:18–22.

19. Goodwin FK (2002), Rationale for long-term treatment of bipolar disorder and evidence for long-term lithium treatment. *J Clin Psychiatry* 63 Suppl 10:5–12.

20. Birmaher B, Brent DA, Kolko D, Baugher M, Bridge J, Holder D, Iyengar S, Ulloa RE (2000). Clinical outcome after short-term psychotherapy for adolescents with major depressive disorder. *Arch Gen Psychiatry* 57:29–36.

21. Brent DA, Holder D, Kolko D, Birmaher B, Baugher M, Roth C, Iyengar S, Johnson BA (1997), A clinical psychotherapy trial for adolescent depression comparing cognitive, family, and supportive therapy. *Arch Gen Psychiatry* 54:877–85.

Chapter 9

1. Martin A, Scahill L, Charney D, Lekman JF, eds. (2003), *Pediatric psychopharmacology: principles and practice.* New York: Oxford University Press.

2. Wilens TE (2002), *Straight talk about psychiatric medications for kids.* New York: Guilford.

3. Kutcher S (1997), *Child and adolescent psychopharmacology,* Philadelphia: Saunders.

4. Werry JS, Aman MG (1999), *Practioner's guide to psychoactive drugs for children and adolescents.* New York: Plenum Medical Book.

5. Barkley RA (2000), *Taking charge of ADHD,* rev. ed. New York: Guilford Press.

6. Green RW (1998), *The explosive child: a new approach for understanding and parenting easily frustrated, chronically inflexible children.* New York: HarperCollins.

7. Kendall PC, ed. (2000), *Child and adolescent therapy: cognitive-behavioral procedures.* New York: Guilford.

Chapter 10

1. Shaffer D, Pfeffer CR (2001), Practice Parameter for the Assessment and Treatment of Children and Adolescents. *J Am Acad Child Adolesc Psychiatry* 40:25–51, supplement.

2. Lewinsohn PM, Klein DN, Seeley JR (1995), Bipolar disorders in a community sample of older adolescents: prevalence, phenomenology, comorbidity, and course. *J Am Acad Child Adolesc Psychiatry* 34:454–63.

3. Goodwin FK, Jamison KR (1990), *Manic-depressive illness.* New York: Oxford University Press.

4. American Psychiatric Association (APA)(1994), Practice guideline for the treatment of patients with bipolar disorder. *Am J Psychiatry* 151(Dec. supplement).

5. Edwards SJ, Pfaff JJ (1996), *The 4R's: managing youth suicidal behavior.* Subiaco, Australia: Ramsay Health Care.

6. Edwards SJ, Growing up with young people. A parent's guide to understanding adolescents and young adults and encouraging their emotional mental health. Australia: Canberra, 1994.

7. Brent DA, Holder D, Kolko D, Birmaher B, Baugher M, Roth C, Iyengar S, Johnson BA (1997), A clinical psychotherapy trial for adolescent depression comparing cognitive, family, and supportive therapy. *Arch Gen Psychiatry* 54:877–85.

8. Linehan MM. (1993), *Cognitive behavior therapy for borderline personality disorder.* New York: Guilford.

9. Miller AL, Rathus JH, Lineham MM, Wetzler S, Leigh E (1997), Dialectical behavior therapy adapted for suicidal adolescents. *J Practical Psychiatry Behavioral Health* 3:78–86.

Chapter 11

1. Kendall PC, ed. (2000), *Child and adolescent therapy: cognitive-behavioral procedures.* New York: Guilford.

2. Barkley RA (2000), *Taking charge of ADHD*, rev. ed. New York: Guilford Press.

3. Green, RW (1998), *The explosive child: a new approach for understanding and parenting easily frustrated, chronically inflexible children.* New York: HarperCollins.

4. Patterson GR (1975), *Families: applications of social learning to family life.* Champaign, IL: Research Press.

5. Patterson GR (1976), *Living with children: new methods for parents and teachers.* Champaign, IL: Research Press.

6. Barkley RA (1997), *Managing the defiant child: a guide to parent training.* New York: Guilford Press.

Chapter 12

1. Schwab Stone ME, Henrich C (2002), School consultation. In *Child and adolescent psychiatry: a comprehensive textbook*, Lewis M, ed. Baltimore: Williams & Wilkins.

2. Overview of ADA, IDEA, and Section 504. ERIC Digest E537. Educational Resources Informational Center (ERIC) Web site. Available at www.ed.gov/data bases/ERIC_Digests/ed389142.html. Also see bpkids.org.

3. An Overview of ADA, IDEA, and Section 504: Update 2001. ERIC EC Digest #E606. Educational Resources Informational Center (ERIC) Web site. Available at www.ldonline.org/ld_indepth/legal/legislative/update_504_2001.html. Also see bpkids.org.

Chapter 13

1. Malloy M (1995), *Mental illness and managed care: a primer for family and consumers.* Arlington, VA: National Alliance for the Mentally Ill.

2. Bazelon Center for Mental Health Law
www.bazelon.org

3. Child & Adolescent Bipolar Foundation
   (847) 256-8525
   www.bpkids.org
4. Federation of Families for Children's Mental Health
   (813) 974-7930
   www.federationoffamilies.org
5. National Alliance for the Mentally Ill (NAMI)
   (703) 524-7600
   NAMI Helpline: (800) 950-6264
   TDD: (703) 516-7227
   www.nami.org

INDEX

ABOUT THE AUTHOR

Boris Birmaher, M.D., professor of psychiatry at the University of
Pittsburgh School of Medicine, is one of the country's top researchers
in the field of child and adolescent bipolar disorder. He, together with
David Axelson, M.D., is also currently the director of Child and Ado-
lescent Bipolar Services at Western Psychiatric Institute and Clinic in
Pittsburgh. Dr. Birmaher lives in Pittsburgh, Pennsylvania.